Japan's Great Stagnation

Japan's Great Stagnation: Financial and Monetary Policy Lessons for Advanced Economies

edited by
Michael M. Hutchison and
Frank Westermann

CESifo Seminar Series

The MIT Press
Cambridge, Massachusetts
London, England

HB
3817
.J37
2006

MIT Press books may be purchased at special quantity discounts for business or sales
promotional use. For information, please email special_sales@mitpress.mit.edu or write
to Special Sales Department, The MIT Press, 55 Hayward Street, Cambridge, MA 02142.

This book was set in Palatino on 3B2 by Asco Typesetters, Hong Kong.
Printed and bound in the United States of America.

Library of Congress Cataloging-in-Publication Data

Japan's great stagnation : financial and monetary policy lessons for advanced economies /
Michael M. Hutchison and Frank Westermann, editors.
    p.   cm. — (CESifo seminar series)
  Includes bibliographical references and index.
  ISBN 0-262-08347-7 (alk. paper)
  1. Recessions–Japan. 2. Monetary policy–Japan. 3. Finance–Japan. 4. Japan–Economic
policy–20th century. 5. Japan–Economic conditions–20th century. I. Hutchison,
Michael M. II. Westermann, Frank, 1970– III. Series.

HB3817.J37   2006
339.50952—dc22   2005058040

10 9 8 7 6 5 4 3 2 1

Contents

Contributors

Yoichi Arai
University of Tokyo

Robert Dekle
University of Southern California

Zekeriya Eser
Gatton College of Business and
Economics
University of Kentucky

Eiji Fujii
University of Tsukuba

Kimie Harada
Chuo University

Takeo Hoshi
University of California
San Diego

Michael M. Hutchison
University of California
Santa Cruz

Takatoshi Ito
University of Tokyo

Ken Kletzer
University of California
Santa Cruz

Nikolas Müller-Plantenberg
Universidad Carlos III de Madrid

Kunio Okina
Bank of Japan

Joe Peek
Gatton College of Business and
Economics
University of Kentucky

Eric S. Rosengren
Federal Reserve Bank of Boston

Shigenori Shiratsuka
Bank of Japan

Mark M. Spiegel
Federal Reserve Bank of San
Francisco

Frank Westermann
University of Munich

Nobuyoshi Yamori
Nagoya University

CESifo Seminar Series in Economic Policy

This book is part of the CESifo Seminar Series in Economic Policy, which aims to cover topical policy issues in economics from a largely European perspective. The books in this series are the products of the papers presented and discussed at seminars hosted by CESifo, an international research network of renowned economists supported jointly by the Center for Economic Studies at Ludwig-Maximilians University, Munich, and the Ifo Institute for Economic Research. All publications in this series have been carefully selected and refereed by members of the CESifo research network.

Hans-Werner Sinn

1

The Great Japanese Stagnation: Lessons for Industrial Countries

Michael M. Hutchison, Takatoshi Ito, and Frank Westermann

1.1 Introduction

Japan was the growth miracle and economic model for successful industrial development during much of the postwar period. The economy's double-digit growth rates, remarkable industrial transformation, export success, and negligible unemployment were the envy of the world. The twenty-first century was expected by many scholars to be the "Japanese century" in terms of international economic and corporate dominance. Japan's economic and social institutions were frequently held up as models to be emulated if other industrial countries wanted to keep up technologically and competitively in the world economy.

The seemingly unstoppable Japanese economy fell abruptly into recession in the early 1990s, beginning a period of either recession or weak economic activity, commodity and asset price deflation, banking failures, increased bankruptcies, and rising unemployment. This has been termed the "great recession" (Knutter and Posen 2001) or "lost decade" (Cargill, Hutchison, and Ito 2000), but more aptly should be called the Great Stagnation—a sustained period of general economic malaise not seen in the industrial world since the 1930s. Though the *depth* of the downturn in Japan over the past fifteen years is not comparable to the 1930s, many other characteristics are similar—the duration of the downturn, persistence of banking problems and financial distress, and a sustained deflation combined with zero interest rates. No other industrial country has experienced this *combination* of economic characteristics for almost seventy years. Moreover the recent period was generally one of strong economic growth and prosperity in other

We thank MIT Economics, Business, and Finance Editor Elizabeth Murry and four anonymous reviewers for helpful comments and suggestions.

industrial countries. The cumulative effect of a decade of economic stagnation in Japan amounts to a very large output loss for the country.

Years of stagnation have left an imprint on the Japanese economy, financial system, and institutional structure. Many features that traditionally characterized the Japanese economic miracle have been affected, with changes not necessarily *caused* by the stagnation of the economy but pushed faster and further than would otherwise have been the case. Key features of the Japanese economic model that have undergone major changes include the traditional life-long employment system, the "iron triangle" of close and cooperative linkages among the government, corporate governance and the banking system, the kei-retsu system, the main bank system, the bank-dominated financial system, and the leadership of the Ministry of Finance and Ministry of Trade and Industry in regulating and directing the economy.

Many key questions about the causes and effects of the Great Stagnation in Japan remain unresolved. What are the factors have made Japan so unique in experiencing this set of economic challenges, and why has the country been so slow to recover? This book considers these questions from the financial perspective and is broadly grouped into three areas: features of the financial and banking system that have contributing to economic stagnation, monetary factors and central bank policy, and the role of international financial factors (exchange rate and balance of payments).

This introductory chapter places Japanese economic stagnation in historical context, contrasting the great success of the economy during much of the postwar period with the weak performance and associated problems seen more recently. We focus on the background and institutional aspects of the financial and monetary system in Japan that both contributed to the downturn and hindered recovery, providing context for the topics that are taken up in the other chapters of the book. We describe the major financial features that characterized the "traditional" Japanese economic model—features that contributed to the success of the economy in earlier times—and show how weaknesses in the system gradually emerged and eventually led to economic decline. The next section describes the progression of Japan from "model economy" to recession, deflation, and banking crisis. Sections 1.3 and 1.4 describe the financial and monetary systems, respectively, and how they have contributed to the onset and continuation of the Great Stagnation. Section 1.5 draws out some policy lessons and makes the analogy between asset price declines and collapse in credit in Japan in the 1990s with the

German experience over the past few years. Section 1.6 considers some policy lessons for other advanced economies, particularly if housing prices should drop dramatically as they have done in Japan over the past fifteen years. Section 1.7 concludes the chapter.

1.2   The Road from Model Economy to the Great Stagnation

The sustained economic stagnation in Japan over the course of the 1990s and first part of this decade was startling and in sharp contrast with the enormously successful performance of the economy during the preceding three decades. Table 1.1 shows that Japan had by far the most rapid economic growth in the industrial world during 1960 to 1973, averaging 9.6 percent real GDP growth annually compared with 4.9 percent for the entire OECD area. Unemployment rates were very low in Japan, averaging just 1.3 percent over the period compared with 3.2 percent in the OECD area, although inflation was relatively high (6.2 percent average) compared with most other industrial countries. This period is oftentimes termed the high-growth period in Japan, and it has brought worldwide attention to the country's economic success.

Following the 1973 oil shock economic growth in Japan and other industrial countries slowed sharply. Real GDP growth in Japan in the subsequent two decades was still quite high by the standards of other industrial economies, averaging about 3.8 percent annually during 1973 to 1989 compared with about 2.7 percent for the OECD area, but clearly reflected capacity limits and other constraints on growth (e.g., labor shortages, high productivity levels, and high technological levels) facing mature industrial economies. The rate of unemployment in Japan over the 1973 to 1989 period was less than half of that prevailing on average in the OECD area, and the rate of inflation averaged only about 2.2 percent annually. During this period Japan caught up technologically with the United States and other leading industrial nations, took international leadership positions in many industries, and its economic influence grew enormously on the world stage. Japan's economy became the envy of the world, frequently heralded as a model for other industrial nations to follow.

Stagnation of the Japanese economy in the 1991 to 2005 period, juxtaposed against such strong performance during the preceding three decades, came as a complete surprise. Real GDP growth averaged only 1.5 percent during this period, about half of that recorded in

Table 1.1
Economic performance in Japan and OECD area, 1960 to 2004

	Real-GDP growth rate	Inflation (CPI)	Unemployment rate
1960–1973			
Japan	9.6	6.2	1.3
United States	3.9	3.2	4.8
Germany	4.3	3.4	0.8
G7 average	4.8	3.9	3.1
OECD average	4.9	4.1	3.2
1973–1979			
Japan	3.6	9.9	1.9
United States	2.5	8.5	6.7
Germany	2.4	4.7	3.4
G7 average	2.7	9.8	4.9
OECD average	2.8	10.8	5.0
1979–1989			
Japan	4.0	2.5	2.5
United States	2.5	5.5	7.2
Germany	1.8	2.9	6.8
G7 average	2.7	5.6	6.9
OECD average	2.6	8.9	7.2
1990–2004			
Japan	1.5	0.5	3.8
United States	3.1	2.7	5.6
Germany	1.5	2.1	7.9
G7 average	2.1	2.1	7.7
OECD average	2.9	6.1	7.4

Source: *Historical Statistics, 1960–1993* (Organization for Economic Cooperation and Development, 1993); *OECD Economic Outlook, No. 76* (Organization for Economic Cooperation and Development, December 2004).
Notes: Macroeconomic performance of Japan and various other industrial countries (average percentage changes). "Germany" is the Federal Republic until unification. G7 includes Japan, the United States, Germany, France, Italy, the United Kingdom, and Canada. OECD includes G7, Australia, Austria, Belgium, the Czech Republic, Denmark, Finland, Greece, Hungary, Iceland, Ireland, Korea, Luxembourg, Mexico, the Netherlands, New Zealand, Norway, Poland, Portugal, the Slovak Republic, Spain, Sweden, Switzerland, and Turkey. Growth rate and CPI inflation rate are annual percentage rates of change between the years indicated. Unemployment rate is unemployment as a percentage of the total labor force and the average of the years indicated.

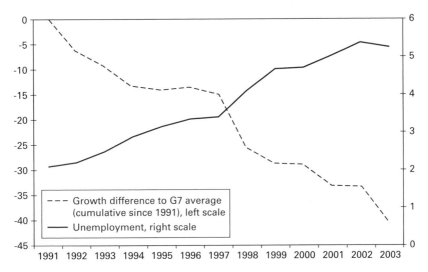

Figure 1.1
Industrial production and unemployment rate. The "growth difference" is the cumulative difference between industrial production in Japan and the average of G7 countries, without Japan, in percentage points. Over the twelve years displayed, the average of the G7 countries grew more than 40 percent faster than Japan. Source: IMF, *International Financial Statistics.*

the OECD. The economic malaise, demonstrated in figure 1.1 by the rise in Japan's unemployment rate and weak industrial production relative to the other major industrial countries, was initially described as a lost decade, but at this writing continues for almost fifteen years. (Signs of an upturn were evident in late 2005, but it is not clear whether this is sustainable.) This is the feature that makes Japan stand out most amongst other industrial countries—the *duration* of stagnation and other economic problems. The financial problem in Japan is related to both the collapse in the stock market and other asset prices—and their failure to recover—and characterized by the burden of nonperforming loans that became institutionalized in the system (figure 1.2). The other key characteristic of the Japanese economic malaise was prolonged deflation in tandem with a sustained period of zero short-term interest rates where the central bank seemingly lost leverage to provide additional monetary stimulus to the economy (figure 1.3).

The challenge in understanding this period of economic stagnation and myriad of problems is to connect the real, financial, and monetary

Thousand yen   Percent

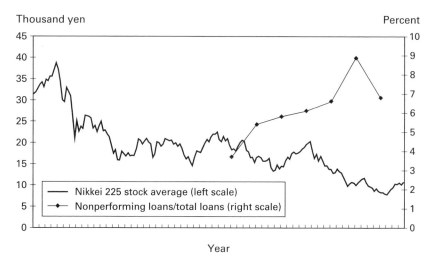

Year

Figure 1.2
Stock market and nonperforming loans. Source: Japan Financial Services Agency.

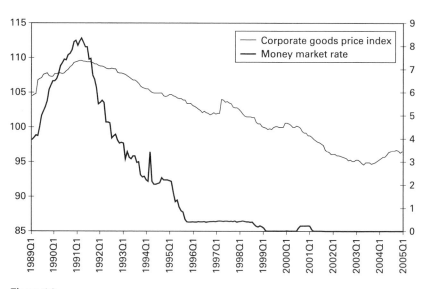

Figure 1.3
Prices and short-term interest rates. Sources: Bank of Japan and IMF, *International Financial Statistics*.

components with common causal factors. Emphasizing these linkages, Japanese Prime Minister Junichiro Koizumi February 23, 2002, directed ministries to formulate *emergency countermeasures to deflation*, stating "while deflation has a varied background, the resolution of the immediate financial problems is indispensable to overcoming deflation" (Ministry of Foreign Affairs of Japan press release, February 27, 2002). At this writing, it still remains unclear when Japan's economy will return to its potential growth path or completely resolve its financial problems.

The Japanese economy's prolonged downturn—the Great Stagnation—provides a fascinating case study of "depression economics" with lessons for many industrial economies today. The magnitude of the Japanese stagnation, of course, is not comparable to the economic disaster affecting much of the world in the 1930s. Fischer (2001), for example, points out that Japanese economic performance of the 1990s was unimpressive but not disastrous, and that policy probably would have been forced to be more decisive had there been a full-blown crisis. It is telling that when the financial system was momentarily at the brink of a full-blown panic, in late 1997 with the collapse of two major financial institutions (Hokkaido Takushoku Bank and Yamaichi Securities Company), there was a flurry of activity to make rapid institutional changes on both the financial and monetary side—and a brief political window of opportunity for institutional change—that helped stabilize the situation. Policy measures have been taken, albeit gradually and hesitantly, to resolve the banking problem in tandem with institutional changes in banking and financial supervision and regulation. However, Japan's economy remains weak and is operating far below potential.

Though the depth of the recession in Japan is not comparable to that seen in many countries during the 1930s, many other characteristics are similar—the duration of the downturn, persistence of banking problems and financial distress, and a sustained deflation combined with zero interest rates. No industrial country other than Japan has experienced this *confluence* of economic events for almost seventy years. Moreover this period was generally one of strong economic growth and prosperity in other industrial countries and the cumulative effect of a decade of economic stagnation in Japan amounts to a very large output loss for the country. Not only does the Japanese stand out by the seeming inability of policy makers to pull the economy out of its stagnation, but the worrisome prospect that other countries could fall into similar dire economic circumstances. We argue in section 1.5 that Germany has several of the characteristics that were associated with the *onset* (preconditions) of the Great Stagnation in Japan.

1.3   Japan's Financial System and the Great Stagnation

1.3.1   Traditional Characteristics of the Japanese Financial System

Several key characteristics of the "traditional" Japanese financial system were important factors in the country's remarkable postwar growth performance, but also contributed to instability as the economy matured. The most important features in this context include the dependence of the economy on the banking system ("indirect" finance), the keiretsu system, "main bank" affiliations, and the nature of bank supervision and regulation. These institutional features, however, failed to evolve quickly enough to keep pace with the transformation, internationalization and modernization with other parts of the economy. The banking crisis of the 1990s and beyond can in large part be traced to a failure of the old financial framework to adapt to new economic realities.

Firms in Japan traditionally acquired credit for investment through the banking system—"indirect finance" was the predominant channel through which funds moved from savers to borrowers. Corporate bond and bill markets, as well as equity markets—direct financial channels—played a small role in raising funds for investment in Japan until the 1980s. The traditional system weakened as open financial markets developed in Japan and, at the same time, many of the largest internationally oriented corporations were both flush with funds from retained earnings (allowing them to largely self-finance investment) and had easy access to world bond and equity markets. The traditional indirect finance system in Japan, similar to Germany and other countries in continental Europe (as opposed to the United States and Great Britain), fostered a high degree of "co-dependence" between banks and firms that was facilitated and encouraged by established legal and institutional structures.

Keiretsu and Main Bank Affiliations in Japan

The keiretsu system, also known as enterprise or industrial groups, has its origins in the pre-war zaibatsu system where business enterprise groups were closely affiliated with, and financed by, banks owned by the same family. In the zaibatsu system, family-owned banks were the only lender and controller of the large business enterprises.

Although these large conglomerates were broken up after the Second World War, some of their features remained in the modern keiretsu system. The rigid structure of the zaibatsu was dissolved after the war but was replaced by a looser structure of company groups with leadership provided by a large bank and the main bank system. In general terms, keiretsu consist of formal and informal links between firms, customers and suppliers, and financial institutions. Key elements were bank dominance of the enterprise groups and in the flows of funds, both of which were special characteristics of Japanese finance during the period 1950 to 1971 (Cargill and Royama 1988). In many ways keiretsu connections facilitate coordinating, financing, and monitoring firm investment. In particular, these tight networks oftentimes have provided Japanese firms with strategic international competitive advantage, easier access to financing during economic downturns, management support from banks, and other benefits (Hoshi et al. 1991).

Two key characteristics of keiretsu, discussed in the next subsection, proved particularly problematic with the economic downturn and fall in asset prices of the 1990s: (1) the system of cross-ownership, across firms and banks, created by large purchases and holding of equity positions, and (2) the predominance of corporate financing coming from the large "city" banks that form the core of each of the large keiretsu groups.

Cross-ownership of shares distinguish Japanese banks, as well as those in Germany, from other most countries. For example, it was illegal in the United States until recently for banks to hold shares in nonbank corporations (under the Glass-Steagall Act) and this practice is subject to considerable regulation in the United Kingdom. The regulatory agencies in many other countries either control the total amount of cross-shareholding or severely limit the extent to which revaluation gains from equity holdings can be included as capital when computing the capital–asset ratios that are relevant to comply with international agreements. Japan allows these unrealized equity revaluation gains to be applied liberally in calculating capital–asset ratios.[1]

Furthermore banks in Japan still commonly have representatives on the boards and in managerial positions of the firms to which they lend. By this means banks are able to exert direct control over the

decision and the management of the firms. In principle, this relationship allows banks to monitor firms more effectively and to steer them
directly in time of financial difficulties. In times of distress the firms
gain from this "main bank" affiliation by maintaining their ability to
borrow and invest. While up to and through the 1980s these features were viewed as one of the key positive attributes of the Japanese economy, more recently researchers have argued than it may
also be responsible for the recent slowdown of economic growth.
Eser, Peek, and Rosengren (chapter 5) analyze how this feature of
the Japanese financial system helps to understand the financial crisis
in the mid-1990s. In particular, they demonstrate empirically that traditional main bank relationships has frequently led to poor lending decisions by banks, especially "ever-greening" of loans. Banks
are lending too much to firms in which they have close ties (through
keiretsu/main bank linkages), oftentimes simply making loans to
allow firms to pay interest on their existing debts, that is, ever-greening
the loans. This way main bank links are diverting funds away from
productive uses (new productive investments) to existing problematic
debtors.

Government Prudential Regulations and Enforcement
Another key feature of the Japanese financial system that eventually
led to serious problems and contributed to the banking crisis was the
traditional practice of supervisory forbearance and the absence of effective prudential regulation of the banking sector. This a key feature in
the model of Dekle and Kletzer (chapter 3). They show that public deposit insurance and weak prudential regulation may have led to the
accumulation of nonperforming assets, banking crises and *permanent*
declines in economic growth.

Over the last two decades banking supervision has gone through
several stages in Japan. The main responsibility for designing and
enforcing regulations was until 1998 held by the Banking Bureau of
the Japanese Ministry of Finance. Officials from this ministry regularly
visited banks and classified loans according to their own subjective
evaluation about the likelihood of repayment. While banks with a
high percentage of "questionable" loans were put on notice, and in severe cases merged with stronger banks, there was no systematic and
tractable early warning system that forced the banks to write off bad
loans at an early stage. Much was left to the discretion of the bank

examiner, and some even retired into executive positions at commercial banks while maintaining close contacts with the Ministry of Finance (a practice referred to as the amakudari system). Supervisory forbearance was typical and a general practice in this regulatory environment.

The Financial Supervisory Agency (FSA) was created in 1998 to address the serious lapses in bank supervision that contributed to the banking crisis. The FSA reported directly to the Financial Reconstruction Commission of the Prime Minister's Office until 2001, when it became a part of the government. The FSA was reorganized as the Financial Services Agency (new) in 2000. The FSA took on many of the supervisory and regulatory responsibilities formerly held by the Ministry of Finance, and was charged with implementing a new system to assess the quality of bank's loan assets. The FSA developed a new non-performing loan classification system that is rigorous and consistent across banks. Slower progress has been made with other reforms and in the area of enforcement. The FSA has proved more successful than the Ministry of Finance especially since 2002 in supervising and regulating banks so as to both resolve the bad loan problem in Japan, force management accountability in the banking system, and avoid future crises from occurring (Hoshi and Ito 2004). It is noteworthy that the FSA was created *after* the banking crisis and, in this context, is constrained in that a tighter assessment of nonperforming loans would lead to banks further abandoning firms in distress, inducing even more bankruptcies and contributing to continued weakness in the economy.

In chapter 4, Spiegel and Yamori show that banks voluntary disclosure of their balance sheet positions is necessary for market discipline in a modern financial sector. If voluntary disclosure is not forthcoming, then government-imposed strict disclosure rules are necessary to ensure financial stability. Spiegel and Yamori show empirically that voluntary disclosure did not work in Japan—weak banks were reluctant to disclose the magnitude of their nonperforming loans while healthy banks voluntarily made public more accurate assessments of their true balance sheet positions. Moreover the Ministry of Finance did not strictly enforce disclosure rules. The authors find that stricter disclosure rules enforced by the Ministry of Finance would have helped to avoid the Japanese banking crisis, or at least limit its magnitude. The authors also provide concrete policy options for efficient regulation of the Japanese economy in future.

1.3.2   The Banking Crisis and Pubic Bailouts in Japan: A Chronology of Events

The evolution of the banking crisis in Japan may be highlighted in the context of its traditional financial characteristics. The burst of the stock market bubble, starting on the first trading day of 1990 and continuing into the mid-1990s, led to significant losses for the banks because of their large equity holdings associated with their main bank relationships. The simultaneous decline of real estate prices further led to bankruptcies and debt service problems of private corporations in the real-estate related sectors. At this initial phase, the magnitude of the nonperforming loans problem was difficult to assess due to the lack of disclosure of the banks.

The first public awareness of the seriousness of Japan's banking problems emerged publicly with the failure of a number of small financial institutions in 1995, most notably the *Jusen* (housing) finance companies. The *Jusen* were created in the mid-1970s as subsidiaries of banks, securities firms, and life insurance companies. They provided household credit and, in the 1980s, turned to real estate finance. The *Jusen* collapsed with the downturn in the economy, especially hard-hit by the drop in the real estate property market. The initial failure of *Jusen* and some small banks in the mid 1990s led to questions about whether the banks would be bailed out by the government and, if so, who would ultimately assume the losses and bear responsibility.

Insolvent banks initially were merged with another healthy private bank (a practice known as the *convoy system*) and, in 1995, 685 billion yen of public funds where used for this purpose. This was the first major public bailout of a financial institution in Japan. Because of a lack of explicit burden sharing rule when insolvent financial institutions fail, this injection only came after severe disagreements among the Ministry of Finance, the Ministry of Agriculture, Forestry and Fishery, and private banks. These internal disputes prevented a more decisive solution of the nonperforming loans problem and ultimately led, by the end of 1997, to the second phase of the banking crisis with the failures of much larger financial institutions, most notably the Hokkaido Takushoku bank and Yamaichi Securities. By November 1997 Japan was on the edge of financial panic (Cargill, Hutchison, and Ito 2000).

In order to prevent a full-blown financial crisis, the government provided a total of 1.8 trillion yen to 21 financial institutions in the form of preferred shares and subordinated debt. The long-term credit bank (LTCB) and the Nippon Credit Bank also were nationalized in 1998. These public rescue measures were not sufficient, however, and the government injected another 7.5 billion yen into 15 banks in March 1999. These monies, combined with extensive guarantees of deposits and a strengthened deposit insurance system for assisted mergers, helped stem the crisis.

In the following years banks used this buffer of capital to write off some of the nonperforming loans on their balance sheets. A wave of mergers also accompanied this period of financial consolidation. Most prominently three large banks, Fuji, Daiichi-Kangyo, and the Industrial Bank of Japan, joined to form the Mizuho Financial Holdings in 1999. The last remaining zaibatsu, Sakura and Sumitomo joined to form the Mitsui-Sumitomo Financial group (completed in 2002). Some recovery in the stock market, due largely to the worldwide boom in IT shares, facilitated financial consolidation as it created unrealized capital gains to banks.

In March 2001, however, the stock market declined sharply again with the burst in the IT bubble. The Nikkei stock index fell 50 percent from its peak. Under these circumstances even additional capital injections in 2001 and 2002 (2 trillion yen each) were still insufficient to restore the solvency of bank balance sheets, and they were pushed to the limit of their operational capabilities. In April 2003, stock prices fell to below one-fifth of their peak in 1989. Two more banks failed in 2005.

In the present situation banks are continuing to face three major challenges. First, there remains a problem of nonperforming loans in the banking system, although substantial progress has been made in recent years. For example, in mid-2005 the FSA officially declared the bad-loan crisis to be over (*Financial Times*, May 25, 2005). Although the "crisis" atmosphere and urgency may be over, nonperforming loans still weigh down bank balance sheets. Signs of a recovering economy in 2005 should help on this front. Second, maintaining the 8 percent capital adequacy ratio—required by FSA to meet the international Basle accord—remains a challenge for most banks. Part of the 8 percent rule was satisfied using unrealized capital gains from banks' stock holdings. Recent losses in their stock portfolios, however, have had the reverse effect and have put additional pressure on banks' capital positions. (The analogy to the German banking system is discussed in detail in the end of the chapter.) Third, the proportion of deterred tax assets is becoming an increasingly large share of bank capital. As the provision to bad loans is conducted from profits after taxes, the taxes that are paid at the time of provisioning will be repaid by the government in case the loans turn out to be nonperforming ex post. This tax credit can be deducted from profits in the future (when the next income taxes are due). A major current problem of the banking system is that the majority of the banks capital consists of either direct capital injections from the government or deferred tax credit assets.

Ito and Harada (chapter 2) demonstrate that it is possible to monitor the magnitude of the banking problems in Japan using private market indicators, not just official statistics on nonperforming loans published by the FSA or balance sheet disclosures provided by the banks themselves. They show that institutional changes have made the "Japan premium" (the extra interest charged on international borrowing by Japanese banks) less useful as an indicator of the probability of banks defaulting on their obligations, but that credit derivative spreads are very informative. In this context, Ito and Harada demonstrate empirically that the bank fragility is still very much in evidence more than ten years since these problems first came to light in Japan.

1.4   Monetary Policy: Background and Institutions

1.4.1   Background

Monetary policy in Japan during the postwar period has undergone a number of distinct phases.[2] The first distinct phase of monetary was the Bretton Woods system of fixed exchange rates when Japan's real GDP was consistently growing at double-digit rates. The key policy anchor for almost twenty years in Japan, operating between 1950 and 1971, was the exchange rate peg at 360 yen per dollar. Monetary policy during this period, working together with active foreign exchange intervention and controls on international capital movements, was directed to maintaining the fixed exchange rate. A secondary objective—pursued only when it didn't conflict with the exchange rate peg—was managing aggregate demand through occasional changes in the official discount rate and borrowed reserves.

Policy was largely passive during the Bretton Woods phase in the sense that monetary policy changes were in large part directed to maintaining the fixed exchange rate peg. The instruments of policy, against a background of tightly regulated financial markets and a bank-dominated lending system, were primarily "window guidance" (i.e., quantitative limits on commercial bank lending), quantitative limits on Bank of Japan (BOJ) loans to commercial banks (i.e., discount loans), and changes in the discount rate (i.e., the interest rate charged for discount loans). The BOJ alternated between periods of tight and loose monetary policy depending on whether the balance of payments was in deficit or surplus (Ito 1992). "Fine-tuning" of aggregate demand was not a major issue—the Japanese economic miracle was in full swing and attempts at limiting aggregate demand growth to slow inflation and maintain the exchange rate peg were the main monetary policy concerns.

The breakup of the Bretton Woods exchange rate system in 1973, and the loss of the exchange rate anchor, presented a major challenge to the BOJ.[3] A period of high inflation (the "wild inflation") at this time—averaging about 16 percent during 1973 to 1975—was caused by a major oil shock, an episode of very simulative fiscal policy and, at least initially, an accommodative policy stance by the Bank. High inflation occurred in tandem with a sharp recession, and this confluence of events was in large part responsible for labor strife and social discord that proved disastrous for the economy and threaten the foundations of the Japanese model of economic cooperation.

To combat inflation and stabilize the economy, the BOJ embarked on a new "money-focused" monetary policy in the mid-1970s that emphasized steady moderate growth in the broad monetary aggregate (M2 + CDs) and predictability in the form of publicly announced monetary growth forecasts. Interbank interest rates were the primary operating instrument of policy, supported by occasional changes in the discount rate. With financial liberalization in the economy, and the development of financial markets, interest rates became the most important mechanism through which monetary policy actions were transmitted to the economy.

The primary emphasis of the money-focused policy was to control inflation, and it was enormously successful in doing so. The rate of growth of the monetary aggregates declined steadily, and inflation followed suit, from 1975 to 1979. Inflation declined from double-digit rates in 1974 and 1975 to only 3 percent by 1979. This policy, with some modifications, was largely in place from the mid-1970s until the mid-1990s.

The main policy challenge in the late 1980s was setting the course of policy in a highly unusual economic environment—low inflation by conventional measures such as the consumer price index combined with very rapid economic growth and an unprecedented boom in asset prices (e.g., equities, land, commercial real estate, and other assets). This remarkable period is now termed the "asset price bubble," of course, but the BOJ at the time observed low inflation and was reluctant to tighten policy. By May 1989, however, the BOJ finally acted. Policy was tightened over the subsequent fourteen months and, in five steps, the discount rate was eventually raised by 3.5 percentage points.

1.4.2   Steps to Ease Monetary Policy during the Great Stagnation[4]

The stock market collapsed in Japan in 1990 and land and real estate prices started to decline in 1991.[5] Following the fall in asset prices, the economy slowed, and weakness in the banking system began to emerge—the Great Stagnation had begun. Monetary policy during this period was changed several times, starting with a gradual reduction in interest rates using the conventional money-focused framework. As deflation and economic stagnation continued unabated, the BOJ was eventually forced to abandon its traditional approach to policy and introduced more radical measures such as "zero interest rate policy" (ZIRP) and "quantitative easing."

With signs of increasing weakness in the economy and the downward movement in asset prices, the BOJ began to lower interest rates in July 1991 with a 50 basis point decrease in the official discount rate. Over the next four years, as the economy continued to stagnate, the BOJ reduced the official discount rate eight more times until it stood at only 0.5 percent (September 1995) and the interbank interest rate (uncollateralized overnight call rate) was reduced in tandem. The target for the interbank interest rate, the primary operating instrument of the BOJ, stood at only 0.25 percent by late 1998.

February 12, 1999, marked the start of the zero interest rate policy (ZIRP) when the BOJ stated that it wanted to "encourage the uncollateralized overnight call rate to move as low as possible." The BOJ made it clear, however, that this was an extraordinary move and was done reluctantly. This policy lasted for eighteen months, and in August 2000 the BOJ lifted the ZIRP, claiming "Japan's economy has reached the stage where deflationary concern has been dispelled." The government opposed this move, however, pointing out that deflation had not abated and the economy was still weak.

Economic condition started to deteriorate as soon as the BOJ lifted the ZIRP with industrial production declining 5 percent over the subsequent four months. The BOJ was reluctant to publicly announce a

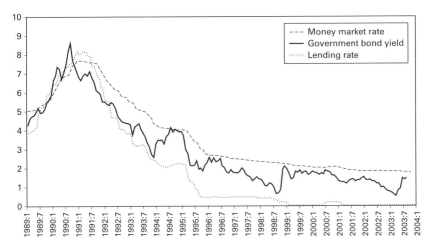

Figure 1.4
Interest rates in Japan. Source: IMF, *International Financial Statistics*.

return to the ZIRP, in part for political reasons, for by doing so would
be an acknowledgment that abandoning the policy had been a mistake.
However, the BOJ responded in other ways. In February 2001, the
Bank reduced the official discount rate, which had been constant at
0.50 percent since 1995, to 0.35 percent, and also created a "Lombard-
type" lending facility that provided funds to financial institutions at
the official discount rate. At the end of the month it lowered the discount rate to 0.25 percent and moved the overnight call rate effectively
to zero (0.15 percent).

Lending rates and government bond yields also declined to unprecedented low levels (figure 1.4). The low interest rates seen in Japan over
the past six years are unprecedented for any industrial country since
the 1930s.

In March 2001, the BOJ introduced its policy of "quantitative
easing," at the same time that the Bank lowered the interest rate to
zero (consisting of bank reserves and current account balances of
exempted institutions). At this time the BOJ began targeting the outstanding balance of banks' current accounts (consisting of required
and excess reserves of commercial banks). The BOJ initially announced
a target of around ¥5 trillion with the objective of pushing the overnight call rate to zero. The BOJ also announced that this procedure
would continue "until the consumer price index (excluding perishables, on a nationwide statistics) registers stably a zero percent or an

increase year on year." The target current account balance (held at the BOJ) was raised three times in 2001, twice in 2002, three times in 2003, and again in January 2004.

The BOJ also announced other policy measures at the time of quantitative easing. In particular, the BOJ gradually increased the amount of outright purchase of long-term government bonds over this period from to ¥400 trillion ¥1.2 trillion per month and, in late 2002, introduced a plan of buying ¥2 trillion of stocks held by banks over a two-year period. (The latter was not discussed in the context of monetary policy, in particular quantitative easing, but as a measure to improve the balance sheets of banks.)

1.4.3   Bank of Japan Institutional Changes, and the Political Economy of Monetary Policy

The late 1990s was a turbulent period for monetary policy in that (1) policy had limited effectiveness in stimulating the economy, (2) policy makers were operating in uncharted territory once interest rates fell to zero, (3) the BOJ was under intense political pressure to do more to ease policy, and (4) the BOJ underwent dramatic institutional changes. In particular, the legal foundation of the BOJ went through a major change in 1998 when a change in the central bank law gave it formal independence from the Ministry of Finance.

After the change in the central bank law granting it more independence, the BOJ immediately was at odds with the Ministry of Finance, and the government more generally. The BOJ stated that monetary policy alone could not create an economic recovery. Rather, the BOJ argued that structural reforms in the economy, and particularly in the banking system, were essential to restore economic growth. Their view was that the prolonged recession was a structural problem and Japan needed structural reforms for the economy to recover. Moreover the BOJ was very slow to accept that deflation was a overriding concern for monetary policy. Only when quantitative easing was introduced in early 2001, after several years of deflation, did the BOJ state that its objective was to continue the procedure "until the consumer price index (excluding perishables, on a nationwide statistics) registers stably a zero percent or an increase year on year." The BOJ denied that it was implementing inflation targeting, however, negating a potentially important announcement effect. The government meanwhile announced "antideflationary measures" and encouraged the BOJ to take "bold monetary policy," while the BOJ once again stressed the importance of structural reforms and the need to strengthen the financial system in order to stop deflation.

Governor Masaru Hayami completed the five-year term in March 2003, and Toshihiko Fukui became the new governor of the BOJ. The arrival of Governor Fukui initially did not immediately create an explicit break in the BOJ's policy, but overtime it became clear that a more expansionary stance would be followed. Most important, Governor Fukui clearly stated the BOJ would continue quantitative easing until deflation stopped.

1.4.4   How Stimulative Was BOJ Policy?

It is evident that the Bank of Japan tried to follow a more expansionary policy in the 1990s by successively lowering the call money (interbank) interest rates from the peak of 8.2 percent in March 1991 to virtually zero in March 1999.[6]

The difficultly, of course, is that growth in the broader money aggregate of M2 + CDs—the key monetary policy indicator—has been very low and the economy remains stagnated. The key monetary aggregate (M2 + CDs) rose at only about 1.5 to 2.0 percent (annualized rate) during 2003 and the first half of 2004 despite the monetary base growing at an annualized rate of over 14 percent during this period.[7] Conventional monetary policy instruments—interest rates and base money growth—have also been ineffective in stopping the Japanese deflation. Japanese deflation continued in 2003 and 2004 as the GDP deflator fell at an annual rate of about −2.5 percent and continued at this pace during the first half of 2005.[8] The Japanese price level has been declining by several measures since the mid-1990s.

The empirical evidence reported in Arai and Hoshi (chapter 6) suggests both a structural (downward) shift in the money multiplier in the late 1990s and a structural break in the monetary transmission mechanism. A major channel of the monetary transmission mechanism is through the banking system, and this channel has been stymied since 1995. Growth in the broad monetary aggregates—money created through the banking system—has been very weak, and there has been a sharp absolute decline in the amount of bank credit.

Moreover Fujii (chapter 8) demonstrates empirically that one means of combating deflation—through depreciation of the yen exchange rate—has lost much of its effectiveness.[9] In any case, the yen is not under pressure to depreciate but rather to appreciate. Müller-Plantenberg (chapter 9) provides empirical evidence that pressure on the yen to appreciate is likely to continue, since it is closely tied to the surplus in Japan's balance of payments. He concludes that depreciation of the yen exchange rate is not a viable option to ease deflation and pull the economy out of stagnation.

Arai and Hoshi argue that the BOJ, despite its attempts to employ conventional instruments of monetary policy to stimulate the economy, fell short in its efforts. In particular, they argue that the Bank could have expanded base money even further and made a firmer public commitment to combating deflation—perhaps by formally introducing an explicit positive inflation target for an extended period. Okina and Shiratsuka (chapter 7) document that that the ZIRP had the effect of flattening the yield curve at the short- and medium-term duration. They interpret this as evidence of market confidence that the BOJ was committed to the ZIRP and that it would continue for a sustained period. The question arises, however, why longer term rates were not affected by the BOJ's policy actions. Okina and Shiratsuka suggest that the ZIRP was not able to offset strong underlying deflationary pressures, and hence longer term rates proved insensitive to the BOJ policy stance. An alternative explanation, consistent with Hutchison (2004) and Arai and Hoshi (chapter 6), is that the BOJ was not as expansionary as it could have been and that a stronger institutional commitment to the ZIRP would have been possible.

1.5   Lessons for Advanced Economies

There is no exact analogy between the financial problems facing Japan and other industrial countries today. Research to date has drawn out the similarities of the Japanese experience with industrial countries during the Great Depression (Cargill et al. 2000; Hutchison 2004). This comparison only goes so far, however, since Japan's output performance, while disappointing, does not compare with the full-scale economic collapse of the 1930s.

What then are the lessons that may be applied to other industrial countries in a modern setting? One clear lesson from the Japanese experience, also highlighted in other chapters of this volume, is to make concerted efforts to avoid the onset of the problem or, at the least, take aggressive policy measures to move out of stagnation—recession, deflation, and banking sector dysfunction—before monetary and fiscal policies become paralyzed as effective stabilization instruments.

1.5.1   Is Germany Following in the Footsteps of Japan?

In terms of avoiding the onset of the problem, recent developments in the banking sector of Germany and elsewhere in Europe are worrisome. In this respect the Germany economy at present is reminiscent of the *beginning* of the banking crisis in Japan in the early 1990s. While the magnitude of the problem might differ in Japan in the early 1990s and Germany today, the timing between the fall in equity prices, collapse in credit, and emergence of a "capital crunch" and weak performance of the real economy is remarkably similar. Moreover both countries faced special situations with respect to the macroeconomic environment and to the regulatory characteristics of the banking system at these times. There is no indication at present that Germany has a weak bank supervisory structure and an emerging nonperforming loan problem of the sort or magnitude that characterized Japan in the early 1990s. On the other hand, Japan was in a stronger economic position in 1990—stronger real growth, a more profitable and competitive industrial sector, better fiscal balance, and exceptionally low unemployment—than Germany was in 2001. And the collapse of the Japanese economy was not only completely unexpected, but its weak performance has lasted for fifteen years. Might an already weak Germany economy follow the path of Japan into a Great Stagnation?

In both Japan and Germany lending booms ended in stock market crashes—1990 in Japan and 2001 in Germany—while banks aimed to achieve the international agreements on capital adequacy requirements (i.e., the Basle I and Basle II accords). Japanese as well as German Banks also hold substantial amounts of equity in nonbank firms in which they also have outstanding loans. As Ito and Sasaki (2002) points out, changes in stock prices in these banking systems—in contrast to other OECD countries—directly translate into fluctuations in banks' balance sheets and capital positions. A fall is stock prices therefore reduces the risk-based capital–ratio (Basle I), reduces the ability of banks to lend, and induces a "credit crunch."

Aggregate credit volume, shown in figures 1.5 and 1.6, has stagnated in Germany since the first quarter of 2001 and closely mirrors the

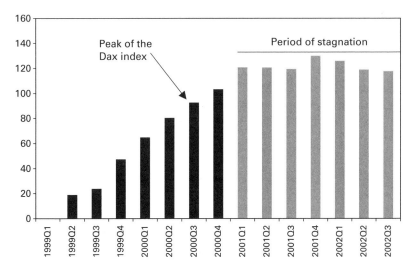

Figure 1.5
Bank credit in Germany.

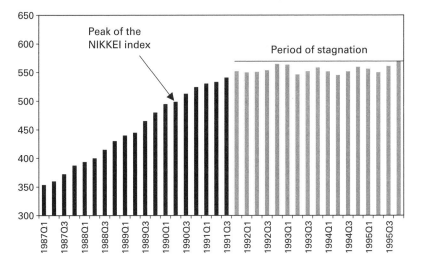

Figure 1.6
Bank credit in Japan. Shown are the accumulated changes of bank credit to domestic enterprises and economically independent individuals. Sources: Statistische Beihefte zum Monatsbericht, *2002, Bankenstatistik, I. Banken in Deutschland, 7. Kredite an inländische Unternehmen und Privatpersonen*, reihe 7 + 11, p. 34, and IMF, *International Financial Statistics.*

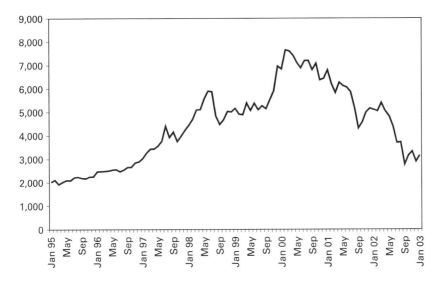

Figure 1.7
German stock market index, DAX.

development of credit in Japan at the beginning of the 1990s. In both Germany and Japan a stock market crash preceded the collapse in aggregate credit by between one and two years (figures 1.7 and 1.8). Moreover the decline in asset values was not a gradual incremental change but rather a large discrete fall that reduced value of the major aggregate stock indexes by about 60 percent in both of the two countries.

Falling stock prices do not only affect the banks directly via their balance sheets, but also indirectly reduce their ability to meet the required capital–ratios. In principle, there are two ways to increase the capital–ratio: either by raising additional capital or by reducing lending and shifting asset to "zero-risk-weight" government bonds. The indirect effect of the stock market crash is to make the former option more difficult. As the new issues of equity are highly correlated with the stock prices themselves in the two countries, the difficulty of raising new capital in the stock market makes the reduction of lending the only alternative for maintaining the required capital asset ratio.

Perhaps even more informative than the volume of aggregate as an indicator of a bank credit crunch is the development of an important substitute for bank credit–short-term commercial paper.[10] If changes

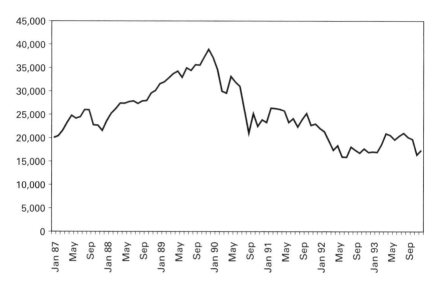

Figure 1.8
Japanese NIKKEI 225 index.

in aggregate credit were mainly due to changes in the *demand* for credit, then all substitutes of bank credit would be expected to display fairly similar fluctuations. In particular, commercial paper held and issued by firms should therefore also decline during an aggregate decline in the demand for credit. As figure 1.9 shows, however, there was no decline in commercial paper in Germany after aggregate credit began to stagnate. On the contrary, the beginning of the credit crunch and the structural discontinuity in aggregate lending coincide with a boom in alternative sources of financing. This suggests that *supply side* changes played an important role, adversely affecting firms in a credit crunch situation.

Similar developments occurred in Japan, although changes in the composition of external finance are less clear than in Germany. Net issues of commercial paper boomed in Japan since the introduction of the market in 1988, shown in figure 1.10, but the short time series makes the experience more difficult to interpret. Nonetheless, the pattern after the crash is strikingly similar to Germany.

Finally, figure 1.11 shows the results of the Tankan Survey in Japan, which asks firms about the perceived lending attitude of the banks. This question can be answered by each firm as "lax," "normal," or "right," and it is aggregated into an indicator that shows the percent-

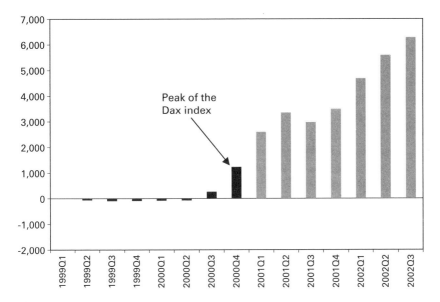

Figure 1.9
Commercial paper in Germany (increment of stocks since 1999). Shown are the accumulated changes of the net issuance of short-term commercial paper, up to four years. Source: Deutsche Bundesbank, Statistische Beihefte zum Monatsbericht, *Kapitalmarktstatistik, 2002.*

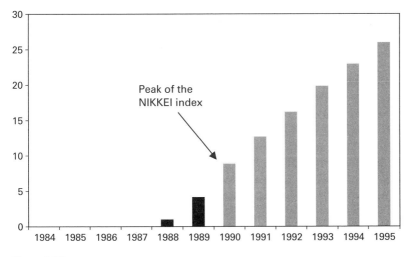

Figure 1.10
Commercial paper in Japan (increment of stocks since 1984). Shown are the accumulated changes of the net issuance of short-term commercial paper. Source: TANKAN, Short-term Economic Survey of All Enterprises in Japan.

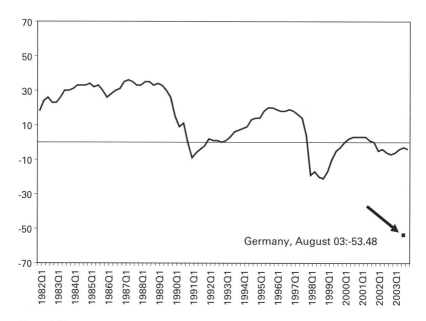

Figure 1.11
Lending attitudes of banks in Germany and Japan. In the TANKAN and IFO surveys, banks' attitudes toward lending are evaluated by firms on a scale ranging from "accommodating" to "severe." Sources: TANKAN, *Short-term Economic Survey of All Enterprises in Japan*, and Ifo Institut.

age of the firms that answer accordingly on a scale of 50 (accommodating) to −50 (severe). Cargill, Hutchison, and Ito (2000), Hutchison (2000), and others use this indicator to show that Japanese firms are strongly affected by the credit crunch even today. Only recently, however, has a comparable indicator become available in Germany. The Ifo Institute, a think tank that conducts regular surveys on the business climate in Germany, started asking the question about credit conditions in exactly the way as that used in Japan for the Tankan Survey.[11] The first results, from August 2003, show that Germany firms indeed perceive the recent slowdown in credit to be partly attributable to supply side factors (figure 1.11). In particular, it is telling that from the perspective of firms, the credit situation in Germany is *severe*.[12]

By contrast, the property price bubble that occurred in Japan in the 1980s is not evident in Germany. German property price increases have been relatively modest compared with other European countries (or with Japan in the 1980s), shown in figure 1.12, and do not indicate that a sharp correction is imminent.

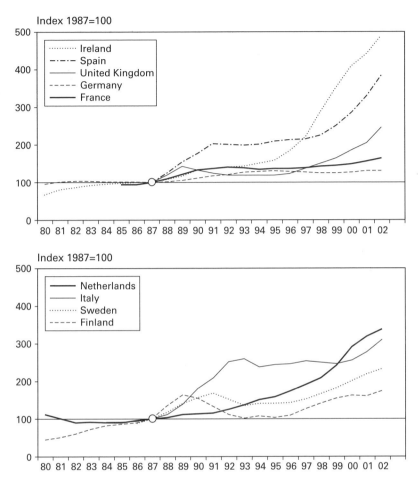

Figure 1.12
Housing prices in European countries. Index 1987 = 100. Sources: EEAG Report 2005.
Principal data from Deutsche Bundesbank, ECB, Nationwide Building Society (UK), and
Ifo Institut calculations.

1.5.2   Real Property Price Declines and Financial Distress: A Problem for Advanced Economies?

In the 1980s and 1990s a number of advanced economies experienced severe bank crises similar to that of Japan—Finland (1991–94), Italy (1990–94), Norway (1987–93), Portugal (1986–89), Sweden (1990–93), and the United States (1984–87). Japan's experience seems to fit with the general characterization of the causes of these banking crises in at least two ways (Hutchison and McDill 1999): macroeconomic instability (boom and bust cycles in asset prices and real output) and weakness in financial structure (financial liberalization, deposit guarantees, and weak supervision and regulation).

However, the slow response of the regulatory authorities to resolve the banking problems—and their subsequently long duration—makes Japan a very special case. Only in mid-2005, after a decade of banking problems, did Japan's Financial Services Agency declare that the bad-loan crisis was "officially" over (*Financial Times*, May 25, 2005). Most observers are not so sanguine, having heard overly optimistic statements by the Japanese Ministry of Finance many times before about the magnitude of bad loans in the banking system. Nonetheless, it is evident that banking problems in Japan are less severe today than just a few years ago, as the sector has gradually responded to widespread bank restructuring, government bailouts of the industry, and improvements in the overall economic environment.

As discussed above, a major factor in the banking crises in Japan and elsewhere has been a collapse in the property market. Property prices in Japan continue to decline—after a period of fifteen years—following the remarkable bubble in prices that occurred in the 1980s. Land prices in Tokyo today are less than a third of their peak value reached in 1990. Residential land prices nationwide (average) in Japan are less than half their peak value reached in 1990. It is also noteworthy that the most severe banking crises in the early 1990s were in Scandinavia—and these cases were directly related to price bubbles in the commercial and residential property markets. Residential property prices declined by 38 percent in Finland during 1989 to 93; the banking crisis onset was in 1991. Residential property prices in Sweden declined by 19 percent during 1991 to 93, and the onset of the banking crisis was in 1990. Similarly commercial property prices in the capital of Norway declined by over 40 percent during 1986 to 1991 and the banking crisis started around 1987.

A generalized increase in property prices in Europe, such as Ireland, Spain, and the Netherlands (figure 1.9), and other economies such as Australia and the United States, has raised the specter of future financial instability and other economic problems should there be a sharp housing price correction. If these price rises are unrelated to fundamentals, meaning price "bubbles," then at some point corrections will occur. Similarly, if the rapid rise in prices is related to extremely low interest rate levels—a fundamental determinant, but likely to be temporary— then a return to interest rates more in line with "normal" historical levels will also cause a sharp drop in real property prices. In either case sharp declines in property prices would lead to deterioration in household and bank balance sheets and could induce financial instability.

The lessons from Japan for other countries in these cases are clear. First, an adequate supervisory and regulatory structure should be in place to monitor and accurately measure bank performance and loan portfolios in a timely manner. Second, the authorities need to be able to act quickly and decisively if bank problems arise. This difference in response is perhaps most striking between Japan and Sweden. Japan responded very slowly, taking the better part of a decade to fully implement structural changes in the banking system. By contrast, Sweden in early 1990 acted quickly to the bank crisis—within several months—with far-reaching nationalizations, management changes, and public funds infusion. The result in Sweden was a rapid and low-cost solution of the banking problem. The outcome in Japan— combined with a number of other causal factors discussed above— was the Great Stagnation.

1.6 Conclusion

The problems in the financial system that emerged in the early 1990s were recognized too late and initially not acted upon. The political impasse slowing the restructuring of the banking system and reluctance by a newly independent Bank of Japan to act quickly and aggressively on monetary stimulus were just two of the hindrances to economic recovery. Adverse financial developments stood at the center of Japan's economic morass. These observations, and the Japanese experience generally, provide some important cautionary tales for other advanced economies.

Recent declines in asset prices and the collapse in bank credit in Germany present worrying signs, especially because the two countries share many of the same institutional characteristics in their financial structures. There is also the potential for sharp price declines in real property markets in many advanced economies, following a pattern similar to that seen in Japan over the past fifteen years. Recent jumps in property prices in Australia, Ireland, the Netherlands, Spain, the United Kingdom, the United States, and elsewhere present the worrisome prospect that a price bubble has formed and may be followed by sharp price declines. Substantial stress on the financial system and a drag on the real economy would likely occur if real property prices collapse in other advanced economies.

Japan has been faced with economic stagnation for fifteen years, partly because its financial system was initially vulnerable and partly because its government and central bank failed to take aggressive actions when problems first arose. Other advanced countries, starting from much worse economic circumstances than seen in Japan at the beginning of 1990, cannot afford to follow the same passive approach.

Each chapter in this book sheds light on a particular aspect of the financial problem facing Japan today, and highlights how the factor contributed to the onset and duration of the Great Stagnation. The first part of the book focuses on the financial system, and the second part emphasizes monetary policy and central banking issues. The third part of the book looks at international financial factors. All the chapters consider analytical as well as empirical perspectives to issues at hand. In addition they consider policy implications arising from the analysis and provide insights into ways that Japan can help move its economy forward. Taken as a whole, the contributions to this book demonstrate the key importance of financial factors in fostering robust economic growth and healthy economies. Unfortunately, they also demonstrate the enormous costs to the economy from having a dysfunctional financial system. Hopefully the chapter analyses in this book will provide a better understanding of the financial problems that have pulled down the Japanese economy for the past fifteen years and help other countries avoid the same fate.

Notes

1. In particular, the so-called Basel criterion sets the risk-based capital–asset ratio of banks doing substantial business internationally at 8 percent. Japan and Germany allow banks to apply 45 and 35 percent of equity unrealized capital gains, respectively, in calculating their capital base for this ratio.

2. See Cargill, Hutchison, and Ito (1997, 2001) for detailed reviews of Japanese monetary policy.

3. See Hutchison (1986) for a description of this policy and its introduction.

4. This subsection draws on the working paper version of Arai and Hoshi's chapter 6 in this volume. We thank them for allowing us to summarize their institutional background section.

5. The Nikkei stock price index reached 38,915 on the last business day of 1989. The index dropped to around 20,000 by October 1990 and below 15,000 by summer 1991. This represents a decline of more than 60 percent.

6. The collateralized overnight interest rate (end of month) was lowered from 0.34 in December 1998 to 0.22 in January 1999 and 0.07 in February 1999. The rate was raised to the 0.20 to 25 range for a few months in late 2000 and early 2001, but again lowered to below 0.01 for most of 2001 and through September 2004.

7. The monetary base (percent changes from a year earlier in average amounts outstanding) rose 25.7 percent in 2002, 16.4 percent in 2003, 13.8 percent in 2004Q1, and 6.1 percent in 2004Q2.

8. Nominal GDP rose 0.3 percent in 2003 and at a similar annual rate in the first half of 2004. Real GDP growth, by contrast, indicated some recovery of the economy in 2003 and early 2004. (2003 real GDP growth was 3.2 percent.)

9. He estimates that a 10 percent depreciation of the yen exchange rate led to roughly a 1 percent rise in the price level in Japan in the 1980s but only a 0.5 percent increase in the 1990s.

10. Kashyap, Stein, and Wilcox (1993) employ this indicator for the United States. They find that firms substitute commercial paper for bank credit after contractionary monetary policy of the Fed, and interpret this as evidence of the credit channel of monetary policy.

11. In particular, firms are asked whether they perceive the lending conditions of financial institutions to be "accommodative," "not so severe," or "severe."

12. Nearly 2000 firms that participated in the survey and, on a scale from −100 to +100, assigned an average value of −53 (midpoint between "not so severe" and "severe" credit condition) to this question. This value is lower than the values Japanese firms have given in any point in the past twenty years, which included a stock market crash and a major banking crisis. Country fixed effects probably play a role in the results, as cultural and historical influences are important when answering such a question and the differences in levels should not be overinterpreted.

References

Cargill, T., M. Hutchison, and T. Ito. 1998. *The Political Economy of Japanese Monetary Policy*. Cambridge: MIT Press.

Cargill, T., M. Hutchison, and T. Ito. 2000. *Financial Policy and Central Banking in Japan*. Cambridge: MIT Press.

Fischer, S. 2001. Comments on Knutter and Posen. *Brookings Papers on Economic Activity* 2: 161–66.

Hoshi, T., and T. Ito. 2004. Financial regulation in Japan: A sixth year review of the Financial Services Agency. *Journal of Financial Stability* 1: 229–43.

Hoshi, T., and A. Kashyap. 2001. *Corporate Finance and Governance in Japan: The Road to the Future.* Cambridge: MIT Press.

Hoshi, T., A. Kashyap, and D. Scharfstein. 1991. Corporate structure, liquidity and investment: Evidence from Japanese industrial groups. *Quarterly Journal of Economics* 106 (1): 33–60.

Hutchison, M. 2004. Deflation and stagnation in Japan: Collapse of the monetary transmission mechanism and echo from the 1930's. In R. Burdekin and P. Siklos, eds., *Fears of Deflation and the Role of Monetary Policy: Some Lessons and An Overview.* Cambridge: Cambridge University Press.

Ito, T. 1992. *The Japanese Economy.* Cambridge: MIT Press.

Ito, T., and Y. Sasaki. 2002. Impacts of the Basel capital standard on Japanese banks' behavior. *Journal of the Japanese and International Economics* 16: 372–97.

Kashyap, A., J. Stein, and D. Wilcox. 1993. Monetary policy and credit conditions: Evidence from the composition of external finance. *American Economic Review* 83 (1): 78–98.

Knutter, K., and A. Posen. 2001. The Great Recession: Lessons for macroeconomic policy from Japan. *Brookings Papers on Economic Activity* 2: 93–160.

Krugman, P. 1998. It's Baaack: Japan's slump and the return of the liquidity trap. *Brookings Papers on Economic Activity* 2: 137–205.

2

Bank Fragility in Japan, 1995 to 2003

Takatoshi Ito and Kimie Harada

2.1 Introduction

The objective of this chapter is to identify, analyze, and compare differnt indicators of bank fragility in order to determine which one best measures the financial health of the Japanese banks. Since the 1997 to 1998 crisis period the Japan premium—the premium charged to Japanese by Western interbank lenders—has been the most commonly used measure of Japanese bank fragility in the literature. During the 2001 to 2003 crisis period, however, the Japan premium did not rise substantially, as it did before, and therefore failed to measure Japanese bank fragility. Interviews with market participants revealed that Western banks now require Japanese banks to post cash collateral instead of paying a premium on for interbank loans. As a consequence the Japan premium no longer reflects the markets assessment of Japanese bank fragility.

In this chapter we propose that the credit derivative indicator is a better indicator of bank fragility. The credit derivative spread reflects pricing in the derivatives market for credit risk, which is a more direct measure of the markets assessment of the probability of a particular bank to fail. Although the credit derivative spread has been used in this capacity by market participants, it has not been used in the academic literature. In conclusion we hope to show that, starting in about the year 2000, the Japan premium no longer measured financial fragility in Japanese banks, and that a new measure—the credit derivative spread—more accurately reflects bank fragility in Japan.

Before going into detailed analysis of credit derivative spread, we want to put bank fragility in Japan into the perspective of the Japanese macroeconomic stagnation. Low growth, asset price collapse, bank failures, and deflation are only a few phenomena that characterize the so-called lost decade of Japan. The average growth rate from 1992 to 2002 was just about 1 percent. Many stock and land prices in the spring of 2003 were one-fourth to one-fifth of the peak in 1989 and 1990, and at about the same level of twenty years ago. The nominal GDP has been deflating since 1997, and it shrank by 5 percent in five years. Many financial institutions do not have sufficient core capital, and fragility in financial institutions makes expansion of bank loans less likely and puts a full recovery of the Japanese economy at risk. It is generally believed that bank fragility has been a drag on the Japanese economy.

As deflation has continued in the last eight years, many consumers and business executives have begun to expect that deflation will continue for some time. The long-term (ten-year) government bond yield fell significantly below 1 percent in 2002 to 2003, reflecting a pessimistic outlook on the economy and the expectation of continuing deflation in the future. Deflationary expectations constrain consumption and investment. Low domestic demand keeps the GDP gap high and forces prices to decline even further. Thus deflation feeds back on itself through deflationary expectations.

On the asset side, a sharp decline in asset prices has made many borrowers practically insolvent. Many consumers in owner-occupied housing with large mortgages have found themselves in severe relocation difficulties, as the their values of their houses (minus mortgages) turned negative. Corporations that took large bank loans to invest in real estates became insolvent on balance sheets and hurt their core businesses. Consequently they are unable to invest in housing or plants and machines, even at the zero interest rate. Banks that lent to these borrowers are suffering from nonperforming loans. With deflation, corporations' nominal earning power declines, and they find it difficult to service past debts. Deflation also means that past debts in real terms become larger and larger. Interested corporations have to sell assets to keep businesses going, or they must apply for protection from creditors and restructure their debt. With weak balance sheets, corporations cut prices to win customers. Asset price deflation causes further asset price deflation.

Now that the Japanese economy is trapped in a deflationary cycle, choosing monetary and fiscal policy measures to put the economy on the recovery track has been difficult. The short-term interest rate has been driven down to zero, but deflation means that the *real* interest rate is still positive. The zero bound limited the power of conventional monetary policy. Despite the zero bound of interest rate, monetary easing has continued in the last few years through quantitative easing. The monetary base increased by 20 to 30 percent in 2002, with ample liquidity injection, but there were no signs of an end to deflation as of the summer of 2003.

The banking system, burdened by large nonperforming loans and a weak capital base, is trying to retrench rather than expand. They have put assets into government securities rather than lending to corporations.

Fiscal policy has been applied to stimulate the economy, but repeated large packages in the last ten years raised the debt to GDP ratio to 140 percent, the worst among the G7. Even with the strong stimulus of 6 percent of GDP deficit financing, the GDP growth rate remains at around 1 percent. Further fiscal stimulus with deficit financing seems to be a sure way to cause a fiscal melt down sooner rather than later.

Many hypotheses have been put forward to explain the poor performance of the Japanese economy during the 1990s and well into the 2000s. But there is no doubt that one of the most important problems has been the weakness of the banking system. Without improving the health of the banking system, the chance of a strong recovery of the Japanese economy is remote. Conversely, unless corporations become profitable again and the problem of deflation is solved, nonperforming loans problem will not be subdued.

The solution to the troubled economy has to be multidimensional, mobilizing monetary, fiscal, and banking policies at the same time. This chapter focuses on the banking sector problem. In particular, in the chapter we will review market indicators of financial vulnerability from 1995 to 2003: the stock prices of banks, the so-called Japan premium, and the credit derivative spread. (For earlier studies on the Japanese financial sector problem, see Horiuchi 1999; Ueda 2000; Cargill, Hutchison and Ito 2000; Kashyap 2002.) This chapter is the first in the literature to analyze the characteristics of the credit derivative spread. We will argue that the Japan premium was a good indicator of bank vulnerability from 1997 to 1999, while the credit derivative spread became the indicator of choice after 2000.

The rest of the chapter consists of the following sections. Section 2.2 will briefly review the continuing saga of the financial crisis in Japan, starting from 1995. Section 2.3 describes and analyzes the daily series of the three indicators of bank vulnerability. In section 2.4 we look at nonperforming loans and other bank health indicators that are available from semi-annual bank balance sheets. Section 2.5 examines the

relationship between three indicators that are used to measure the
health of the Japanese banks. Section 2.6, concludes the chapter.

2.2   A Brief Review of Japan's Banking Crisis Using Marketwide Stock Price Index

The stock prices of Japanese commercial banks used to more closely
follow the marketwide stock price index. Before the bubble burst,
banking was an industry with few risks. Banks took deposits and lent
money to companies with a steady spread. They avoided too great a
fluctuation in profits, since deposit rates were regulated and there was
no hard competition with respect to lending rates. Because the weight
of capitalization of the banking sector was reasonably high, the banking sector index (BINDEX) and the overall stock price index (TOPIX)
behaved similarly for the purely statistical reason that a large part of
TOPIX was indeed banking.

Figure 2.1 shows the time series of TOPIX and BINDEX. The two
indexes moved closely together until the mid-1990s. However, in the
second half of 1995, these indexes started to deviate from each other.
The BINDEX surpassed TOPIX, the first obvious sign that the banking
sector was in serious trouble. The first sign of nonperforming loans

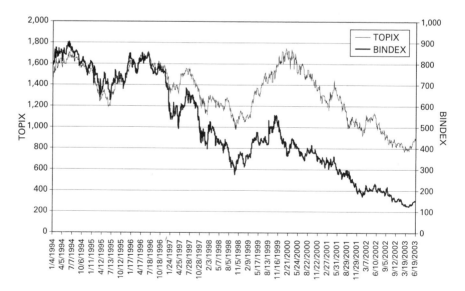

Figure 2.1
TOPIX (*left scale*) and bank index (*right scale*).

also emerged at this time and the first set of medium-size financial institutions failed in 1995. The deviation of BINDEX from TOPIX seemed to have widened in 1997 and 1998, and then again after 2000. These deviations also reflect the banking crisis of 1997 to 1998 and continued weakness of the banking sector after 2000. The relationship between the bank stock price index and the overall stock price index seems to be a good indicator of the market perception of the banking sector's financial soundness.

Bank stock prices declined in the mid- to late 1990s as the bank failures accumulated. The next set of figures show the behavior of BINDEX, the Nikkei 225, the stock price of failed banks, and the weighted average of the stock prices of banks with credit rating of Baa3 and Baa2 (in the case of Hyogo Bank, the weighted average of the stock prices with lower ratings was Baa2 and Baa1, since there were no banks with credit ratings of Baa3 at that time). Figure 2.2 shows the "before" and "after" of the failure of Hyogo Bank in August 1995, figure 2.3 shows the same information for the case of the failure of Hokkaido Takushoku Bank in November 1997, and figure 2.4 shows the experience of the Long-Term Credit Bank of Japan (LTCB) in 1998. When the Hyogo Bank failed, other bank's stock prices, even those with low credit ratings, did not show any effects compared to the over-all stock price index. The failure must have been judged by the market

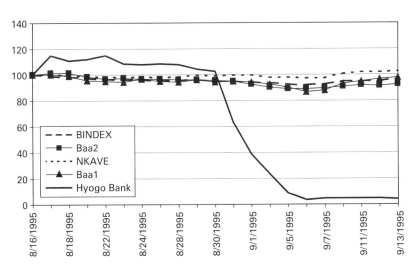

Figure 2.2
Hyogo Bank failure, August 30, 1995.

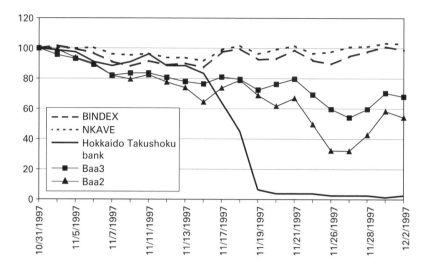

Figure 2.3
Hokkaido Takushoku Bank failure, November 17, 1997.

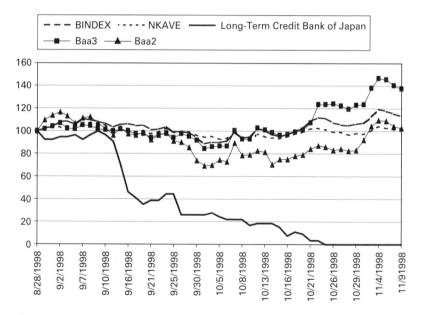

Figure 2.4
Nationalization of Long-term Credit Bank of Japan, October 23, 1998.

as an isolated event.[1] When Hokkaido Takushoku Bank failed in November 1997, other bank stock prices fell sharply, and weaker bank (Baa2, Baa3) stock prices fell more than other banks. There are two possible reasons for this. First, Hokkaido Takushoku Bank was a large bank with a nationwide branch network. It was much bigger than Hyogo Bank, so the impact to the industry was more serious. Second, by this time market participants seem to have recognized the fragility of the banking sector as a whole. Many had concerns about the possible spillover effect to other banks the emerged from the failure of the Hokkaido Takushoku Bank.[2] In contrast to the Hyogo Bank, or the Hokkaido Takushoku Bank, the case of the LTCB failure was not a surprise by the time it was announced. The Diet had debated how to deal with the failing bank, and they passed a law to nationalize the LTCB and to protect creditors and depositors of the bank. There was less concern about the spillover effects to other banks. The response of other bank's stock prices reflects this. Later in the year Nippon Credit Bank (NCB) was nationalized under the same scheme, and the reaction of other bank stocks was once again muted.

2.3   Three Market Indicators of Bank Fragility

2.3.1   Summary of Indicators

Banks are considered to be "fragile" when their capital base is deteriorated (a low capital–adequacy ratio), when a large portion of their loan is nonperforming (future losses), or when potential losses from other sources are apparent (exposures to interest rate risk, currency risk, loan guarantees, and others). However, the true position of each bank is hard to observe in a timely manner. For example, disclosure of nonperforming loans is conducted only twice in a year, and the self-assessment in classifying bad loans is often questioned. Market participants—interbank counterparties, stock market investors, and derivative speculators—are trying to estimate risks and to reflect those risks in pricing every minute of the trading day. They use all the information available at the time to assess the bank's vulnerabilities.

It is commonly observed that the fragility of Japanese banks is reflected in the three indicators: (1) the Japan Premium (for interbank borrowing), (2) the credit derivative (credit default swaps), and (3) bank stock prices. However, each indicator may depend on different (or a combinations of) risks. Perceptions of increased risk of default will raise indicators 1 and 2 and will lower indicator 3.

Looking at the credit derivatives is the most direct way to measure credit risk, since it is pricing the default probability. Stock prices reflect the residual values of company assets as well as the discounted sum of future profit streams. Even if the event of failure is remote, stock prices fluctuate due to changing prospects of profitability, reflecting both market- and economywide shocks as well as individual bank shocks. The Japan premium reflects the probability of interbank default. However, an interbank default may occur even for a solvent bank if, for some reason, a bank cannot obtain (dollar or yen) liquidity. On the other hand, interbank liability may be protected at the end, even in the event of bank failure. Interbank credits are considered to have a higher priority in repayments than equity stake holders.

The Japan premium entered the spot light as an indicator of Japanese banks' vulnerability in 1997 and 1998. Western banks required higher interest rates when Japanese banks wanted to borrow in the offshore interbank market. The premium was much higher in the US dollar interbank market than it was in the yen interbank market. This was interpreted to reflect the risk of Japanese banks not being able to obtain enough dollars to repay the interbank loans, as their soundness was questioned. In 1997 and 1998 Japanese banks had to pay nearly 100 bps (basis points) more than US and European banks to borrow dollars.

When the vulnerability of Japanese banks reappeared in 2001 and 2002, there was no significant increase in the LIBOR rate for Japanese banks, however. The magnitude of the Japan premium in 2001 and 2002 was at most 10 bps. However, the low Japan premium does not necessarily prove that the markets were less pessimistic about Japanese banks this time compared to the period 1997 to 1998. First, weaker banks disappeared from the data or exited from the market, either by withdrawing from the interbank market or by being merged with other healthier banks. Second, the remaining banks were required to put up cash collaterals to obtain interbank funds. Collaterals protect creditors from losses even in the event of counterparty (Japanese bank) failure. Third, even in the three cases of Japanese banks failure in 1997 and 1998, interbank obligations were repaid promptly. The Western banks could have remained optimistic about Japanese regulators' competence and willingness to carry out interbank obligations promptly.

2.3.2 *The Japan Premium*

The Japan premium is the difference between the rate at which an individual bank can borrow in the euro-dollar or euro-yen market and the market average rate (excluding Japan) measured on LIBOR euro-yen rates. In other words, the Japan premium is a premium imposed on Japanese banks' borrowing rate by US and European banks in the euro-dollar and euro-yen market. In Ito and Harada (2000) the Japan premium is defined as the difference between the euro-dollar TIBOR (the Tokyo interbank offered rate, or the euro-dollar interbank borrowing rate in Tokyo) and the euro-dollar LIBOR (the London interbank offered rate, or the euro-dollar interbank borrowing rate in London), since by construction, TIBOR reflects the rate among Japanese participants, while LIBOR reflects the rate changed by the Western banks on the Japanese banks.

It reflects counterparty risk based on the Western banks' belief that Japanese banks have a higher risk of default, especially in the dollar market. In particular, the dollar liquidity was a concern at the time of the 1997 and 1998 crises. In this chapter the Japan premium is defined as the difference between the interbank euro-yen rate quoted by Japanese banks and the average of the rate quoted by the non-Japanese banks in the euro-yen LIBOR samples. The reason we used the euro-yen rate rather than the euro-dollar rate is the availability of samples. There are very few banks to sample in the euro-dollar market.[3] We have learned from interviews with market participants that, since the spring of 1999, Japanese banks have paid cash collaterals in interbank transaction. Default risk is therefore no longer reflected in the Japan premium. We define the Japan premium in the following way:

$$JP_{it} = LIBOR3M_{it} - LIBOR3M_t,$$

where JP_{it} is the Japan premium of bank i, $LIBOR3M_{it}$ is the euro-yen three-month interbank rate quoted by bank i, and $LIBOR3M_t$ is the euro-yen three-month market rate at time t.

2.3.3 *Credit Derivatives*[4]

Credit derivatives are over-the-counter financial contracts that have payoffs contingent on the charges in the credit of a firm. This measure also reflects default risk, as the other indicators pointed out above.

Default risk of a firm, bonds, loans, or other credit contracts can be transferred by a credit derivative agreement. Total return swaps, credit default swaps, and credit-linked notes are the three major products in the market, where credit risks are traded. Among them, credit default swaps are the financial contracts that provide insurance against credit-related losses and are the most commonly traded product in the Japanese market. The basic structure of credit default swaps are described in the appendix at the end of this chapter.

Methodology
The average of offer and bid rates denominated in the US dollar market, posted by brokers, are used for the close of the Tokyo market. When both bid and offer rates are missing for day t, we used the data of day $t - 1$. When either a bid or an offer rate is missing, the value is substituted between observation days so that the bid and offer would not be reversed. When missing days continue for a couple of days, we eliminated the period form our samples. However, there were only few days missing since June 1998. Samples are from the Bank of Tokyo Mitsubishi (now Mitsubishi-Tokyo Financial Group), Fuji Bank, Daiichi Kangyo Bank, Industrial Bank of Japan (which now merged into Mizuho Financial Group), Sanwa Bank (later UFJ Holdings), Sumitomo Bank (later Sumitomo Mitsui Financial Group), and Sovereign Japan. The credit derivative spread reflecting Japanese bank's probability of default risk is

$$CDS_{it} = BANK_{it} - JAPANsovereign_t,$$

where CDS_{it} is the credit derivative spread of bank i, $BANK_{it}$ is credit default premium of bank i, and $JAPANsovereign_t$ is sovereign premium at time t. The credit derivative spread is the price of insurance versus the credit risk for a particular bank. It is calculated by the average of the insurance buyers' price and the insurance providers' price (bid and offer, which are in the form of basis points) minus the average measure of bid and offer of sovereign risk is calculated. This chapter's innovation is in using this calculation of the cost of risk as a direct measure of a bank's soundness.[5] The benchmarks of the credit derivatives market are available from July 2003 forward.[6] The norm for the Japan premium is zero, meaning in normal conditions Japanese banks should pay no more than other banks to borrow. This also applies to the norm for the CDS. It should be zero for an individual bank that is equal to a market benchmark that express the average premium of Japanese firms in Japanese credit derivatives market. During our sample period no benchmark was available, so sovereign Japan rates are used as a proxy for the market risk.

2.3.4   Bank Stock Prices

The individual bank stock price relative to the market is constructed by subtracting TOPIX from individual bank stock value. That is, the specific bank stock price is controlling for general stock price movements. The bank stock price movements and the market index are defined as the relative stock price index:

$$STOCK_{it} = \log(stock)_{it} - \log(TOPIX)_t,$$

where $STOCK_{it}$ is the log difference of the bank i's stock price and the market index $TOPIX_t$ at time t. The movement of specific bank stock prices relative to other sectors can be examined. The stock price indicator used is the difference between the rate of change of an individual bank stock and the rate of change of the TOPIX. The measure captures whether an individual bank's stock fell by more than the overall index, which may reflect the effect of risk.[7]

2.4   Deposits and Nonperforming Loans

In this section we look at different aspects of the Japanese financial system by focusing on less frequently available data. Deposits may show depositors' behavior in response to bank fragility if depositors are concerned about the possibility of bank failure. Although deposits are explicitly and implicitly protected, a bank failure may cause temporary inconvenience. Deposit shift is a strong signal that a bank is having a serious trouble. Another indicator of bank fragility is the bank's nonperforming loan ratio, as banks continued to struggle with nonperforming loans in the second half of the 1990s.

2.4.1   Changes in Deposits

The blanket deposit guarantees implemented in June of 1996 eroded market discipline among depositors and even provided incentives for them to disregard the risk of bank failure.

The Deposit Insurance Corporation (DIC) was established in 1971. DIC covers deposits in deposit taking institutions—commercial banks, long-term credit banks, trust banks, regional banks, shinkin banks, and credit cooperatives. There were no bank failures and no DIC payouts until in the beginning of the 1990s. In 1991, for the first time in the postwar period, resources from DIC were used to assist in the mergers of insolvent depository institutions. By 1995 DIC's reserves were almost exhausted. Despite the DIC resource constraint, the Ministry of Finance announced in 1996 that all bank deposits would be guaranteed until March 31, 2001, by using a special fund financed by government bonds (for details, see Cargill, Hutchison, and Ito 2000).

The Deposit Insurance Corporation Law was first revised in 1996 to expand its role in financial markets. The revised law allowed the DIC to pay off depositors and represent depositor interests in the bankruptcy proceedings. It also was allowed to purchase bank assets, thereby removing the payoff ceiling. For the enhanced role, the premium was raised from 0.012 to 0.084 percent in 1996 and to 0.094 percent in 2002. As it was revised (the law was revised three more times in 1998, 2000, and 2001), a series of strengthening measures were taken for the DIC. The blanket guarantee by the government until March 31, 2001, was extended by one year to March 31, 2002, and it prevented bank runs. However, it could have increased moral hazard among depositors.

Table 2.1 shows three categories of major banks and their deposit asset ratios, capital asset ratios, and bad loan asset ratios from September 1998 midyear to March 2001 that is the end of the fiscal year 2000. Depositors did respond to deposit insurance and the blanket guarantee. In April 2002 the blanket guarantee for time deposits accounts were lifted and replaced by regular deposit insurance (with a ceiling of 10 million yen). Depositors have fled from time deposit accounts to demand deposit accounts that were kept under the blanket guarantee. The total balance of time deposit accounts declined by 15 percent from July 2001 to July 2002, while demand deposits increased by 36 percent during the same period. It was also the case that larger banks collected more deposits than smaller banks. Thus for some events the loss or gain of deposits reveals the depositors' assessment of a banks' health. However, the frequency of such deposit shifts is very low, so that it is difficult to use deposits in a regression analysis.

2.4.2 Disclosed Nonperforming Loans

The Ministry of Finance officially redefined categories of nonperforming loans in January 1998. The amount under the new definition was

Table 2.1
Deposits and nonperforming loans

	1998 September	1999 March	1999 September	2000 March	2000 September	2001 March
Deposit/asset ratio						
DKB	58.4%	54.6%	59.7%	56.0%	59.5%	57.1%
Sakura Bank	60.5	62.5	65.5	62.3	62.4	61.7
Fuji Bank	59.2	50.5	52.5	51.5	53.3	49.8
Bank of Tokyo Mitsubishi	55.5	53.5	56.0	56.3	52.6	51.0
Sanwa Bank	57.0	56.5	61.4	61.6	59.9	58.8
Sumitomo Bank	53.5	51.1	52.9	52.7	52.0	46.1
Capital/asset ratio						
DKB	2.8	4.4	4.6	4.7	4.9	4.7
Sakura Bank	2.6	4.4	4.5	4.6	4.3	4.2
Fuji Bank	2.3	3.8	3.8	3.9	3.8	3.5
Bank of Tokyo Mitsubishi	2.5	3.5	3.6	3.8	3.9	3.2
Sanwa Bank	2.9	4.1	4.4	4.7	4.1	3.5
Sumitomo Bank	2.1	3.2	3.3	3.4	3.2	2.7
NPL/asset ratio						
DKB	1.7	4.4	3.9	3.5	3.1	3.3
Sakura Bank	3.1	3.6	3.6	3.4	3.3	2.8
Fuji Bank	3.3	3.1	2.8	2.7	2.7	2.5
Bank of Tokyo Mitsubishi	2.5	3.0	2.7	2.6	2.6	3.8
Sanwa Bank	2.8	2.9	3.1	2.9	2.7	2.7
Sumitomo Bank	2.7	4.3	3.9	4.1	4.3	2.7

far larger than the previous estimates. The new loan categories were based on possible risk assessment in addition to previous overdue and bankrupt borrowers by individual banks. This classification scheme has become the standard for assessing the nonperforming loan problem in Japan. The nonperforming loan data in table 2.1 are based on this classification.

Banks are required to classify their outstanding loans into four categories: class I consists of loans with little or no risk of default, class II consists of loans with some risk that requires monitoring, class III consists of loans that are unlikely to be repaid, and class IV consists of loans to bankrupt borrowers that are unrecoverable. There was, however, a question as to whether internal estimates of problem loans under the classification scheme would be accurate.

Despite their poor performance major banks continued paying dividends and the management remained the same. Many suspected that banks' classification of bad loans was questionable in some cases, and provisioning for nonperforming loans was inadequate. The suspicion was that banks wrote off bad loans and recognized new bad loans only as much as they could afford without jeopardizing the minimum profits to justify paying out shareholders. Consequently official nonperforming loans ratios are not a good indicator for bank fragility.

2.5   Correlation among Indicators

2.5.1   Daily Indicators for Each Bank

Although we cover the period from June 1998 to May 2003, there was a major change in the scenery of Japanese banking. After mergers of several banks and trust banks, the four major banking groups emerged. Because of the mergers some banks cannot be compared before and after these mergers. Therefore we break the sample into two: the First half from June 1998 to September 1999, and the second half from April 2001 to May 2003 (for analysis in subsections 2.5.2 and 2.5.3, the first period is June 1998 to September 1999 and the second period is April 2001 to September 2002).

Three indicators for each bank in our sample are shown in figure 2.5 (panels a–f) for the first period and figure 2.6 (panels a–d) for the second period. STOCK represents level of the banks stock price, LIBOR (in the figures, LIBOR is denoted by LIBOR3) is the Japan premium, the difference between the individual bank's euro-yen three-month interbank rate and the market rate, and CDS denotes the credit derivative spread, the credit default premium of bank i minus the sovereign premium. LIBOR in the figures is ten times larger than the original level for convenience.

In the first period the three indicators of all six banks show a similar time-series pattern. (1) The Japan premium (LIBOR) shows quite a dramatic increase from June to November 1998, and then decreased gradually in April 1999, just after the second round of capital injection. (2) Credit derivative spreads showed a similar pattern, but peaking slightly earlier than the LIBOR, and they also decreased more gradually than the LIBOR. (3) Stock prices had a sharp decline from June to

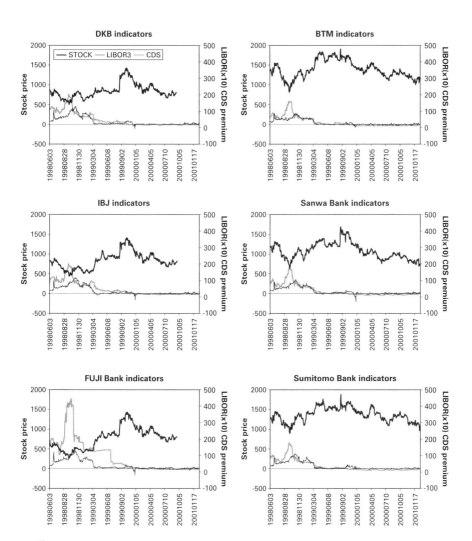

Figure 2.5
Correlations among first period indicators.

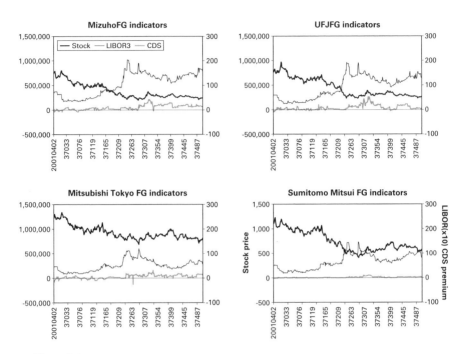

Figure 2.6
Correlations among second period indicators.

September or October 1998, and then started to recover. After April
1999 all indicators are more or less calm. (4) The Japan premium and
the CDS basically disappeared after April 1999, when the second capital injection was completed, except for Fuji, IBJ, and DKB, which had a
return of a high LIBOR in the summer and fall of 1999. The correlations
among the three indicators are fairly high between June 1998 and April
1999.

An examination of these three indicators reveals that the market had
discriminated based on the quality of these banks. The indicators tend
to agree on the health of individual banks:

1. In the first period, Fuji Bank was considered to be the riskiest
among the six. It had the highest LIBOR, the highest CDS, and the
largest stock price decline. In the second period, Mizuho was the worst
in terms of the stock price change, the peak level of LIBOR (tie with
UFJ), and the peak level of the CDS.

2. The market regarded the Bank of Tokyo Mitsubishi to be the strongest among the six in the first period and among the four in the second

period. For all of the three indicators, in both periods (except in the stock price decline in the first period), the Bank of Tokyo Mitsubishi is performing the best.

3. The timing of the peaks of LIBOR and CDS, and also the drop in stock prices tend to coincide for all banks. This indicates that a shock was common to the banking sector, but vulnerability and sensitivity to the shock was different among different banks.

In the second period the CDS increased markedly in December 2001 for all four financial institutions, Mizuho (spread of up to 204.5), Mitsubishi Tokyo (120), UFJ (192), and Mitsui Sumitomo (145.5). Stock prices had declined steadily from the spring of 2001 to February 2002. The degree of decline was the largest for the Mizuho (72.8 percent) and UFJ (70.1 percent), and the least for Mitsubishi Tokyo (43.5 percent).

The soundness evaluated by the markets did not change even after most major banks consolidated and formed four financial groups. The Bank of Tokyo Mitsubishi has been the best and Fuji, currently Mizuho, has been the riskiest, according to the market.[8] Bank consolidation did not seem to change fundamentally the financial health of merging banks.

Table 2.3 presents a statistical summary of the levels of STOCK, LIBOR, and CDS. The table reveals the following characteristics of the market indicator movements: the banks that had high CDS values (average and maximum) in either first or second period tended to have higher LIBOR (average and maximum) levels and the sharpest drop in stock prices ((maximum − minimum)/average). The averages of LIBOR and CDS were smaller in the second period except CDS of DKB and IBJ. The averages of CDS for DKB and IBJ were smaller before their merger, but CDS for two banks became larger in the second period. The ranges for the LIBOR and the CDS were much smaller in the second period than those in the first period. The standard deviations of the LIBOR became smaller in the second period, but standard deviations of the CDS did not change over time.

The worst bank in terms of the CDS average was the Fuji Bank in the first period, and the Mizuho in the second period. The Mizuho is a product of a three-way merger of Fuji, IBJ, and DKB. The three banks were the weaker three of the six in the first period. A merger of three weaker banks turned out to be one large weak bank, at least in the eyes of the market.

Table 2.2
Statistics summary

	STOCK				LIBOR peak		CDS peak		Credit rating 1999/4/1 FITCH
	Level March 31, 1997	Level lowest	Decline (%)	Lowest date	Level	Date	Level	Date	
First sample: Level (March 31, 1997), lowest level, and date									
DKB	1,310	505	−61.45	October 1, 1998	45.38	November 10, 1998	203	August 24, 1998	A
IBJ	1,260	440	−65.08	October 1, 1998	39.38	November 5, 1998	200.5	September 28, 1998	A−
Fuji Bank	1,430	259	−81.89	October 1, 1998	45.38	November 10, 1998	446.5	October 12, 1998	A
BTM	1,930	811	−57.98	October 1, 1998	27.97	June 30, 1998	160.5	September 29, 1998	A
Sanwa Bank	1,330	632	−52.48	October 2, 1998	35.25	November 5, 1998	183	October 5, 1998	A
Sumitomo Bank	1,470	894	−39.18	October 2, 1998	38.75	November 5, 1998	180.5	September 29, 1998	A
	Level April 2, 2001	Level, lowest in the spring 2002	Decline (%)	Lowest date	Level	Date	Level	Date	2001/4/1 FITCH
Second sample: Level (April 2, 2001), lowest level, and date									
Mizuho FG	736,000	200,000	−72.83	February 6, 2002	5.25	March 12, 2002	204.5	December 19, 2001	A
Mitsubishi Tokyo FG	1,220,000	689,000	−43.52	February 6, 2002	3.25	March 28, 2002	120	February 6, 2002	A+
UFJ FG	766,000	229,000	−70.10	April 5, 2001	5.25	December 19, 2001	192	December 19, 2001	A
SMFG	1,114	407	−63.46	February 6, 2002	4.25	March 12, 2002	145.5	February 5, 2002	A

Table 2.3
Statistics summary

	STOCK					LIBOR					CDS				
	Average	Range	Standard deviation	Minimum	Maximum	Average	Range	Standard deviation	Minimum	Maximum	Average	Range	Standard deviation	Minimum	Maximum
First half															
DKB	847	925	184	505	1,430	8.77	56.62	11.35	−11.25	45.37	52.65	189.50	43.59	13.50	203.00
IBJ	836	970	214	440	1,410	7.47	55.62	10.86	−16.25	39.37	52.61	187.50	43.61	13.00	200.50
Fuji Bank	772	1,171	271	259	1,430	9.83	61.62	11.69	−16.25	45.37	106.02	431.00	102.37	15.50	446.50
Bank of Tokyo Mitsubishi	1,419	1,099	224	811	1,910	4.99	35.38	7.93	−7.42	27.96	38.07	150.50	33.70	10.00	160.50
Sanwa Bank	1,116	1,053	198	632	1,685	6.67	56.50	9.24	−21.25	35.25	41.29	172.50	37.32	10.50	183.00
Sumitomo Bank	1,387	986	174	894	1,880	7.93	41.12	10.07	−2.37	38.75	40.96	170.00	36.72	10.50	180.50
Second half															
Mizuho FG	385,167	603,000	151,467	200,000	803,000	1.03	5.25	0.97	−1.00	4.25	104.56	170.25	46.84	34.25	204.50
Mitsubishi Tokyo FG	928,292	651,000	135,726	689,000	1,340,000	0.56	5.71	0.72	−2.46	3.25	50.71	103.00	23.26	17.00	120.00
UFJ FG	453,136	741,000	187,461	229,000	970,000	0.83	6.25	1.00	−1.00	5.25	91.73	167.25	45.47	24.75	192.00
SMFG	742	822	205	407	1,229	0.83	6.25	1.11	−1.00	5.25	66.32	127.25	31.28	18.25	145.50

Table 2.4
Correlation of (log(stock) − log(TOPIX)) and CDS

	Days	DKB (Mizuho)	IBJ (Mizuho)	Fuji (Mizuho)	BTM (MTFG)	Sanwa (UFJ)	Sumitomo (SMFG)
June 1998–September 1999	315	−0.588	−0.686	−0.76	−0.88	−0.763	−0.793
October 1999–September 2000	216	0.662	0.7	0.81	0.713	0.705	0.557
April 2001–September 2002	352	—	−0.807	—	−0.283	−0.903	−0.821

Table 2.5
Correlation of LIBOR and CDS

	Days	DKB (Mizuho)	IBJ (Mizuho)	Fuji (Mizuho)	BTM (MTFG)	Sanwa (UFJ)	Sumitomo (SMFG)
June 1998–September 1999	315	0.656	0.655	0.661	0.651	0.719	0.724
October 1999–September 2000	216	0.501	0.362	0.394	0.432	0.431	0.704
April 2001–September 2002	352	—	0.556	—	0.451	0.529	0.583

2.5.2   Correlation among Indicators

Next correlation coefficients among the three indicators are presented and interpreted. The correlation between stock prices and credit derivative spread are expected to be negative. This is confirmed during the period of bank turmoil. However, during the period of the IT bubble, from 1999 to the spring of 2000, stock prices of banks rose more than the market average, because banks hold a wide range of stocks, including IT-related stocks. The CDS, representing credit risk, behaved differently from stock price movements. The market participants in credit derivatives were not impressed by the stock price increases. The correlation of the LIBOR and the CDS is shown in table 2.5. The correlation is expected to be positive, as both represent the vulnerability of bank financial health. This prediction is confirmed in the data.

The correlation coefficient in the first period is uniformly higher than those in the second and third periods, suggesting that LIBOR represented better credit risk more in the first period. As suggested earlier in the chapter, LIBOR direct relationship to credit risk disappeared after April 1999—because either collaterals were used or counter-parties believed interbank liabilities would be honored even in the case of a bank failure.[9] Banks that are rated weak by credit rating agencies tended to have higher correlations in the second period, especially in relation to stock prices and credit derivative spread (-0.807 for Mizuho, -0.903 for UFJ, -0.821 for SMFG, and -0.283 for MTFG). Long-term credit ratings for Mizuho, UFJ, and SMFG were merely "A," whereas the rating of MTFG was "A+" at the end of March 2001 as shown in table 2.2.

2.5.3 Panel Analysis

A panel regression is conducted using the methods described below. The dependent variable is either one of the following:

$JP_{it} = LIBOR3M_{it} - LIBOR3M_t,$

$STOCK_{it} = \log(stock)_{it} - \log(TOPIX)_t.$

As an independent variables we used CDS, the call rate, and dummy variables defined as follows: $CDS_{it} = BANK_{it} - JAPANsovereign_t,$ Call = call rate, uncollateralized overnight.[10] For the interest rate we used daily observations of the overnight uncollateralized call rate. The data were taken from the Toyo Keizai Monthly Statistics (2003). Both CDS and Call are expected to correlate positively with the Japan premium and negatively with the STOCK. Call rate is a proxy for monetary policy so that an increase in call rate implies the tighter monetary policy and liquidity in the market, and it may lead to a higher probability of bank failures.

Tables 2.6, 2.7, and 2.8 report results of the panel analysis. The regression results of the OLS regression, with the fixed effect estimators, are reported in table 2.6. Stock prices are affected negatively by CDS, and the coefficient is statistically significant. The Japan premium tends to be higher when the CDS is higher, and the coefficient is also statistically significant for both of the periods. In equations (1) and (2), we examine whether CDS, as the fundamental default indicator, influences stock prices and the Japan premium. The impact of CDS on the Japan premium in the second period is about one-eighth of that in the first period (0.101 for the first half and 0.013 for the second half). This evidence is consistent with our conjecture that the Japan premium became very small in the second period, as a result of the collateral that was

Table 2.6
Panel analysis: Fixed effect

	JP (1)	STOCK (2)
First half variable		
CDS	0.101***	−0.0003***
	(0.00269)	(0.000032)
Call	21.858***	0.043***
	(1.02847)	(0.012244)
R^2	0.593	0.678
F_1	41.238***	72.446***
F_2	30.491***	1,058.4***
Second half variable		
CDS	0.013***	−0.001***
	(0.00064)	(0.000034)
Call	−4.839**	−0.113
	(2.24037)	(0.119043)
R^2	0.304	0.999
F_1	4.9716***	198.76***
F_2	10.803***	38,603***

Note: Asterisks ***, **, and * denote the significance at 1, 5, and 10 percent levels respectively.

used or because of the market participants believed that a failure does not imply default in the interbank market. The impact of CDS on STOCK increased (this is reflected in the larger coefficient in magnitude) in the second period (−0.0003 for the first half and −0.001 for the second half). In fact the magnitude of the coefficients of CDS in the second period is about four times as large as in the first period. Stock prices, representing profitability, are more sensitive to the default risk in the second period. Therefore, unlike the Japan premium, the default factor in stock prices has increased in the second period compared to the first period. The signs of the call rate are sometimes not consistent with our priors.

Table 2.7 and Table 2.8 present the results of the OLS regression, with pooled and random effect estimators, respectively. Most of the results of Table 2.6 carry over to tables 2.7 and 2.8. The sensitivity of stock prices to CDS is similar for the first sample period, and stock prices are negative (significantly) and smaller in the first period. The reaction of the Japan premium to CDS is also the same. It is positive and significant for the first and second period, and much smaller in the second half.

Table 2.7
Pooled OLS

	JP (1)	STOCK (2)
First half variable		
Intercept	−0.463***	−0.103***
	(0.1726)	(0.00328)
CDS	0.089***	−0.001***
	(0.0024)	(0.000046)
Call	24.485***	0.211***
	(1.0083)	(0.0192)
R^2	0.574	0.142
F Statistic	38.945***	480.57***
Second half variable		
Intercept	−0.248	2.398***
	(0.0540)	(0.0816)
CDS	0.011***	0.002***
	(0.00055)	(0.00083)
Call	−7.254***	5.842*
	(2.201)	(3.3251)
R^2	0.288	0.007
F Statistic	6.9767***	23,771***

Note: Asterisks ***, **, and * denote the significance at 1, 5, and 10 percent levels respectively.

An important finding is that the evidence that the Japan premium is becoming insensitive to CDS is robust against different methods of panel regression. The conventional wisdom, that the Japan premium lost its value as an indicator of default probability of Japanese banks, is therefore confirmed in our study. However, it is important to stress that the Japan premium and stock prices do react to changes in CDS, which is a direct measure of default probability of Japanese banks. Although the magnitude of CDS as well as that of the Japan premium was lower in 2001 and 2002, compared to in 1998, this does not necessarily mean that reputations of Japanese banks recovered. The stocks prices and the interbank markets did react to the changes in the pricing of default risk of Japanese banks, although with lower sensitivity.

2.6 Concluding Remarks

The banking sector has been a weak link in the Japanese economy. It is not at all clear whether the weak economy produced weak banking, or

Table 2.8
Panel analysis: Random effect

	JP (1)	STOCK (2)
First half variable		
Intercept	−0.738	−0.122***
	(0.6076)	(0.0416)
CDS	0.100***	−0.0003***
	(0.00267)	(0.000032)
Call	21.989***	0.043***
	(1.0264)	(0.012243)
R^2	0.572	0.137
Hausman test	3.9776**	3.3594*
Second half variable		
Intercept	−0.139*	2.733***
	(0.0841)	(0.6231)
CDS	0.013***	−0.001***
	(0.00063)	(0.000034)
Call	−5.221**	−0.113
	(2.23067)	(0.11904)
R^2	0.288	0.005
Hausman test	3.3645*	0.21855

Note: Asterisks ***, **, and * denote the significance at 1, 5, and 10 percent levels respectively.

vice versa, but any solution to the problem of stagnation must include decisive actions to address problems in the banking sector, including low capital ratios, high nonperforming loans ratios, low loan-deposit spreads, capital losses from stock holdings, and high deferred tax assets.

Market participants attempt to assess a true risk of bank failure, and to price transactions in the interbank market and the stock market accordingly. The credit derivative spread is the most direct measure of the market participants' perception of the risk of bank insolvency and default. The Japan premium also is also an indicator of default probability in the interbank market. However, in this case defaults can occur due to liquidity problems, in addition to insolvency problems. Stock prices of banks reflect not only default but also future profitability. Insolvency is only an extreme case of cumulative losses.

Credit derivative spreads became a better measure than the Japan premium for bank fragility in recent years. Higher credit derivative spreads tend to be associated with lower stock prices and a higher the

Japan premium. Various specifications of panel regressions produced similar results that confirm this conclusion. The negative correlation between credit derivative spread and stock prices, and the positive correlation between credit derivative spread and the Japan premium, tend to hold both in time series and in cross section. As we argue in the chapter, the Japan premium ceased to be a good indicator of bank fragility after 2000 because lenders started requiring Japanese banks to put up cash collateral, an unusual step for interbank transactions. When the credit derivative spread was used as the fundamental default indicator, its impact on the Japan premium was one-eighth of that in the earlier period, when the Japan premium was believed to be the best indicator of default probability. Although the change in the Japan premium still reflects market perceptions of the Japanese banks' vulnerability in obtaining liquidity, its sensitivity has declined substantially. Most of the results given by different methods of panel regressions point to the same conclusion, confirming our hypothesis, as well as market participants' belief.

Many argue that bank fragility contributed significantly to the stagnation of the Japanese economy. Quantifying the banks fragility has been difficult, however. The chapter compared three indicators of bank fragility, two of which are well known and have been used in the literature. Use of credit derivative spreads for measuring bank fragility presents a promising new research direction, and we propose it as a better measure of the soundness of the Japanese banking system.

Appendix: Credit Derivatives[11]

A credit default swap (CDS) is a bilateral contract in which the credit protection buyer pays a premium on a predetermined amount in exchange for a contingent payment from the credit protection seller to cover losses following a specified "credit event" on a specific asset, which is called reference asset. Credit events generally follow the definitions promulgated by the International Swaps and Derivatives Association (ISDA). Standard credit events are: failure to pay, bankruptcy, acceleration, repudiation or moratorium, and restructuring. (Restructuring is no longer marketed as a credit event in the Japanese credit derivatives market, following a 2001 controversy in the US market.) The premium, notional principal, reference asset, credit instrument, and credit events, as well as other terms of the contract, are negotiated between the protection buyer and the seller. A protection buyer pays the LIBOR plus a spread to a protection seller. The main protection sellers of CDS are foreign securities companies and hedge funds, not Japanese banks, while Japanese banks participate as protection buyer. A protection seller has to pay obligations to the protection buyer if a credit event occurs. Since the regular trading unit of a notional principal is 10 million dollars, multiplying 10 million dollars by a spread gives the payment that a protection buyer pays. This is settled by either bonds or in cash.

In Japan the credit derivatives market become active around the beginning of 1998, relatively late in comparison to other developed countries. The market is still immature, but it has advanced considerably since banks started relying on securitized products constructed with derivatives such as collateralized debt obligation (CDO) and collateralized loan obligations (CLO). These instruments let the banks shift credit risk off their balance sheets while keeping the loans themselves, which count as assets, on them (*Financial Times*, September 15, 2003). In a synthetic CDO a bank as a credit protection buyer takes default risk of a firm or a portfolio by a credit derivative. (For the relationship between synthetic CDO and credit derivatives, see FITCH's Structured Finance Reports or R&I, Japanese top rating agency's papers which are provided on their homepage. For the relationship between credit derivatives, as well as credit risk, and financial market behavior, see Neal 1996.)

An example is taken from Hull and White (2000). Suppose that two parties entered into a five-year credit default swap over Bank A on March 1, 2000. Assume that the notional principal was $100 million, and the buyer agreed to pay 90 basis points annually for protection against default by the reference entity. If Bank A (the reference entity) does not default (i.e., there is no credit event), the buyer receives no payoff and pays $900,000 on March 1 of each of the years 2001, 2002, 2003, 2004, and 2005. If a credit event occurs, a substantial payoff from the seller to the buyer is likely. Suppose that the buyer notifies the seller of a credit event (e.g., a failure of Bank A) on September 1, 2003 (halfway through the fourth year). If the contract specifies physical settlement, the buyer has the right to sell $100 million par value of the reference obligation (e.g., Bank A's debt instrument) for $100 million. If the contract requires a cash settlement, the calculation agent would poll dealers to determine the midmarket value of the reference obligation on a predesignated number of days after the credit event. If the value of the reference obligation proved to be $35 per $100 of par value, the cash payoff would be $65 million (65 percent of the notional principal of $100 million). In the case of either a physical or cash settlement, the buyer would be required to pay to the seller the amount of the annual payment accrued between March 1, 2003, and September 1, 2003 (approximately $450,000 or half the amount of annual payments of $900,000, since the credit event occurred halfway into 2003), but no further payments would be required.

Notes

We are grateful for the helpful discussions and insightful comments of Professor Jenny Corbett.

1. We examined other two bank failures in 1995 and 1996: Taiheiyo Bank and Hanwa Bank. These failures had similar characteristics, and no effect on other bank stock prices was observed.

2. In November 1997 the Sanyo Securities and the Yamaichi Securities also failed. A similar strong pattern of spillovers to bank stock prices are observed for these cases.

3. The euro-yen LIBOR is calculated by the British Bankers' Association as the average of the yen interbank offered rates. Although the premium in the dollar market was more pronounced than that in the euro-yen market, as described in Saito and Shiratsuka (2001), the euro-yen LIBOR is used in this chapter because throughout the sample period only one referenced Japanese bank was in the euro-dollar market, the Bank of Tokyo Mitsubishi. The referenced banks of the euro-yen LIBOR comprised sixteen banks, five of them being Japanese banks (the Bank of Tokyo Mitsubishi, Sumitomo Mitsui Banking Co., Mizuho Corporate Bank, UFJ Bank, and the Norinchukin Bank). Because the highest four and the lowest four banks are eliminated from the average calculation of the LIBOR, it can be safely assumed that the LIBOR is not influenced by the Japan premium.

4. We wish to acknowledge Mr. Saeki Nobukazu of Mitsubishi Tokyo Financial Group and Ms. Kawai Yuko of RP Tech for their kind help in answering our questions on the structure of the credit derivatives market.

5. Our sample period reflects the availability of the CDS data since the start of the market at the beginning of 1998. The premium of credit derivatives of sovereign Japan were not high compared with those of the other banks. Sovereign Japan usually traded below 50 bp while some banks' charged more than 300 bp.

6. Foreign securities companies started calculating credit derivative benchmarks for the first time in July 2003. The benchmark is "TRAC-X Japan (presently called iTraxx)." Several other benchmarks are available as of 2005.

7. Excess returns are not used as a measure of stock price movements because the difference between the stock prices can be negative for any one bank. BINDEX, the index of bank stock prices, is not used because each bank is huge and can capture most of the industry index.

8. The capital ratios of banks disclosed publicly were all above a critical mark of 8 percent and differences among banks were not significant. However, market participants did not seem to have trusted these numbers. The capital ratios in 2000 to 2003 included the deferred tax assets and capital introduced earlier by the government. Capital ratios adjusted for these elements were widely examined in the research publications of investment banks and securities firms as well as in academic work.

9. This information is obtained from the hearings we had with market participants. By "collaterals," we do not mean those under CSA (Collateral Support Annex, which is official transaction based on the regulation of ISDA). Rather, collaterals in this instance were part of a swap arrangement whereby for a certain period the Japanese yen was swapped by Japanese banks for the US dollar. The "Japanese premium" is hidden in the interest rates involved in this swap arrangement.

10. We have also examined panel regressions with a dummy variable that takes the value 1 before the second capital injection in March 1999, and zero after April 1999. The regression results were almost the same as the results presented in this chapter. The dummy variable was included to control for a possible regime change in bank financial soundness. However, the regression results are not shown because of the following econometric reason: As long as a dummy variable is used in the panel regression, the fixed effect model has a bias. For the level data that we use in our regression, the fixed effect model is preferable because it produces the same result as the panel regressions in differenced form.

11. From Hull and White (2000), FITCH (February 6, 2001), "Synthetic CDOs: A Growing Market for Credit Derivatives," R&I (June 30, 2003); "The Relationship between Ratings and Default: The Broad-Definition Default Ratio and the Rating Transition Matrix," Mitsubishi Tokyo Financial Group's presentation material, and *Financial Times* article (September 15, 2003).

References

Cargill, T., M. M. Hutchison, and T. Ito. 2000. *Financial Policy and Central Banking in Japan.* Cambridge: MIT Press.

Horiuchi, A. 1999. Financial fragility and recent developments in the Japanese safety net. In T. Bos and A. T. Fetherston, eds., *Advances in Pacific Basin Financial Markets*, vol. 3, Greenwich, CT: JAI Press, pp. 45–72.

Hull, J., and A. White. 2000. Valuing credit default swaps 1: No counterparty default risk. Mimeo.

Ito, T., and K. Harada. 2000. Japan premium and stock prices: Two mirrors of Japanese banking crises. NBER Working Paper 7997.

Kashyap, A. K. 2002. Sorting out Japan's financial crisis. NBER Working Paper 9384.

Neal, S. R. 1996. *Credit Derivatives: New Financial Institutions for Instruments for Controlling Credit Risk.* Kansas City: Federal Reserve Bank.

Ueda, K. 2000. Causes of Japan's banking problems in the 1990s. In T. Hoshi and H. Patrick, eds., *Crisis and Change in the Japanese Financial System.* Norwood, MA: Kluwer Academic, pp. 59–81.

Saito, M., and S. Shiratsuka. 2001. Financial crises as the failure of arbitrage: Implications for monetary policy. *Monetary and Economic Studies* (special issue): S239–70.

Toyo Keizai. 2003. Toyo Keizai Monthly Statistics.

3

Japan

G21, 042
628, 622
612
E44, 047
E20

Deposit Insurance, Regulatory Forbearance, and Economic Growth: Implications for the Japanese Banking Crisis

Robert Dekle and Kenneth Kletzer

3.1 Introduction

Since the early summer of 2003 Japan has started to recover from its long recession. With this recovery the nonperforming loan problems of the major banks appears to be abating. The major banks were helped by large injections of equity from the government and a recovering economy that boosted profits, allowing the major banks to increase their loan-loss reserves and capital–asset ratios. However, difficulties persist with the regional banks, which have been slow to write off their nonperforming loans. Moreover the growth prospects for the Japanese economy are still uncertain. The persistent difficulties facing the banking sector are a legacy of weak government financial regulation and prudential supervision. This chapter considers the possibility that public policy toward the financial system is the root cause of the Japanese banking and growth crisis.

A simple endogenous growth model with a bank-centered financial system is presented and solved for equilibrium in closed form. Three stylized facts about the Japanese financial system are incorporated into the assumptions of our model economy. Domestic investment is financed primarily by bank loans and equity issues. The government provides deposit insurance guarantees to the holders of domestic bank deposits. Prudential regulation and enforcement are weak, leading to rises in the nonperforming assets held by banks and the deposit insurance liability of the government over time. In our model, banks can accumulate nonperforming loans against deposit liabilities when the government guarantees deposits and fails to monitor additions to bank loan-loss reserves.

In the theoretical model, production displays constant returns to a single accumulable factor, capital, and is subject to idiosyncratic productivity shocks. Bank financing of investment by firms dominates direct lending by savers to firms. Bank loans are derived as constrained optimal contracts under standard information assumptions. Productivity shocks are independent across a continuum of firms, and there is no aggregate uncertainty. In equilibrium the asset portfolios of both banks and households (which hold both deposits and corporate equities) are perfectly diversified. Our analysis focuses on how public sector deposit guarantees and regulatory forbearance lead to the accumulation of nonperforming bank assets, deposit insurance liabilities, and falling growth rates in the endogenous growth model. We show how a banking crisis can evolve endogenously as investment and output growth decline in the absence of systemic shocks.

Weak prudential regulation is interpreted in our model as a failure of the government to enforce loan-loss reserve accumulations by banks against nonperforming corporate loans or, equivalently, the writing off of nonperforming assets. In this case banks are able to make dividend payments to their shareholders against the interest contracted on both performing and nonperforming assets. Deposit insurance allows the banks to transfer resources from the government to their shareholders. With regulatory forbearance, the output growth rate falls gradually in equilibrium as nonperforming bank loans grow in the economy. The longer the government fails to intervene, the lower the growth rate falls toward zero. If the government fails to intervene before a critical date, the banks will be unable to meet the deposit withdrawal demands of households for consumption leading to a banking crisis. A banking crisis arises endogenously under perfect foresight in our model.

The dynamics for output, consumption, and investment under regulatory forbearance and deposit insurance predicted by the model are compared to the recent experience of the Japanese economy. A feature of our model is that we can solve for the equity values of the banking sector and the nonbank corporation sector. A prediction special to our model is that the relative value of bank stocks to the aggregate stock market falls ahead of a banking crisis, while the value of corporate equity can be rising. The model also predicts a collapse in the market for collateral at the moment of the crisis. We also compare these implications to the data for Japan. Our empirical work begins with a test of the maintained hypothesis of perfect foresight. We compare the experience of Japan to the model and test the relationships in our model using structural vector autoregressions.

We argue that the data are consistent with our simple dynamic model that assumes that asset prices correctly reflect fundamentals. We show that for Japan's recent economic history, fundamentals are important in explaining Japanese stock returns and that the role of bubbles in affecting stock returns may be small or superfluous. We show that these results hold even for the 1980s, when Japanese equity prices skyrocketed. The data on Japanese macroeconomic aggregates, consumption, investment, and growth are also roughly consistent with the comparative dynamics of our model.

Given that Japanese stock prices roughly correspond to fundamentals, we test the theoretical prediction in our model that the ratio of the value of bank equities to the overall stock market declines before the crisis, and ahead of other macroeconomic aggregates. Our causality tests are consistent with our theory: the ratio of the value of bank equities to the overall stock market precedes the movement in other macroeconomic aggregates, for example, the investment–output ratio.

The model of banking crises presented here complements the traditional view of Japan's banking crisis in the 1990s. The traditional view places blame for Japan's banking crisis on the manner of financial sector deregulation initiated in the middle of the 1970s.[1] In that view, as alternative financial instruments were introduced, large, internationally oriented firms began to raise funds directly in the domestic and foreign bond markets. As the large banks started to lose their highest quality corporate borrowers in the late 1980s, they began lending to smaller firms. When in the late 1980s Japan's asset-market boom collapsed, the Japanese economy began its prolonged stagnation, and the nonperforming assets of the banking system rose rapidly. Despite the rise in direct borrowing by major corporations, Japanese financial intermediation is dominated by commercial banks. Cargill, Hutchison, and Ito (1997) and Cargill (1999) emphasize, as we do, the importance of explicit and implicit deposit guarantees and of regulatory forbearance in the creation of the crisis. This chapter contributes a formal model of credit market dynamics that complements our earlier paper, Dekle and Kletzer (2003).[2]

Our model is one of the few general equilibrium models that analyze the Japanese financial and growth crisis of the 1990s. Banking crises affect capital accumulation and economic growth, whereas low growth rates exacerbate banking crises. Because of the endogenous mutual relationship between banking crises and growth, partial equilibrium models are severely limited. Three other papers analyze the Japanese economy in the 1990s using a general equilibrium framework. Hayashi and Prescott (2002) present and calibrate a real business cycle model for Japan to show how the decrease in labor supply and total factor productivity growth can account for the growth slump of the 1990s. Hayashi and Prescott argue that credit constraints were not important for reducing investment rates, but they also suggest that weakness of the banking sector might have played a role in lowering the productivity of investment. As in our model, Barseghyan (2002) emphasizes delays in government bailouts of the banking system in an overlapping generations model. In his model, when the government delays bailouts, banks use new deposits to meet the withdrawals by old depositors, as in a Ponzi scheme. Barseghyan calibrates his model to Japanese data and finds a favorable comparison to Japanese growth in the 1990s. The third paper is our earlier model (Dekle and Kletzer 2003) of endogenous banking crises, which presents a somewhat different model and empirical analysis for Japan.

The next section discusses the stylized facts about the Japanese financial system that motivate the simple assumptions of our analysis. Sections 3.3, 3.4, and 3.5 present the endogenous growth model, analyze the effects of weak prudential supervision in the presence of deposit insurance, and show how a banking crisis can occur in turn under perfect foresight. Sections 3.6 and 3.7 show how our model is consistent with the data and present some econometric analysis supporting the main implications of our model. Section 3.8 concludes.

3.2   Three Characteristics of the Financial System of Japan

The theoretical model of this chapter incorporates three characteristics of the Japanese financial system into its assumptions. These assumptions are central to the dynamics of economic growth and domestic financial markets before and after a banking crisis that are derived in the model. The first is the predominance of commercial bank intermediation of corporate finance, modeled as arising from the informational advantage of banks over other lenders. The second is the prospect of government-provided deposit insurance, or public sector bailouts of the domestic banking sector. The third is supervisory forbearance and the absence of effective prudential regulation of the banking sector. In this section we review these three aspects of the financial system of Japan to support the use of our assumptions.

Bank loans comprise an exceptionally large share of Japanese corporate and other firm debt by international comparison. Typically only large, well-capitalized firms have been able to funds on bond markets. Small- and medium-sized domestic firms continued to rely on bank financing through the 1990s (see Hoshi and Kayshap 2001). The fraction of small- and medium-sized business loans to total loans increased from 73 percent over the period 1977 to 1986 to 78 percent over the period 1987 to 1990, as reported by Ogawa and Kitasaka (2000). This reliance on bank financing was especially prevalent for small- and medium-sized firms in the service, construction and real estate sectors. Between 1987 and 1990, while bank loans to the manufacturing sector increased by 1 percent, loans to the service, construction, and real estate sectors rose by 14, 7, and 18 percent, respectively (Ogawa and Kitasaka 2000).

Japanese bank deposits have been implicitly guaranteed by the government, traditionally through the "convoy system," or "purchase and assumption," rescue, in which a healthy bank is encouraged by the government to provide assistance to a troubled one. Recently, however, the government has provided implicit guarantees through direct injections of capital to troubled banks.

The government's system of explicit and implicit guarantees implies that no deposits, large or small, were ever at risk in postwar Japan. Before 1991, the official policy was that there would be "no failures of financial institutions." Since 1991, banks have failed; for example, from 1991 to 1995, eleven small banks were formally declared insolvent. However, the guarantees meant that no depositor ever lost any funds.

In our model the failure of authorities to monitor the accumulation of nonperforming assets and holding of loan-loss reserves by banks until the deposit insurance liability of the government has reached either a critical level leads to financial crises and falling GDP growth.

Awareness of the problems with the existing bank supervisory regime led the government to move financial supervision and examination from the Ministry of Finance to the new independent Financial Supervisory Agency in 1996. The government also tried to replace discretion of supervisors by a rule-based scheme, the Prompt Corrective Action system, in 1998. Under Prompt Corrective Action, regulators are required to intervene quickly at poorly capitalized banks. For example, regulators are required to close a bank if the bank's capital–asset ratio falls below zero.

Initially these institutional changes led to improvements in prudential supervision and enforcement. The Financial Supervisory Agency
moved to examine the books of all banks, which led to the immediate
closure of five smaller banks. However, as the immediate financial
crisis subsided, the regulations were redefined to make them less
restrictive. The introduction of the Prompt Corrective Action policy
was delayed a year. Accounting standards were changed so that banks
could make their financial statements appear better than they were.
Some banks that should have been closed under the statutes were
allowed to continue operating because the closure of these banks
would add to local unemployment.

3.3   A Model of Growth and Banking Crises

This section presents a general equilibrium model of endogenous
growth with bank-intermediated investment to show how publicly
funded deposit insurance and prudential supervisory or regulatory
failures combine to affect investment and output growth. The model
differs from our earlier model (Dekle and Kletzer 2003) in a number of
respects. There are two important innovations in this chapter. The first
is that we use an open economy with a banking sector that faces competition for deposits at a given real rate of interest. The second is the
production structure. Together these lead to a significant qualitative
difference in the dynamics leading up to a bank liquidity crisis.

3.3.1   Production and Bank Lending

Output is produced from capital alone using a constant returns to scale
technology with stochastic productivity. There is a continuum of firms,
indexed across the unit interval, and productivity shocks are independent and identically distributed across firms and over time for each
firm. The net output for a typical firm is given by

$$y_t^j = \alpha_t^j k_t^j,$$

where y_t^j, k_t^j, and α_t^j denote output, the capital stock, and the realized
net productivity for firm j at time t, respectively. There is no depreciation for simplicity, and investment is assumed to be irreversible (this
assumption is used later). For simplicity, productivity realizations, α_t,
are distributed uniformly over the common interval, $0 \leq \alpha_t \leq \alpha$. With
a continuum of firms, aggregate output is not stochastic and is given by

$$y_t = \frac{\alpha}{2}k_t,$$

where y_t and k_t denote aggregate net output and the capital stock at time t, respectively.

Savings is undertaken by a continuum of households who acquire bank deposits and hold equities in firms and banks. All households are identical and infinitely lived so that there is no trade in firm or bank equity in equilibrium. Capital accumulation is debt-financed, and any firm income net of interest is immediately paid in dividends to firm shareholders. A standard informational asymmetry motivates the predominance of bank lending over direct lending by households and generates conventional loan contracts. Firms observe their productivities in each period at no cost, but lenders can only observe it at a positive cost. Banks are able to make these observations at a lower cost than households so all lending is intermediated by banks in equilibrium. Townsend (1979) and Diamond (1984) show that the standard loan contract is optimal in this context (in a static setting).[3] For algebraic simplicity, the costs of observing a corporate borrower's output is proportional to firm's capital (e.g., auditing costs rise with firm size).

The expected net return for a one-period bank loan to a firm is given by

$$\frac{1}{\alpha}\int_{r^\ell}^{\alpha}\ell_t^j(1+r_t^\ell)\,d\alpha_t + \frac{1}{\alpha}\int_0^{r^\ell}(1+\alpha_t-\gamma)k_t^j\,d\alpha_t - (1+r)\ell_t^j, \tag{1}$$

where r_t^ℓ is the loan rate of interest, r is the deposit rate of interest, γ represents auditing costs and ℓ_t is the size of the loan. Under our assumptions, if a firm has no accumulated unpaid past net interest, the firm's debt, ℓ_t, just equals its capital stock, k_t. The equilibrium rate of interest, r', charged to a single-period loan in a competitive market in this case is given by

$$r'\left(1 - \frac{1}{2}\frac{r'}{\alpha} - \frac{\gamma}{\alpha}\right) = r. \tag{2}$$

With positive probability, r'/α, the earnings of the firm will fall short of the net interest on the loan in period t. The loss to the bank is accounted for by the interest rate spread, $r' - r$, in equation (2).

The interest rate that maximizes a lender's expected return in this economy is $\alpha - \gamma$ (per unit of firm capital). The interest charged can reach this level if banks rollover unpaid interest obligations into longer term loans increasing interest charges as a share of firm revenues. Under perfect competition, the initial interest rate charged to firms would be less than r'. However, rolling over unpaid interest in this economy increases the future probability that firm revenues will be less than interest costs. This means that the probability that banks bear and pass on intermediation costs, γk, rises with rollovers. Therefore, in present value, intermediation costs are minimized under single-period contracts.[4] Since these are deadweight costs (passed on to firms in interest with competitive banking), short-term contracts charging an interest rate equal to r' are efficient in this economy. Additional institutional assumptions could be made to get long-term contracts, but the only effect on the balanced growth path of this economy would be quantitative, the interest rate would be $\alpha - \gamma$ rather than r'. We use the constrained optimal contract for this standard model.

The aggregate dynamics of the economy are easy to analyze because there is no aggregate uncertainty with a continuum of firms. The portfolio of each of a finite number of banks is fully diversified with the continuum of firms drawing productivity realizations from independent and identical distributions. In the balanced growth path, the flow of aggregate net output equals $[(\alpha/2) - (\gamma r'/\alpha)]k_t$, and the capital stock evolves according to the resource constraint,

$$\dot{k} = \left(\frac{\alpha}{2} - \frac{\gamma r'}{\alpha}\right)k_t - c_t,$$

where c_t is aggregate consumption. Aggregate flow profits of the corporate sector are given by

$$d_t = \frac{1}{\alpha}\int_{\hat{r}}^{\alpha}(\tilde{\alpha} - r')k_t\,d\tilde{\alpha} = \frac{(\alpha - r')^2}{2\alpha}k_t,$$

which is paid in dividends to households for holding shares of corporate equities.

3.3.2 Household Consumption and Saving

The representative household seeks to maximize its utility,

$$U_t = \int_t^{\infty}\frac{c_s^{1-\sigma}}{1-\sigma}e^{-\rho(s-t)}\,ds,$$

with respect to its consumption plan given its flow budget identity,

$$\dot{a} = ra_t + d_t + x_t - c_t,$$

the conventional solvency constraint,

$$\lim_{s \to \infty} e^{-r(s-t)} a_s \geq 0,$$

and initial deposit holdings, a_t. x_t represents bank dividends. The number of firms and banks is fixed so that equity shares cannot be accumulated in the aggregate, hence by the representative household in equilibrium.

Households completely avoid any corporate dividend income risk by holding a fully diversified portfolio of corporate stocks with a continuum of firms realizing independent productivity shocks. In equilibrium at each date, a proportion $(1 - r'/\alpha)$ of each bank's loans pay interest r' per unit of capital, and a proportion r'/α pay average interest $(1/2\alpha)r'^2$. In addition the flow cost of bank intermediation is equal to the current auditing costs, $(r'/\alpha)\gamma k_t$.

The assumptions that allow complete diversification of productivity risk by households as shareholders and depositors allow us to show how inadequate bank monitoring and prudential regulation with deposit insurance affect investment, output growth, and asset prices. Incomplete risk diversification opportunities or incentives, as emphasized in the agency models proposed by Dekle and Kletzer (2002a, b), could raise the social costs created by inadequate supervision and regulation of intermediaries or firms.[5]

3.3.3   Benchmark Equilibrium

We take the case where the government requires banks to hold reserves against any loan losses they accumulate and enforces this regulation continuously as a benchmark. In equilibrium the losses of banks on a proportion r'/α of the total loan portfolio, equal to

$$\left(\frac{1}{2\alpha} r'^2 + \frac{r'}{\alpha} \gamma - r \frac{r'}{\alpha} \right) k_t,$$

are offset by surpluses on a proportion $(\alpha - r')/\alpha$ given by

$$\frac{\alpha - r'}{\alpha} (r' - r) k_t.$$

With continuous loan-loss reserving enforced, the banks' profits on some loans just match write-offs on other loans. The profits of each bank are always zero, and the value of bank equity is always zero. The government accumulates no liabilities associated with deposit insurance or other guarantees to the banking system, implicit or explicit.

The equilibrium path for the economy is found by maximizing representative household utility with respect to the consumption plan given the aggregate resource constraint,

$$\dot{k} = \left(\frac{\alpha}{2} - \frac{\gamma r'}{\alpha}\right)k_t - c_t, \tag{3}$$

and the predetermined capital stock under perfect foresight. The parameter restriction,

$$\left(\frac{\alpha}{2} - \frac{\gamma \hat{r}}{\alpha}\right) - \left(\frac{r - \rho}{\sigma}\right) > 0,$$

ensures the existence of a solution. Under perfect foresight, equilibrium consumption is given by

$$c_t = \left(\frac{\alpha}{2} - \frac{\gamma r'}{\alpha} - \frac{r - \rho}{\sigma}\right)k_t, \tag{4}$$

and the equilibrium growth rate of consumption, capital and output is

$$\frac{\dot{c}}{c} = \frac{\dot{k}}{k} = \frac{\dot{y}}{y} = \frac{r - \rho}{\sigma}. \tag{5}$$

The growth rate remains constant over the entire infinite horizon. In this case net household savings just equals economywide capital accumulation,

$$s_t = \frac{r - \rho}{\sigma}k_t = \dot{k}_t. \tag{6}$$

Imposing the assumption that $r > \rho$ allows positive investment and output growth. Note that the gross earnings on household bank deposits equal rk_t, and net withdrawals from bank deposits equal $[r - (r - \rho)/\sigma]k_t$. Bank deposits, a, grow at the same rate as output, $(r - \rho)/\sigma$.

The aggregate value of corporate equity is given by the present value of dividends, discounted at the household's opportunity rate of interest,

$$V_t^f = \int_t^\infty d_s e^{-r(s-t)}\,ds = \int_t^\infty \frac{(\alpha - r')^2}{2\alpha} k_s e^{-r(s-t)}\,ds$$

$$= \frac{(\alpha - r')^2}{2\alpha} k_t \left(r - \frac{r - \rho}{\sigma} \right)^{-1}, \tag{7}$$

which rises proportionally with the capital stock and output.

3.4   Growth with Deposit Guarantees and Regulatory Forbearance

To analyze the effects of weak prudential supervision in the presence of publicly funded deposit insurance, we assume that government regulators do not enforce loan loss reserve requirements. They do not audit the balance sheets of the banks and require reserving against accumulated losses on individual loans. This allows banks to keep uncollected interest on their balance sheets as performing assets without using the profits earned on other loans to cover the losses. By doing so, the banks can pay dividends from current loan profits without subtracting current loan losses.

If the liability of shareholders to the holders of bank deposits is limited, banks have an incentive to accumulate nonperforming assets and pay out dividends from current loan income. When a bank becomes insolvent, shareholders are spared from liability, so the value of shareholder equity is bounded from below by zero. As a bank accumulates losses as nonperforming loans without also saving the surplus, $r' - r$, from repaid loans, these losses will be borne eventually by shareholders, depositors, or the government through a depositor bailout. If depositors bear the cost and cannot monitor the bank's accounts,[6] then the rate of interest received by depositors will be driven down and the growth rate of the economy declines.

In our case the government provides deposit insurance but does not audit the bank loan portfolios or monitor loan-loss reserves. By accumulating nonperforming assets and paying dividends equal to the loan income from performing assets, a bank accumulates a deposit insurance claim against the government. The liabilities of the banking system equal the total deposits of savers, and its assets equal the sum of the corporate sector capital stock and the total deposit insurance claim against the government. That is, the accumulated loan losses are assets, but they are claims against the government's deposit insurance plan rather than against the corporate sector. The deposit insurance liability of the government is a public debt held by the banks. The assets of the banking sector, which are equal to its deposit liabilities, are the sum of k_t and government debt, b_t. Total household interest-bearing assets equal bank deposits, so $a_t = k_t + b_t$ in equilibrium. The deposit insurance claim of the banks against deposits contrasts with bonds or other forms of public debt issued by the treasury. The deposit insurance liability of the government is created endogenously by the banking sector.

So that banks pay positive dividends in equilibrium, some form of imperfect competition in banking needs to be introduced. This model does not require us to be very articulate about imperfect competition. For simplicity, we let banks compete in individual initial loans but pay out dividends against individual loan profits and accumulate deposit insurance claims against accumulated individual loan losses with a fixed number of banks. The loan rate of interest is r' as defined by equation (2). If banks compete away any profits by offering lower interest rates to the corporate sector, the deposit insurance liability of the government will finance dividends to corporate shareholders in exactly the same amount as will go to the bank shareholders here. Since all shares are held by the representative household, nothing but the division between bank dividends and corporate dividends is affected by our assumption.

We consider two simple institutional constraints on the flow of dividends that a bank can pay at each date. One is that if the bank cannot meet its net withdrawal demand at any time, it is illiquid and the government immediately intervenes. The second constraint is that banks cannot accumulate nonperforming assets faster than the flow of unpaid interest obligations, which equal

$$\left(\frac{1}{2\alpha} r'^2 - r \frac{r'}{\alpha} \right) k_t \tag{8}$$

in the aggregate. This is the same as loan profits minus the costs of intermediation given by

$$\left(r' - r - \frac{\gamma r'}{\alpha} \right) k_t. \tag{9}$$

Total dividends paid to bank equities will equal this amount in equilibrium until regulatory authorities stop allowing the public sector deposit insurance liability to grow. Deposit insurance is a subsidy to shareholders, and banks maximize the value of shareholder equity under limited shareholder liability by making these lump-sum transfers as fast as possible. In this economy, bank dividends are a transfer from the public sector to bank shareholders. The additional institutional assumption is that banks cannot claim larger deposit insurance losses than the deposit cost of accumulated unpaid interest on corporate loans.

We first allow banks to accumulate losses for a fixed period of time, from $t = 0$ to T. At time T, the government intervenes and stops further accumulation of nonperforming loans by the banks. Public sector liabilities, b_T, are determined in equilibrium given T, or conversely. The analysis is the same if the government halts the accumulation of deposit insurance liabilities at some time, T, or at some maximum liability, b_T.

Bank dividends,

$$x_t = \left(r' - r - \frac{\gamma r'}{\alpha} \right) k_t,$$

grow with the capital stock until date T. The capital stock grows as the difference between bank deposits and the deposit insurance claim of the banks. The deposit insurance liability of the public sector grows as

$$\dot{b} = rb_t + x_t \tag{10}$$

for $0 \leq t \leq T$. The value of bank equity evolves according to

$$\dot{V}^b = rV_t^b - x_t. \tag{11}$$

At time T, dividends drop permanently to zero, so V^b must converge to zero at time T. Initially deposit insurance liabilities (equivalently, nonperforming loans) are zero, so that $b_0 = 0$. The sum of the public sector liability and banking sector equity, $b + V^b$, grows as

$$\dot{V}^b + \dot{b} = r(V_t^b + b_t) \tag{12}$$

for $0 \leq t \leq T$. For this period the government does not recognize or cover its deposit guarantee liabilities.

The solvency constraint for the public sector implies that after time T, the government must collect revenue to meet its obligation, b_T. In this economy the government does not have access to lump-sum taxes and imposes a tax on interest income (the interest received on deposits) at a constant proportionate rate, τ. The deposit rate of interest from time T on is $\hat{r} = (1 - \tau)r$. The flow-budget identity for the public sector from T onward is

$$\dot{b} = rb_t - \tau r(k_t + b_t) = \hat{r}b_t - \tau rk_t, \tag{13}$$

and the intertemporal budget constraint for the government is

$$\int_0^T x_t e^{-rt}\, dt + e^{-rT} \int_T^\infty \tau rk_t e^{-\hat{r}(t-T)}\, dt = e^{-rT}b_T + e^{-rT} \int_T^\infty \tau rk_t e^{-\hat{r}(t-T)}\, dt = 0. \tag{14}$$

To simplify the mathematics only, τ is taken to be constant. For the same reason τ is chosen so that the government is solvent and the ratio of government liabilities to deposits stays constant. This keeps the after-tax rate of interest, $\hat{r}$, and the ratio b/k constant for $t \geq T$.

The equilibrium growth path is derived assuming perfect foresight. That is, households correctly anticipate the future tax on interest earnings imposed at time T. The flow-budget identity for the representative household is given by

$$\dot{k} + \dot{b} = r(k_t + b_t) + x_t + d_t - c_t \qquad \text{for } 0 \leq t \leq T \tag{15}$$

and

$$\dot{k} + \dot{b} = \hat{r}(k_t + b_t) + d_t - c_t \qquad \text{for } t \geq T. \tag{16}$$

Maximizing household utility leads to the equilibrium growth rates of consumption,

$$\frac{\dot{c}}{c} = \frac{r - \rho}{\sigma} \qquad \text{for } 0 \leq t \leq T \tag{17}$$

and

$$\frac{\dot{c}}{c} = \frac{\hat{r} - \rho}{\sigma} \qquad \text{for } t \geq T. \tag{18}$$

Equilibrium consumption is found by integrating the aggregate resource constraint (3) and is given by

$$c_t = \left[(1 - e^{-\theta(T-t)})\theta^{-1} + e^{-\theta(T-t)} \left(\theta + \frac{r - \hat{r}}{\sigma} \right)^{-1} \right]^{-1} k_t \qquad \text{for } 0 \leq t \leq T, \tag{19}$$

where

$$\theta = \frac{\alpha}{2} - \frac{\gamma r'}{\alpha} - \frac{r - \rho}{\sigma}$$

and

$$c_t = \left(\theta + \frac{r - \hat{r}}{\sigma}\right) k_t \qquad \text{for } t \geq T. \tag{20}$$

Consumption as a share of the capital stock rises monotonically, while the national savings rate falls, over time up to date T.

The capital stock grows as

$$\frac{\dot{k}}{k} = \left(\frac{\alpha}{2} - \frac{\gamma r'}{\alpha}\right) - \frac{c_t}{k_t}$$

$$= \left(\frac{\alpha}{2} - \frac{\gamma r'}{\alpha}\right) - \left[(1 - e^{-\theta(T-t)})\theta^{-1} + e^{-\theta(T-t)}\left(\theta + \frac{r - \hat{r}}{\sigma}\right)^{-1}\right]^{-1}$$

$$\equiv \varphi(T - t, \tau) \tag{21}$$

for $0 \leq t \leq T$ and

$$\frac{\dot{k}}{k} = \frac{\hat{r} - \rho}{\sigma} \qquad \text{for } t \geq T. \tag{22}$$

The function $\varphi(T - t, \tau)$ is decreasing in t for $t \leq T$, equals $(\hat{r} - \rho)/\sigma$ for $t = T$, and converges to $(r - \rho)/\sigma$ as $T - t$ goes to infinity. Under perfect foresight the investment rate and growth rate of output fall as non-performing bank assets rise. The constraint that banks must remain liquid before date T is not binding if $\hat{r} - \rho > 0$.[7] In the next subsection we consider the possibility that this inequality does not hold.

To calculate the value of bank equity, recall that shareholder value is maximized if banks pay out the largest possible dividends up to time T, $[r' - r - (\gamma r'/\alpha)]k_t$. The stockmarket value of the banking sector under perfect foresight is given by

$$V_t^b = \int_t^T \left(r' - r - \frac{\gamma r'}{\alpha}\right) k_s e^{-r(s-t)} \, ds$$

$$= \left(r' - r - \frac{\gamma r'}{\alpha}\right) k_t \int_t^T e^{\int_t^s (\varphi(T-v, \tau) - r) \, dv} \, ds. \tag{23}$$

Differentiation of equation (23) shows that the ratio of bank equity to the current capital stock, V_t^b/k_t, or to gross domestic output,

$V_t^b / [(\alpha/2 - (r'/\alpha)\gamma)k_t]$, falls monotonically to zero up to time T. The total value of bank equity is given by

$$V_t^b = \left(r' - r - \frac{\gamma r'}{\alpha}\right) k_0 \int_t^T e^{\int_0^s \varphi(T-v,\tau)\,dv} e^{-r(s-t)}\,ds. \tag{24}$$

Aggregate corporate equity is given by the present value of dividends as

$$
\begin{aligned}
V_t^f &= \int_t^T d_s e^{-r(s-t)}\,ds + e^{-r(T-t)} \int_T^\infty d_s e^{-\hat{r}(s-T)}\,ds \\
&= \int_t^T \frac{(\alpha - r')^2}{2\alpha} k_s e^{-r(s-t)}\,ds + e^{-r(T-t)} \int_T^\infty \frac{(\alpha - r')^2}{2\alpha} k_s e^{-\hat{r}(s-T)}\,ds \\
&= \frac{(\alpha - r')^2}{2\alpha} k_t \left[\int_t^T e^{-\int_t^s (r - \varphi(T-v,\tau))\,dv}\,ds \right. \\
&\qquad \left. + \left(\hat{r} - \frac{\hat{r} - \rho}{\sigma}\right)^{-1} e^{-\int_t^T (r - \varphi(T-v,\tau))\,dv} \right]. \tag{25}
\end{aligned}
$$

After date T, the value of corporate equity grows at the same rate as the capital stock and output, $(\hat{r} - \rho)/\sigma$. Up to time T, it also grows proportionately with k_t and output if $\sigma = 1$, but grows faster than k_t if $\sigma > 1$ and more slowly than k_t if $\sigma < 1$. Thus, for an intertemporal elasticity of substitution of one-half ($\sigma = 2$), typically assumed in calibrated growth models, the value of corporate equity rises faster than gross domestic output up to time T.[8] Although the value of corporate equity is continuous at T under perfect foresight, the growth rate of corporate equity suddenly falls at time T to $(\hat{r} - \rho)/\sigma$ for $\sigma > 1$. This is verified by differentiating equation (25).

The model predicts that the value of bank equity will fall in proportion to gross domestic output before the government realizes its deposit insurance losses in the banking sector. The value of corporate equity rises faster than output before time T, and grows with gross domestic output thereafter. A decline in the value of bank equities foreshadows the banking crisis, but a decline in corporate equity does not under perfect foresight.

3.5 A Banking Crisis under Perfect Foresight

In the model economy, banks accumulate claims against the government in the form of unrealized deposit insurance liabilities as they accumulate nonperforming loans without offsetting loan-loss reserves on their balance sheets. These public sector liabilities held by the banks balance the difference between their total liabilities to depositors and the real assets (capital) of corporate debtors. In paying dividends from what would otherwise be additions to loan-loss reserves, banks create transfer payments from the government to the shareholders. Eventually the government must raise tax revenue to pay for these transfers and does so by taxing depositors. The transfers are possible because the public sector guarantees deposits, either explicitly or implicitly, without adequately monitoring and controlling the growth of its deposit guarantee indemnity or the accumulation of nonperforming loans by banks with positive equity values.[9]

An interpretation of the government's policy is that the government forebears regulation and enforcement until its insurance liability reaches some threshold (b_T). To an extent this characterizes the policies followed by many governments that have subsequently faced banking crises. It is clearly not an optimal policy if monitoring is costless. In the model economy banks can meet household deposit withdrawal demand, given by equation (19), as long as $\hat{r} \geq \rho$. The longer it takes the government to stop the growth of its deposit insurance liabilities, the larger is its debt when it finally does intervene and begins to finance its insurance losses by taxing interest. The longer regulatory authorities forebear (that is, the larger is T), the lower will the rate of investment and the growth rate of output be after time T.

To show this, we begin with the government's intertemporal solvency constraint (from equation 14) written as

$$0 = e^{-rT}b_T + e^{-rT}\int_T^\infty \tau r k_t e^{-\hat{r}(t-T)}\, dt \tag{26}$$

$$= e^{-rT}b_T + e^{-rT}k_0 e^{\int_0^T \varphi(T-v,\tau)\, dv}\tau r\left(\hat{r} - \frac{\hat{r}-\rho}{\sigma}\right)^{-1}. \tag{27}$$

Equation (27) can be rewritten using the solution for $e^{-rT}b_T$ from integrating the growth equation for the government's deposit insurance liability, equation (10). This is

$$e^{-rT}b_T = \int_0^T \left(r' - r - \frac{\gamma r'}{\alpha}\right)k_s e^{-r(s-t)}\, ds$$

$$= \left(r' - r - \frac{\gamma r'}{\alpha}\right)k_0 \int_0^T e^{\int_t^s (\varphi(T-v,\tau)-r)\, dv}\, ds. \tag{28}$$

The solvency constraint becomes

$$\left(r' - r - \frac{\gamma r'}{\alpha} \right) \int_0^T e^{\int_t^s (\varphi(T-v,\tau)-r)\,dv}\,ds$$

$$+ e^{\int_0^T (\varphi(T-v,\tau)-r)\,dv} \tau r \left(\hat{r} - \frac{\hat{r}-\rho}{\sigma} \right)^{-1} = 0, \tag{29}$$

where $\hat{r} = (1 - \tau)r$. Total differentiation with respect to T and τ shows that τ, and public debt, b_T, are increasing in T. The long-run growth rate,

$$\frac{\dot{y}}{y} = \frac{\dot{k}}{k} = \frac{\hat{r}-\rho}{\sigma},$$

falls as the tax rate rises.

For a long enough period of regulatory forbearance, public debt will rise sufficiently so that the tax rate must be raised to the point where the after-tax interest rate on deposits falls below the subjective rate of discount and the long-run equilibrium growth rate is negative. In this case household savings will be negative, and households will withdraw deposits on net from the banking system. These net withdrawals will force the banks to reduce lending to corporations forcing corporations to scrap capital. Our assumption that investment is irreversible (as an extreme case of downward investment adjustment costs) imposes an upper bound on τ, and therefore on T.

The growth rate of the economy given by equation (21) falls continuously until time T to its long-run level given by $[r(1-\tau) - \rho]/\sigma$. If $r(1-\tau) < \rho$, then the growth rate falls to zero at some time $\bar{T}$ before date T. At date $\bar{T}$ the banking system will able to just meet the withdrawal demands of depositors using the interest paid by corporations less costs of intermediation,

$$\left(r' - \frac{\gamma r'}{\alpha} \right) k_t.$$

The growth of deposits, the capital stock and gross domestic output all reach zero at time $\bar{T}$. If the deposit insurance liability of the government continues to rise after the growth rate reaches zero at time $\bar{T}$, the anticipated tax rate on interest must also rise. In this economy (in contrast that in Dekle and Kletzer 2003), the before-tax deposit rate of interest can rise. Bank returns on loans are maximized when the loan rate of interest reaches $\alpha - \gamma$, implying a maximum before-tax deposit rate of interest given by

$$r^* = \frac{(\alpha - \gamma)^2}{2\alpha}.$$

Corporate profits fall to

$$d^* = \frac{\alpha^2 - (\alpha - \gamma)^2}{2\alpha}k,$$

while unpaid interest rises from

$$\frac{r'^2}{2\alpha}k \quad \text{to} \quad \frac{(\alpha - \gamma)^2}{2\alpha}k,$$

where k is constant since the growth rate is zero. The social costs of intermediation also rise to $\gamma(\alpha - \gamma)/\alpha$ so that total dividends that are paid out under regulatory forbearance decline. As the before-tax rate of interest rises, however, the after-tax rate of interest must remain equal to the discount rate, ρ. At time $\hat{T}$ the interest rate reaches r^* with a tax rate given by $r^*(1 - \tau^*) = \rho$. The deposit insurance liability of the government reaches b^*, determined by the tax rate τ^*.

After $\hat{T}$, banks will only be able to meet the withdrawal demands of depositors by reducing outstanding loans to corporate borrowers. This requires the repayment of loan principal by firms. The entire banking system faces net withdrawal demand at $\hat{T}$ in equilibrium, so that no firm can reduce its debt to one bank by borrowing from another. An existing or new firm cannot buy all or part of the firm's capital either, since it is not able to get a loan from a bank to finance its purchase. In this economy, banks become illiquid at time $\hat{T}$ because they have no alternative but to face net withdrawals of deposits that cannot be met. A banking crisis must occur, and the government must stop accumulating deposit insurance liabilities.

The capital stock employed by firms can be interpreted as loan collateral in this economy. Prior to the onset of the crisis, one firm can sell its capital to another and repay its loans fully. This makes a market for collateral with an equilibrium price of collateral equal to one. In a crisis, a bank that attempts to reduce its corporate loans to meet deposit withdrawals will discover that its borrowers are unable to repay their loan principals. If banks foreclose loans in the amount of net withdrawal demand by depositors, the collateral on those loans will have a zero price. This is because no firm will be able to borrow to purchase the collateral. The financing is not available because aggregate bank deposits have decreased by exactly the amount of the foreclosed loans.

Loans are not available to potential purchasers of the seized collateral in equilibrium with irreversible investment. There will be no demand for collateral at a positive price in the crisis, even though the marginal productivity of capital is positive.

Thus the market for collateral collapses in a banking crisis. If banks are heterogeneous and become liquidity constrained idiosyncratically, then a decline in the value of collateral (i.e., a decrease in Tobin's q) could result. Bank heterogeneity could be introduced to the model economy by adding assumptions that lead banks to incomplete diversify their loan portfolios in equilibrium (e.g., allowing a finite number of firms and increasing returns to scale in banking). This would make the deposit insurance liability and current earnings of each bank depend on the particular history of productivity shocks for its corporate clients. Over time some banks would earn less from lending than others and might eventually be unable to meet the withdrawal demands of depositors from their net earnings on loans. Banks that do well could acquire borrowers as banks that do poorly shrink.

However, in the presence of deposit insurance with regulatory forbearance, banks that do well pay out dividends to shareholders only over a finite horizon just as in our model of homogeneous banks. New loans generate future dividends for shareholders only until the accumulation of deposit insurance liabilities by the government stops. Therefore we can expect the value of collateral to fall as more and more banks become insolvent up to the onset of a banking crisis or the end of regulatory forbearance (the interpretation of what happens if T is less that $\hat{T}$). Alternatively, with continuously enforced loan-loss reserves, the price of collateral, q, would remain equal to one in this economy.

For many years the government of Japan dealt with the problem of troubled banks through the "convoy system," under which weak banks would be merged with strong banks. Under the convoy system the losses of a weak bank are absorbed by the shareholders of the strong bank. An interpretation is that the shareholders of a strong bank absorb the equivalent of the deposit insurance liability in these forced mergers. In this interpretation of the convoy system the dividends paid to the shareholders of the weak bank are eventually financed by transfers from the shareholders of the strong bank rather than from taxpayers.

This interpretation also suggests that the convoy system should break down. The managers of the strong banks face the same incentives to accumulate deposit insurance claims as do the shareholders of the weak banks. In a heterogeneous economy their loan portfolios perform well ex post, so their net asset incomes are higher those that of weaker banks, whereas the convoy system taxes the higher returns to pay for (past) dividends paid to the shareholders of the weaker banks. It transfers equity from the owners of stronger banks to weaker banks in expectation. When a bank becomes a convoy leader, its shareholder value falls. Therefore the maximization of shareholder returns implies that a bank should avoid becoming a convoy leader by paying out all the dividends it can over the same horizon as the rest of the banking sector.

In the fiscal policy adopted in our discussion of the analytical model, the tax rate, τ, was constant after date T. This kept the public debt to output ratio constant. Alternative fiscal policies under which the government delays raising revenue or adopts a time-varying tax rate could also be used. For example, regulatory authorities could intervene in the banking system at time T' with public sector deposit insurance liability equal to $b_{T'}$, and fiscal authorities could wait to raise taxes until time $\hat{T}$. The tax rate imposed at time $\hat{T}$ will need to be sufficient to service the accumulated public debt $e^{r(\hat{T}-T')}b_{T'}$. With irreversible investment the growth rate goes to zero at time $\hat{T}$ if the tax rate implied by this debt level reduces the after-tax rate of return to deposits to the household discount rate. Other possible policy responses include imposing taxes so that b stays constant as the economy grows or b is reduced to zero over some finite horizon. In these cases the tax rate varies over time. If the deposit insurance liability declines in proportion to output, then the tax rate falls over time and the growth rate of output will rise again. Under these types of fiscal responses our model would imply a temporary, perhaps sharp, fall in the growth rate of gross domestic output, followed by a recovery.

The model makes two policy assumptions: the deposit insurance liability is not continuously borne by the banks through insurance premium payments and is ultimately financed by a proportional tax on deposits. Both of these are essential to the equilibrium dynamics. The first assumption fits Japan where very little of the cost of risky portfolio choices are borne by bank shareholders. Correct pricing of risk for risk-taker would be the opposite of regulatory inadequacy and forbearance modeled here. Using lump-sum taxes would eliminate the growth effects in the model with a representative agent. In an overlapping generations model the endogenously growing deposit insurance liability could still depress growth if it is financed through lump-sum taxes that redistribute across generations. Intergenerational redistribution in an overlapping generations model also implies that current generations can benefit through the accumulation of public sector liabilities at a cost to future generations. This gives a simple model for motivating regulatory forbearance in the first place.[10]

3.6   Empirical Tests of Asset Prices and Fundamentals

Before we apply our model to the Japanese experience, we first test whether asset prices correctly reflect economic fundamentals. This is because our model imposes perfect foresight, ruling out bubbles and implying that all asset prices reflect fundamentals. The stock market values of corporations (equation 25) and of the banking sector (equation 24) are assumed to equal the present discounted value of dividends. The deposit insurance liability of the government depends on the growth of stock market values (13), and since the flow-budget identity for the representative household depends on this deposit insurance liability (government debt), the behavior of consumption and other real variables in our model depends on the assumption that stock prices reflect fundamental values. Thus it is important to ascertain whether bubbles exist and whether stock values reflect fundamentals. Here we perform some tests, showing that for Japan's recent history, our assumption that asset prices reflect fundamentals is basically correct.

Campbell, Lo, and MacKinlay (1997, p. 260) and others argue that bubbles in stock prices are inconsistent with stationary stock returns if the dividend process follows a linear process with a unit root. They also show that prices and dividends, and prices and earnings should be cointegrated. In fact rational bubbles in stock prices may imply that the series of stock prices, stock returns, dividend–price ratios, and earnings–price ratios follow an explosive process, in which the series keep on increasing to infinity (see the appendix to this chapter).

3.6.1   Unit Root Tests for Bubbles in Stock Prices, Dividends, and Earnings

The validity of these stationarity relationships can be seen in figures 3.1 through 3.3, and in table 3.1. Although the relations in equations (1) through (3) are expressed in terms of levels, Campbell, Lo, and

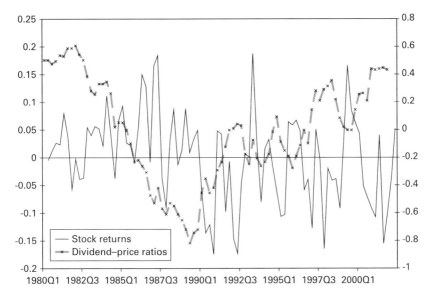

Figure 3.1
Stock returns and the dividend–price ratio.

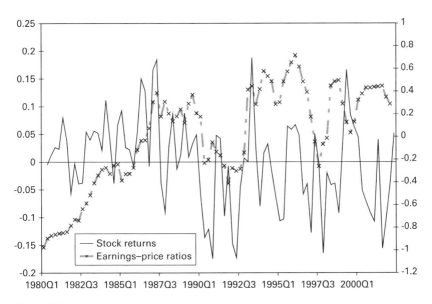

Figure 3.2
Stock returns and the price–earnings ratio.

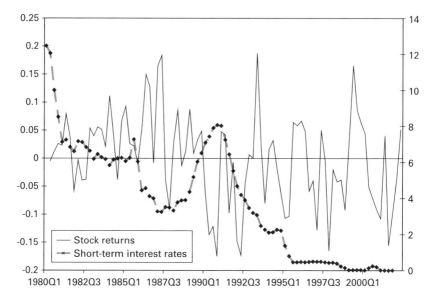

Figure 3.3
Stock returns and short-term interest rates.

Table 3.1
Phillips-Perron unit root statistics

Dates	1980Q2–2002Q2	1980Q2–1990Q4	1991Q1–2002Q2
Stock returns	−6.1***	−3.2*	−5.3***
Dividend–price ratio	−1.5	−0.98	−1.5
Price–earnings ratio	−2.3*	−1.7	−2.3*

Note: Rejection of null hypothesis of unit root: *** significant at 1 percent level, ** significant at 5 percent level, * significant at 10 percent level.

MacKinlay (1997, p. 261) show that they are also valid in terms in logs, if dividends follow a loglinear process. From figures 3.1 through 3.3 we can see that log stock price changes look like a stationary series. This is corroborated in the Phillips-Perron unit root tests of table 3.1, which shows, for all periods, a rejection of the hypothesis that log stock price changes are nonstationary.

If log prices and log dividends are cointegrated, then the log dividend–price ratio should be stationary. From figure 3.1, however, the log dividend–price ratio looks like a nonstationary series. Phillips-Perron unit root tests show that for the 1980Q2 to 2002Q2 and 1991Q1 to 2002Q2 periods, we can reject the null hypothesis of nonstationarity at the 10 percent level, although for the 1980Q2 to 1990Q4 period, we cannot reject the null hypothesis of nonstationarity.

Similarly, from figure 3.2, the log price–earnings ratios looks like a nonstationary series. Phillips-Perron unit root tests show that for all periods, we cannot reject the hypothesis that the log price–earnings ratio is nonstationary.

Finally, since short-term interest rates are used to discount future dividends, we examine the behavior of short-term interest rates (the call rate) in figure 3.3. Short-term interest rates appear to be stationary until the end of 1991. Clearly, since 1992 short-term interest rates appear nonstationary.

Overall, these results suggest that while the evidence for the existence of bubbles is not compelling, we cannot entirely reject the existence of bubbles, especially in the 1980Q2 to 1990Q4 period when there is no cointegration between stock prices and dividends or earnings. However, the balance of evidence suggests that our fundamentals assumption is reasonable.

3.6.2   Fundamentals, Bubbles, and the Predictability of Stock Returns

If stock returns are predictable from fundamentals, then bubbles, even if they exist, are small, and are probably not important in affecting stock returns. Table 3.2 shows some long-horizon regressions, relating stock returns on various fundamentals at horizons of one quarter, four quarters (one year), and twelve quarters (three years). The fundamentals we examine are the log price-earnings ratio, the log dividend–price ratio, and the short-term interest rate. As it is well known, forecast accuracy increases remarkably as the horizon increases. The coefficients, R^2, and t-statistics all increase as the forecast horizon increases. For example, as the current log price–earnings ratio increases, stocks become overvalued, and this overvaluation is corrected after four quarters or so. That is, high log price–earnings ratios imply low stock returns, at medium to long horizons. The coefficients on the log–price earnings ratios are negative. A high current log dividend–price ratio implies increasing stock returns. Finally, high current short-term interest rates predict high stock returns at long-horizons.[11]

Table 3.3 depicts the relationship between fundamentals and stock returns in a VAR framework. It appears that some fundamentals have explanatory power, over and beyond lagged stock returns. Both the

Table 3.2
Long-horizon regressions of stock returns on log price–earnings and log dividend–price ratios, and short-term interest rates

	Forecast horizon		
	One quarter	Four quarters	Twelve quarters
Log price–earnings			
Coefficient	−0.0076	−0.15	−0.58
R^2	0.0017	0.099	0.39
t Statistic	−0.41	−2.29	−5.18
Log dividend price			
Coefficient	−0.017	0.18	0.73
R^2	0.067	1.95	0.45
t Statistic	−0.77	0.09	5.53
Short-term interest			
Coefficient	0.0027	0.017	0.059
R^2	0.011	0.056	0.17
t Statistic	−0.096	1.36	3.05

Notes: Standard errors are Newey-West. Sample: 1980Q2–2002Q2.

dividend–price and the price–earnings ratios have high explanatory power. The moderately high R^2 values suggests a modest degree of forecastability for quarterly stock returns. In the last column of table 3.3 we added first-differences of the variables that are included in our vector autoregression estimates in section 3.7. The first difference of lagged credit (actually the credit–GDP ratio) is highly significant, although none of the other variables are significant. The R^2 value of 0.29 again suggests a moderate degree of forecastability.

Overall, these results suggest that fundamentals have good forecasting power, especially at long-horizons. Furthermore fundamentals appear to have forecasting power, over and beyond lagged stock returns. These results suggest that fundamentals are important in explaining Japanese stock returns, and that the role of bubbles in affecting stock returns may be small or superfluous.

3.7 Application of the Model to the Japanese Economy in the 1990s

In the theoretical model a banking crisis and growth collapse develops endogenously in the absence of effective prudential regulation in an economy without aggregate production risk and under perfect fore-

Table 3.3
Fundamentals and stock returns

Constant	0.022	0.036	−0.0007
	(0.95)	(1.96)	(−0.69)
Stock returns (−1)	0.13	0.22	—
	(0.81)	(1.51)	
Stock returns (−2)	−0.11	−0.84	—
	(−0.92)	(−0.69)	
Dividend-price (−1)	−0.29	—	—
	(−2.21)		
Dividend-price (−2)	0.33	—	—
	(2.55)		
Price-earnings (−1)	—	0.17	—
		(2.09)	
Price-earnings (−2)	—	−0.25	—
		(−3.04)	
Short-term interest (−1)	0.0053	0.0063	—
	(0.39)	(0.49)	
Short-term interest (−2)	−0.0053	−0.16	—
	(−0.39)	(−1.14)	
Ch. (INVEST(−1))[a]	—	—	0.0057
			(0.21)
Ch. (INVEST(−2))	—	—	0.0062
			(0.22)
Ch. (CRED(−1))[b]	—	—	8.89
			(1.35)
Ch. (CRED(−2))	—	—	18.84
			(2.85)
Ch. (LANDPRIC(−1))[c]	—	—	0.00017
			(0.41)
Ch. (LANDPRIC(−2))	—	—	−0.00035
			(−0.89)
R^2	0.27	0.29	0.29
Adjusted R^2	0.19	0.22	0.19

Notes: Dependent variable: stock returns. Sample: 1980Q2–1997Q4. t Statistics in parentheses.
a. First difference of the lagged investment–output ratio.
b. First difference of the lagged credit–output ratio.
c. First difference of the lagged land price.

sight. Idiosyncratic production risk across firms creates individual loan losses that can be exactly offset by profits on other loans but are not offset when banks are able to pay out dividends against deposit insurance liabilities subsidized by the government. We argue that the practice of prudential supervision and regulation in Japan over the last two decades matches our assumptions very well. In this section we consider how well the predictions of the model fit Japanese economic performance.

The model predicts dynamics for investment, consumption, output, bank credit growth, asset prices and the value of collateral assets before and after the crisis that can be compared to the data. Some empirical implications of the model are as follows:

1. As the banking system accumulates a deposit insurance claim in the form of nonperforming corporate loans against which dividends were paid, the growth rate of output decreases steadily to its post-crisis level and consumption rises as a share of output under perfect foresight.

2. The stockmarket value of the corporate sector can grow more rapidly than output before the crisis is realized for the empirical plausible case of inelastic intertemporal substitution ($\sigma > 1$).

3. The stockmarket value of the banking sector will decline before the crisis, implying that we should observe a decrease in the value of bank stocks relative to the aggregate value of the stock market before the banking crisis.[12]

4. The value of collateral in the model equals $q_t k_t$, which grows proportionately with output until output growth falls to zero in a banking crisis and the market for collateral collapses.[13]

Two of the many simplifying assumptions of the model are important to reconsider for comparing its equilibrium dynamics to the empirical record for Japan. The first is the assumption of full information under perfect foresight. In equilibrium the output share of investment decreases gradually to its long-run value and consumption rises steadily to its long-run share before the banking crisis. Households and firms may be imperfectly informed and receive information over time about the health of the banking sector or future fiscal policies under rational expectations. When there is news about bank balance sheets or the government's expected response to deposit insurance losses, investment and GDP growth can change suddenly. The second issue is that aggregate productivity for Japan fluctuates. A temporary adverse aggregate productivity shock would lead to a permanent rise in nonperforming loans held by the bank sector, moving the beginning of a crisis forward in the model economy. Therefore such a shock would have a permanent effect on GDP growth under rational expectations.

It is difficult to identify the beginning of the banking crisis in Japan. At least two dates can be suggested readily. In 1992 the Japanese Ministry of Finance first acknowledged rising nonperforming bank loans publicly. This followed the beginning of the sharp deterioration of Japanese economic performance in the early 1990s. The second possibility is 1997 to early 1998, when several financial institutions, including banks (Nippon Credit Bank and Hokkaido Takushoku) and major securities companies (Sanyo and Yamaichi securities), collapsed. At the same time the East Asian financial crisis of 1997 and 1998 provided a major international shock to the Japanese economy. In the interpretation of the model, either or both of these dates could be times when households and firms receive news about problems in the banking sector. The realization that banks have large and growing nonperforming assets in the early 1990s could reveal information that starts investment and output growth on the adjustment path predicted by the model as the banking sector deteriorates further. The accumulation of deposit insurance losses would not have ended yet, so that date T in the model would not have been reached. Therefore we need to remain agnostic about the timing of the onset of the banking crisis.

3.7.1 Output Growth, Consumption, and Investment

The growth rate of GDP declines leading up to the banking crisis in equilibrium for the model. Figure 3.4 (from Dekle and Kletzer 2003) shows a significant decline in the GDP growth rate for Japan over the three years, 1990 through 1992. Although we cannot make a judgment about when the future costs of bank bailouts were recognized by investors and savers, the decline in the growth rate to lower levels that persist (and worsen) to the present is consistent with the model.

The growth rate of consumption does not fall before the 1990s, but begins to decline as the GDP growth rate fell in 1990. Figure 3.4 also shows a slight rise in consumption as a share of GDP beginning in 1990. This is also consistent with the model because consumption growth does not fall as much as output growth does. In response to economic performance the government of Japan increased transfer payments to households in the 1990s. This could contribute to a

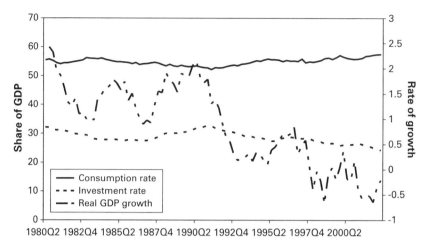

Figure 3.4
Consumption and investment–GDP ratios, including GDP growth rate.

smaller contraction in household consumption as a share of GDP and could help sustain consumption growth. Hayashi and Prescott (2002) argue that regulatory changes in the 1980s reduced the incentives of households to supply labor, leading to a rise in leisure consumption by about 20 percent. If consumption of goods and leisure are complements, then these changes could raise the share of consumption in output.

Figure 3.4 also shows that investment growth does not decline before 1990 as it would if savers and investors anticipated the growth in nonperforming bank loans and public sector liabilities that would be recognized in the early 1990s. The figure shows a decline in the share of investment in GDP after 1990 as predicted by our model. These data are consistent with the interpretation that the news of the impending banking crisis arrives after the end of the 1980s. Indeed, the share of investment in GDP rises in the late 1980s before the onset of the Japanese growth collapse. Our basic model does not imply these dynamics, but a rise in investment share is implied by our agency model (Dekle and Kletzer 2002a, b). That model suggests that extending our current model by allowing adverse selection in investment projects by firms could lead to an increase in the growth rate of the capital stock before a crisis.

A drop in investment may be reflected in investment in research and development or the adoption of technological innovations and be

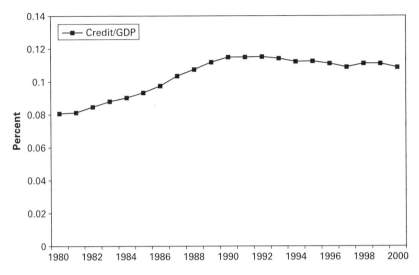

Figure 3.5
Credit growth.

underestimated by the rate of capital accumulation. Investment in new technologies may generate returns over longer average horizons than aggregate capital formation. In Japan, between 1970 to 1980 and 1990 to 1998, total factor productivity (TFP) growth rates dropped from 1.1 percent per annum to 0.2 percent per annum. The decline in TFP was especially sharp in manufacturing, where TFP growth dropped from 4.9 to 0.5 percent per annum. With regards to other measures of productivity, return on equity fell from 12 percent in 1980 to 4 percent in 1998, and the return on invested capital fell from 6 percent in 1980 to 4 percent in 1998. These compare with 1998 returns on equity and invested capital in the United States of 22 and 14 percent respectively.[14]

3.7.2 Bank Credit Growth

Total bank credit in the model equals the sum of firm capital stocks and the deposit insurance claims accumulated by banks, $k + b$. This sum equals the total bank deposits held by households and grow as a share of GDP up to the crisis. Bank credit as a share of GDP should stop rising when a banking crisis occurs and should decline if the deposit insurance liabilities of the government are expected to be cleared in finite time. Figure 3.5 shows that these dynamics correspond roughly to the data for Japan and that there is a distinct change in the growth rate for the ratio of bank credit to GDP in 1991. This is consistent with our dating of the beginning of the banking crisis in the early 1990s followed by a deepening of the crisis in 1997 and 1998.

3.7.3 Nonperforming Bank Loans and Land Prices

An important implication of the model is that the stock market value of domestic banks should be declining up to time T. The stock market value of the corporation sector also grows faster than GDP in equilibrium before the crisis and drop to the growth rate of GDP after the crisis in the model. Because the collapse of the Nikkei bubble of the 1980s would also cause a decline in bank stocks, the distinguishing feature of the model is that the ratio of the value of domestic bank equities to the value of the entire stock market should decline once the private sector realizes the deterioration of the banking sector. The ratio of the stock market value of the banks to the total value of the stock market started to decline sharply in 1987, at least three to four years before the beginning of the crisis, as shown in figure 3.6 (from Dekle and Kletzer 2003). This is consistent with the prediction, special to our model, that the ratio of bank stock values to total stock values leads other macroeco-

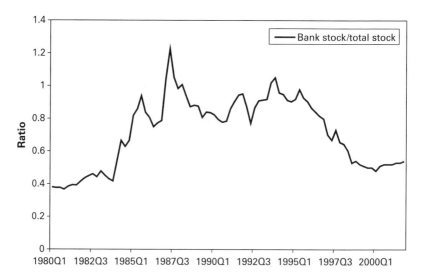

Figure 3.6
Ratio of bank stock value to total stock market value.

nomic aggregate measures. Because asset prices are very responsive to new information regarding future dividend growth and real interest rates, we argue that this offers good evidence in favor of a model based on rational expectations in which consumption and investment are forward-looking.

In the model economy the decline in the quality of bank portfolios leading up to a crisis is gradual and caused by prospective government bailouts. The share of nonperforming loans (NPLs) to total bank loans rises steadily before the crisis. Reliable NPL data are available only after 1992, when the Ministry of Finance first recognized the NPL problem (again, a sudden change in the information of investors and savers). The ratio of nonperforming loans to total bank loans over the 1990s is shown in figure 3.7. Nonperforming loans were 2 percent of GDP between 1992 and 1994, rose sharply to about 5 percent of GDP in 1996, and were 7 percent of GDP in 2000.

Land is not included in the theoretical model, but land is important as collateral for a large proportion of bank lending in Japan. Between 1980 and 1995 about 40 percent of all corporate borrowing was collateralized by real estate (Ueda 2000). The value of the capital stock with irreversible investment in the model, however, parallels the value of other fixed assets that serve as collateral. The total value of collateral suddenly falls in a banking crisis in the model. The dramatic decline in the value of land in Japan during the 1990s parallels the collapse in the

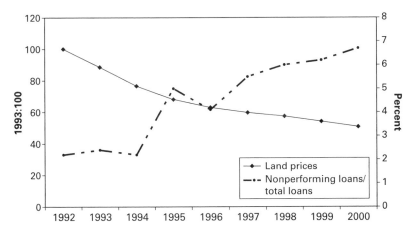

Figure 3.7
Nonperforming loans and land prices.

value of capital predicted by the model. Average land prices in Japan declined by about 60 percent between 1992 and 2000, as shown on figure 3.7. A common hypothesis that the increase in the price of real estate over the 1980s contributed to an expansion in bank credit, which in turn led to higher rates of investment and economic growth.[15] The causality predicted by our model runs the opposite direction.

3.7.4 Vector Autoregression Estimates

Our model yields relationships between the ratio of the value of bank stocks to the total stock market value and subsequent investment, output growth, and bank credit growth. For example, a tightening of prudential supervision and regulatory enforcement will reduce and T. This immediately lowers the bank equity ratio, and subsequently raises the path of investment (as a ratio of GDP) and lowers the growth rate of bank credit to GDP and the present value of collateral assets (as a ratio of GDP).

We test our theoretical prediction that the future paths of investment, bank credit, and the value of collateral respond to shocks to the ratio, but not the converse. We first estimate vector autoregressions (VAR) with the relevant variables, and then perform Granger causality tests to examine whether the bank equity ratio is exogenous in the Granger sense. If so, the bank equity ratio temporally precedes the other variables in our vector autoregression. The VAR is formed using four variables, the bank stock to the total stock market value ratio, the investment to GDP ratio, the bank credit to GDP ratio, and an index of land prices. Although land prices are not modeled directly, our model does capture the value of capital as collateral, which becomes a fixed asset in a crisis. This mimics land prices in a crisis, so we apply the implications of the model for the value of collateral to land prices.

Table 3.4 depicts the VAR results with our four variables: BSTS (the bank equity ratio), CRED (the ratio of bank credit to GDP), INVEST (the investment to GDP ratio), and LANDPRIC (land prices). The optimal lag length of two was chosen by the Akaike Information Criterion. In the BSTS equation, besides its own lagged values, none of the other variables are significant. In the CRED equation, besides its own lagged values, only LANDPRIC lagged once is significant. In the INVEST equation, besides its own lagged values, both LANDPRIC lagged once

Table 3.4
VAR estimates of the model

Equation	BSTS	CRED	INVEST	LANDPRIC
Variable				
BSTS(−1)[a]	1.09	0.00043	0.023	36.71
	(9.75)	(0.15)	(0.0039)	(1.01)
BSTS(−2)	−0.16	0.0022	0.79	−12.29
	(0.11)	(0.75)	(1.28)	(−0.33)
CRED(−1)[b]	1.16	0.76	−8.83	250.9
	(0.25)	(6.62)	(−0.36)	(0.17)
CRED(−2)	−3.42	0.14	2.44	522.7
	(−0.80)	(1.36)	(0.11)	(0.38)
INVEST(−1)[c]	−0.011	−0.00048	0.068	4.63
	(−0.52)	(−0.91)	(0.59)	(0.68)
INVEST(−2)	−0.0021	0.00026	0.0031	−0.15
	(−0.099)	(0.48)	(4.61)	(7.02)
LANDPRIC(−1)[d]	0.000021	0.0000064	−0.0029	1.91
	(0.17)	(2.08)	(−4.51)	(47.6)
LANDPRIC(−2)	0.000055	−0.0000055	−0.0029	−0.95
	(0.45)	(−1.71)	(−4.49)	(23.78)
CONSTANT	0.61	0.014	1.58	−202.96
	(0.33)	(1.71)	(0.89)	(−1.91)
R^2	0.94	0.98	0.98	0.99
Adjusted R^2	0.76	0.77	0.78	0.79

a. Bank stock equity–total stock market equity ratio.
b. Ratio of credit to GDP.
c. Investment to GDP ratio.
d. Land prices.

and twice are significant. In the LANDPRIC equation, none of the other variables are significant.

We next perform Granger causality tests to ascertain whether one variable temporally precedes another. In a VAR framework, Granger causality tests are chi-squared tests of exclusion of all the lags of a particular variable. For example, BSTS Granger causes CRED if BSTS(−1) and BSTS(−2) are jointly significant in the CRED equation, but CRED(−1) and CRED(−2) are not jointly significant in the BSTS equation.

Table 3.5 depicts the results of the Granger causality tests in a VAR framework. In the BSTS equation, none of the variables are significant. In fact, besides lagged BSTS, none of the variables contribute any explanatory power. In the CRED equation, BSTS and LANDPRIC provide good explanatory power. In the INVEST equation, BSTS and

Table 3.5
Granger causality and chi-squared exogeneity tests

	BSTS[a]		CRED[b]		INVEST[c]		LANDPRIC[d]	
Excluded variable	Chi-square	Proba-bility[e]	Chi-square	Proba-bility	Chi-square	Proba-bility	Chi-square	Proba-bility
BSTS	3.41	0.18	5.94	0.05	12.81	0.0016	3.65	0.16
CRED	3.11	0.21	6.11	0.03	0.81	0.62	3.21	0.18
INVEST	2.93	0.23	1.91	0.38	0.73	0.69	3.09	0.21
LANDPRIC	4.13	0.13	5.17	0.07	21.3	0	3.35	0.19

a. Bank stock equity–total stock market equity.
b. Ratio of credit to GDP.
c. Investment to GDP ratio.
d. Land prices.
e. Probability value.

LANDPRIC again provide good explanatory power. In the LAND-PRIC equation, none of the variables are significant.

Taken together, these results are consistent with our theory. BSTS temporally precedes (Granger causes) CRED and INVEST. That is, shocks to BSTS such as a tightening of prudential regulations raises INVEST and CRED. BSTS does not temporally precede LANDPRIC. That is, BSTS and LANDPRIC appear to be simultaneously determined. This is consistent with models in which as asset prices, both equity and land prices respond to correlated future fundamentals.

3.8   Conclusion

Japan has historically had a bank-centered financial system, or relationship banking, where the long-term and tight relationship between banks and corporate borrowers dominated financial intermediation. The efficient functioning of relationship banking requires an effective mechanism to discipline banks to ensure the prudent monitoring of debtor firms. As Horiuchi (2003) notes, it is difficult for outside investors to effectively monitor bank management under relationship banking. For example, it is very difficult for outsider investors to assess the quality of bank loans, creating the need for an agent to monitor and discipline bank managers. Traditionally the bank regulatory authority (in Japan's case, the Banking Bureau of the Ministry of Finance and the Financial Supervisory Agency) serves as monitor of bank portfolios and the actions of bank managers.

We have shown in this chapter that the current difficulties faced by government regulators for resolving the Japanese banking crisis follow from a recent history of regulatory forbearance and the failure to fulfill this monitoring role. In this chapter we presented a model in which regulatory forbearance, accompanied by a high corporate reliance on bank borrowing and government implicit and explicit deposit insurance, can lower the long-run growth rate of the economy and result in an endogenous banking crisis. The model shows that deposit guarantees and slack financial regulation create incentives for banks to make transfers to bank shareholders or depositors that are financed by the public sector, hence taxpayers in the future. The accumulated, unrealized, deposit insurance liability of the government to the banking sector is the public debt used to finance such transfers. Banks accumulate this public debt on the asset side of their balance sheets in the form of nonperforming loans, acknowledged or unacknowledged. In common usage, a banking crisis is not clearly defined. In our model economy the banking sector will deteriorate to the point of a liquidity crisis with certainty unless regulatory forbearance ends and effective prudential regulations are enforced that impose continuous loan-loss reserving, or its equivalent. One may wish to label the event of a rising and irreversible deposit insurance liability for the government that must result in a sharp policy reversible to avoid a crisis for investment finance a banking crisis. This is exactly what happens in our model if the government steps in before the liquidity crisis occurs or not.

In our analysis deposit insurance liabilities affect economic growth because public debt increases lower aggregate wealth in the presence of distortionary taxes. Allowing these debts to accumulate lowers the growth rate further, so postponing regulatory intervention leads to larger declines in GDP growth. This also holds true if the government continues to accumulate net deposit insurance liabilities after a banking crisis begins. The model has two major policy implications. The first is that enforcement of individual loan-loss reserves or loan writedowns eliminates the ability of bank managers to finance transfers to shareholders or depositors from the public sector. The model also supports prompt intervention (e.g., implementation of prompt corrective action in the case of Japan). Because the growth rate of the model economy falls as deposit insurance liabilities rise against dividends paid out to shareholders or depositors, the economy cannot grow out of the problem in an equilibrium.

Appendix

Applying Campbell, Lo, and MacKinlay (1997), with constant interest rates, the stock price can be written as

$$P_t = E_t \sum_{i=1}^{\infty} \left(\frac{1}{1+r}\right)^i D_{t+i} + E_t \frac{B_{t+1}}{(1+r)}, \tag{A1}$$

where P_t is the stock price at time t, D_{t+i} is the dividend at time $t + i$, r is the interest (discount) rate, and B_{t+1} is the bubbles component. The bubbles component is the deviation of the price from the fundamental value of stocks or the present discounted value of dividends.

Equation (A1) can be rewritten as

$$P_t = D_t \sum_{i=1}^{\infty} \left(\frac{1}{1+r}\right)^i + E_t \frac{B_{t+1}}{(1+r)} \tag{A2}$$

if the $E_t D_{t+i} = D_t$, for each i. When there is no bubble component and D_{t+i} follows a random walk, P_t also follows a random walk. Therefore the change in prices, ΔP_t, is a stationary process.

Furthermore, by subtracting a multiple of the dividend from both sides of (A1), we obtain

$$P_t - \frac{D_t}{r} = \frac{1}{r} E_t \sum_{i=1}^{\infty} \left(\frac{1}{1+r}\right)^i \Delta D_{t+1+i} + E_t \frac{B_{t+1}}{(1+r)}. \tag{A3}$$

A random walk in dividends implies that the change in dividends is a stationary process. Thus, from (A3), we can again see that if there is no bubbles component, the stationarity of the change in dividends implies that $P_t - (D_t/r)$ is a stationary process. That is, P_t and D_t are cointegrated. Further, if dividends are a constant fraction of earnings, $D_t = \gamma Q_t$, then (A3) implies that stock prices and earnings are also cointegrated.

All of these relationships—the stationarity of the change in prices, the existence of cointegration between stock prices and dividends, and stock prices and earnings—break down when bubbles exist, and $E_t[B_{t+1}/(1+r)]$ is nonzero. Moreover the existence of rational bubbles imply that

$$\lim_{i \to \infty} E_t \frac{B_{t+i}}{(1+r)^i}.$$

That is, the bubble on stock prices is expected to be nonzero into the infinite future. The intuition is simply that today, people will not pay in excess of the fundamental value of the stock, unless they can expect to unload the stock for higher than fundamental value tomorrow. Likewise, tomorrow, people will not pay above fundamental value, unless they can expect to unload the stock for higher than fundamentals the day after tomorrow, and so on. In fact, with stationary dividends, at each date, people will expect the bubble to increase at a rate greater than the interest rate, to compensate for the probability of bursting. Clearly, (A4), as it enters into (A1) and (A3) will violate the condition that ΔP_t, $[P_t - (D_t/r)]$, and $[P_t - (\gamma Q_t/r)]$ are stationary processes.

Notes

1. This interpretation is explained at length in Cargill, Hutchison, and Ito (1997), Hutchison (1998), Hoshi and Patrick (2000), Hoshi and Kashyap (1999), and Hoshi and Kashyap (2002).

2. Cargill, Hutchison, and Ito (1997) draw a comprehensive picture of the causes of the banking crisis in Japan. They emphasize the role played by monetary policy in precipitating the banking crisis. They suggest that the sudden shift to a tighter monetary policy in 1989 led to asset deflation and the resulting collapse of land prices led to a rise in nonperforming loans. Our nonmonetary model shows how bank lending with inadequate regulation can also lead to a bank crisis.

3. The derivation of simple loan contracts is explained in Freixas and Rochet (1997).

4. Showing this is straightforward for the assumed uniform distribution of firm productivity. It is laborious and beside the point of this chapter.

5. The agency model used in Dekle and Kletzer (2002a, b) is similar to that proposed by Chinn and Kletzer (2001) for the East Asian crisis.

6. Depositor monitoring of each bank's accounts would allow reputational equilibria, for example.

7. This is a consequence of perfect foresight. Suppose that taxes were nondistortionary (lump sum) so that Ricardian equivalence held. The household would save all its dividend income in deposits to pay future taxes, so the increased savings would match the rise in the deposit insurance liabilities. With distortionary taxes the deposit insurance claims of the banking sector net of the future taxes they imply are a negative addition to wealth, adding to the rise in saving.

8. For example, Hayashi and Prescott (2002) assume that $1/\sigma = 0.5$ in their calibrated model for Japan.

9. In our model the positive value of bank equity derives from this policy combination because it allows banks to pay out dividends against uncollected corporate interest.

10. Takeo Hoshi suggested this route for using redistribution from future taxpayers to current depositors and shareholders. Allowing within-generation heterogeneity in a political economy model would also.

11. However, Campbell, Lo, and MacKinlay (1997, p. 265) caution that when expected returns are simply persistent, we can obtain the results in table 3.3 of long-horizon forecastability spuriously.

12. Under perfect foresight corporate stock values grow in proportion to gross domestic product after the crisis for a constant tax rate. If the tax rate varies over time (e.g., to eliminate the deposit insurance liability, b, in finite time), the growth rate of the value of the stock market will be different than the growth rate of output during the transition to the long-run simply because the value of equity is a forward-looking variable. Therefore it

should not be taken as a prediction of our model that the value of the stock market grows with output after time T because its behavior will depend on the policies adopted to resolve the crisis or private sector expectations with respect to these policies.

13. Investment irreversibility is used in the model for analytical simplicity. If smooth adjustment costs to disinvestment were introduced, then a banking crisis would result in corporate bankruptcies and a falling price of capital, q_t. While the model shows that transactions in collateral should drop to zero in a crisis, it also implies that under more general adjustment costs the value of collateral should fall below the growth rate of output in a crisis.

14. The data reported in this paragraph are from Fukao et al. (2002).

15. This is argued, for example, by Ogawa and Kitasaka (2000) and by Ueda (2000).

References

Barseghyan, L. 2002. Nonperforming loans, prospective bailouts, and Japan's slowdown. Unpublished manuscript. Northwestern University.

Bayoumi, T. 2001. The morning after: Explaining the slowdown in Japanese growth in the 1990s. *Journal of International Economics* 53: 241–59.

Campbell, J., A. Lo, and A. C. MacKinlay. 1997. *The Econometrics of Financial Markets*. Princeton: Princeton University Press.

Cargill, T. 2000. What caused Japan's banking crisis? In T. Hoshi and H. Patrick, eds., *Crisis and Change in the Japanese Financial System*. Norwell, MA: Kluwer Academic.

Cargill, T., M. Hutchison, and T. Ito. 1997. *The Political Economy of Japanese Monetary Policy*. Cambridge: MIT Press.

Chinn, M., and K. Kletzer. 2000. International capital inflows, domestic financial intermediation and financial crises under imperfect information. In R. Glick, R. Moreno, and M. Spiegel, eds., *Emerging Market Crises*. New York: Cambridge University Press, pp. 196–237.

Dekle, R., and K. Kletzer. 2002a. Domestic bank regulation and financial crises: Theory and empirical evidence from East Asia. In J. Frankel and S. Edwards, eds., *Preventing Currency Crises in Emerging Markets*. Chicago: University of Chicago Press, pp. 507–52.

Dekle, R., and K. Kletzer. 2002b. Financial intermediation, agency and collateral and the dynamics of banking crises: Theory and evidence for the Japanese banking crisis. Federal Reserve Bank of San Francisco, Conference on Financial Issues in the Pacific Basin Region. September 26–27.

Dekle, R., and K. Kletzer. 2003. The Japanese banking crisis and economic growth: Theoretical and empirical implications of deposit guarantees and weak financial regulation. *Journal of the Japanese and International Economies* 17: 305–35.

Diamond, D. 1984. Financial intermediation and delegated monitoring. *Review of Economic Studies* 51: 393–414.

Diamond, D., and P. Dybvig. 1983. Bank runs, deposit insurance and liquidity. *Journal of Political Economy* 91: 401–19.

Freixas, X., and J.-C. Rochet. 1997. *Microeconomics of Banking*. Cambridge: MIT Press.

Fukao, K., T. Inui, H. Kawai, and T. Miyagawa. 2002. Sectoral productivity and economic growth in Japan: 1970–98. Unpublished manuscript. Hitostubashi University.

Grimes, W. 2001. *Unmaking the Japanese Miracle*. Ithaca: Cornell University Press.

Hamilton, J. 1994. *Time Series Analysis*. Princeton: Princeton University Press.

Hayashi, F., and E. Prescott. 2002. The 1990s in Japan: A lost decade. Unpublished manuscript. University of Minnesota.

Hoshi, T., and A. Kashyap. 1999. The Japanese banking crisis: Where did it come from and how will it end? In B. Bernanke and J. Rotemberg, eds., *NBER Macroeconomics Annual*. Cambridge: MIT Press.

Hoshi, T., and A. Kashyap. 2001. *Corporate Financing and Governance in Japan*. Cambridge: MIT Press.

Hoshi, T., and H. Patrick. 2000. The Japanese financial system: An introductory overview. In T. Hoshi and H. Patrick, eds., *Crisis and Change in the Japanese Financial System*. Norwell, MA: Kluwer Academic.

Horiuchi, A. 2003. A bank crisis in a bank centered financial system—The Japanese experience since the 1990s. Mimeo. Chuo University.

Hutchison, M. 1998. Are all banking crises alike? University of California, Santa Cruz. Working Paper.

Ito, T. 2000. The stagnant Japanese economy in the 1990s: The need for financial supervision to restore sustained growth. In T. Hoshi and H. Patrick, eds., *Crisis and Change in the Japanese Financial System*. Norwell, MA: Kluwer Academic.

Kwon, E. 1998. Monetary policy, land prices, and the collateral effects on economic fluctuations: Evidence from Japan. *Journal of Japanese and International Economies* 12: 175–203.

Ogawa, K., and S. Kitasaka. 2000. Bank lending in Japan: Its determinants and macroeconomic implications. In T. Hoshi and H. Patrick, eds., *Crisis and Change in the Japanese Financial System*. Norwell, MA: Kluwer Academic.

Townsend, R. M. 1979. Optimal contracts and competitive markets with costly state verification. *Journal of Economic Theory* 21 (2): 265–93.

Ueda, K. 2000. Causes of Japan's banking problems in the 1990s. In T. Hoshi and H. Patrick, eds., *Crisis and Change in the Japanese Financial System*. Norwell, MA: Kluwer Academic.

4

Japan
G21
G28
G33
M41

Determinants of Voluntary Bank Disclosure: Evidence from Japanese Shinkin Banks

Mark M. Spiegel and
Nobuyoshi Yamori

4.1 Introduction

In the wake of worldwide financial deregulation and technological development in the financial sector, the task of bank supervision and regulation has become especially difficult. In this environment the benefits of banks voluntarily disclosing their balance sheet positions can be even greater. Self-disclosure provides a channel for enhancing market discipline in the financial sector. Market discipline is expected to play a growing role in bank regulation. It is an important component of the new Basel Banking Committee framework for bank supervision, where it is considered one of the "three pillars" of bank regulation and supervision.[1]

There are a number of papers in the literature that identify empirical examples of market discipline. Flannery and Sorescu (1996), Morgan and Stiroh (2001), and Hancock and Kwast (2001) find a significant positive relationship between US bank bond spreads and indicators of risk to the US banking sector. There are also proposals to require banks to issue subordinated debt to facilitate market discipline (e.g., Calomiris 1999). The motivation behind these proposals is that subordinated debt holders will have an incentive to monitor bank positions and spreads on subordinated debt will provide information of potential use to regulators as well as market participants. Recent evidence indicates that market yields reflect information that differs from that possessed by regulators, suggesting that market discipline can enhance the regulatory environment (De Young et al. 2001; Krainer and Lopez 2002). Moreover the Federal Reserve Board considers market information such as stock prices and interest rate spreads in their bank supervision activities (Federal Reserve Study Group on Disclosure 2000).

Since firm disclosure enhances market discipline, regulatory authorities attempt to design regulations and accounting standards to enhance the level of disclosure. Nevertheless, there is a wide disparity
in disclosure levels across nations. US disclosure standards are considered high relative to the rest of the world, while disclosure rules
in Japan are less stringent.

It is not clear whether private firms would reveal the optimal
amount of disclosure without government intervention. Some argue
that market forces encourage disclosure, so depositors and creditors
would require higher premia or deny funds to banks revealing less
than the optimal level of disclosure. These market forces would then
lead banks to optimal disclosure levels. However, there are also reasons to believe that the level of disclosure chosen by banks on their
own would fall below the optimal level. As the government is usually
a residual claimant on bank assets due to its role as a deposit insurer
and a potential lender of last resort, the private sector has less than full
incentive to monitor the disclosure levels of banks and to discipline
banks for failing to disclose. This would lead us to expect that banks
would not voluntarily engage in full disclosure.

Indeed, there appears to be evidence that they do not. For example,
Gunther and Moore (2000) investigate the impact of bank exams in the
United States on the adequacy of the allowance for loan and lease
losses. They find that bank exams affect the accuracy of financial information released to the public. In the absence of regulatory exams,
banks underestimate the share of nonperforming loans in their balance
sheet.

It should be acknowledged that regulations inducing full disclosure
would not necessarily be optimal. Banks could respond to disclosure
requirements in a number of dimensions, some of which would likely
be unintended. For example, a bank wishing to avoid releasing information to a potential rival may call in loans from a problem debtor
rather than release information on them publicly. Nevertheless, the
general consensus is that the level of disclosure undertaken by Japanese banks is far below the social optimum, although the level of disclosure does appear to be improving over time.[2] For example, Balic,
Bradley, and Kiguchi (2002) conclude that Japanese "disclosure levels
still fall short of the leaders in the Asia Pacific region and the US."[3]
Moreover it is widely believed that the degree of disclosure is particularly suboptimal among Japanese banks. After the burst of the bubble

economy, Japanese banks had large holdings of bad loans, but they did not disclose their holdings in a timely manner, even though market participants requested these figures.

While required Japanese disclosure standards were minimal during the 1990s, some banks did respond to requests for disclosure by voluntarily revealing their asset positions. The characteristics of banks that chose to voluntarily disclose this information is of interest, both as an indicator of the incentives faced by Japanese banks and more broadly as an indicator of the factors that lead to voluntary bank disclosure. The latter question is also relevant to bank regulation outside Japan, such as in the United States, where disclosure standards are so strict that there is usually little heterogeneity in disclosure levels across banks.

In this chapter we examine this question by investigating the degree of disclosure among small Japanese credit associations known as Shinkin banks. We examine the impact of Shinkin bank characteristics in 1998 on their decisions concerning bad loan disclosure in 1996 and 1997. Our sample is unique because disclosure of nonperforming loans by Shinkin banks was voluntary in 1996 and 1997 but became compulsory in 1998. Since individual bank conditions do not change very rapidly, bank conditions in 1998 give us a good indicator of conditions faced by banks in 1996 and 1997, including those banks that decided not to disclose their nonperforming loans.

Using these data, we examine a number of hypotheses concerning the determinants of disclosure decision. Our first hypothesis is that larger Shinkin banks would be more likely to voluntarily disclose. Larger Shinkin banks usually operate in more sophisticated financial environments with depositors that are more adamant about demanding balance sheet information. There may also be economies of scale in the calculation of financial information. Finally, there are regulatory reasons for larger banks to disclose more readily; the National Association of Shinkin Banks (NASB) recommended, but did not require, disclosure by Shinkin banks with deposits exceeding 100 billion yen.[4]

Our second hypothesis is that Shinkin banks would be less likely to voluntarily disclose adverse information. As we discuss below, the relative willingness to disclose adverse information is ambiguous in the literature. Firms may wish to disclose good information to distinguish themselves from their competitors, but they may also feel a need to disclose bad information to avoid exposure to lawsuits. In the case of banks, we believe that the presence of deposit insurance would seem to limit the pressure to voluntarily disclose adverse information, leading us to predict relatively less adverse information disclosure.

Our third hypothesis concerns the impact of financial strength. Traditionally the Ministry of Finance (MOF) executed the "convoy system" regarding Japanese banks,[5] whereby stronger banks were limited in their ability to compete against weaker banks. For example, deposit interest rates were limited to levels consistent with profitability by the most inefficient banks. However, by the time of our sample (March 1996 and 1997), the failures of many financial institutions suggest that the MOF had at least partially abandoned the convoy system.[6] Without the convoy system, a bank could benefit from distinguishing its financial situation from those of its rivals. Our third hypothesis is therefore that institutions with lower leverage levels would be more likely to voluntarily disclose their balance sheet information.

Our final hypothesis concerns market conditions. We would expect a bank that operated in a more competitive market to be more likely to pursue voluntary disclosure for a number of reasons: First, one would expect that a bank in a more competitive market would need to be more responsive to depositor demands for disclosure. Second, one would expect that in a less competitive market, banks would be less likely to voluntarily disclose information that was of potential use to rival banks.[7] Our final hypothesis is therefore that voluntary disclosure would be more prevalent in less concentrated markets.

Our results demonstrate that banks with more serious bad loan problems are less likely to choose to voluntarily disclose. Second, market forces, as measured by the intensity of local competition, did not measurably affect bank disclosure decisions in 1996, but did in 1997. Finally, we find that larger Shinkin banks were more likely to disclose information, in keeping with the corporate literature on disclosure. These results are robust to the inclusion of variables representing regional differences, including past failures in the region and a complete set of regional dummies.

This chapter consists of six sections. Section 4.2 describes the Japanese Shinkin banks. In section 4.3 we examine the history of bank disclosure in Japan. Section 4.4 motivates the hypotheses we study in this paper and discusses our data sources. Section 4.5 discusses our empirical results. Finally, section 4.6 concludes.

4.2   Japanese Shinkin Banks

Japan's Shinkin banks, commonly known as credit associations, are relatively small financial institutions that are privately held by members living or operating near a bank's headquarter or branches. They concentrate their lending on small and medium enterprises in a given region and can only issue up to 20 percent of their loans to nonmembers (Hsu 1999). However, they accept deposits from both members and the public. In 1996 there were 410 Shinkin banks with average outstanding loans of 171 billion yen. The average size of a Shinkin bank is therefore about an eighth that of a regional bank. On average, they have 21 branches and 372 employees (Kano and Tsutsui 2003).

Although they are small individually, the large number of Shinkin banks outstanding implies that as a group they form an important component of the overall Japanese financial system (see table 4.1). As a group, Shinkin banks have more deposits and loans outstanding than either the group of second regional or trust banks.

Moreover, because Japanese Shinkin banks are mandated to provide a large share of the financing of small and medium firms who might have exceptional difficulty obtaining credit elsewhere (Fukuyama 1996), their importance to the financial system may exceed their size. Shinkin banks extended 17 percent of small business loans in March 1996. They also play a particularly important role in rural regions where large banks have few branches.

There may be some concern that since Shinkin banks are privately held and only issue loans to their members, they may deviate from decisions based on profit maximization. However, despite the fact that members elect the CEO of Shinkin banks, they have a lot of autonomy

Table 4.1
Japanese financial institutions, March 1996

Bank type	Number of banks	Deposits (billion yen)	Loans (billion yen)
City banks	10	214,406	215,236
Regional banks	64	168,732	135,998
Second regional banks	65	61,265	53,280
Trust banks	33	17,146	31,584
Shinkin banks	410	97,732	70,201

Source: Bank of Japan, *Economic Statistics Monthly*.

in practice. Moreover most Shinkin bank business is quite similar to that of commercial banks.

Alternatively, there may be some concern that because many depositors in Shinkin banks also own equity in those banks, they will fail to provide the depositor discipline needed for disclosure rules to have an effect on privately held institutions. However, while general evidence on Shinkin banks' deposit sources is unavailable, evidence from individual Shinkin banks that do release their deposit share data indicates that a majority of deposits are obtained from the general public, rather than members. For example, Toyohashi Shinkin, the sixtieth largest shinkin bank, recently disclosed that only 29.2 percent of its deposits came from its members, while the remainder came from the general public. Similarly it was recently revealed that only 30.3 percent of deposits at Adachi Seiwa Shinkin bank were held by its members.[8]

As such, although we admit that Shinkin banks may have unique characteristics because of their status as mutual organizations, we feel comfortable proceeding under the assumption that Shinkin banks do behave in a similar manner to commercial banks and face market discipline from their depositors.

4.3   Disclosure by Japanese Financial Institutions

In the 1980s Japanese banks outperformed US and European banks. Then the downturn in the 1990s deteriorated the financial positions of Japanese banks. When defaults did occur, collateral values (primarily backed by land and real estate) were not large enough to cover losses. This led to the current bad loan problems faced by Japanese financial institutions.

Japanese banks were initially very reluctant to disclose their bad-loan exposure, and disclosure was initially not required by the MOF. However, the public demand for bad-loan disclosures grew as the situation deteriorated. This led to large banks (city banks, long-term credit banks, and trust banks) being forced at the end of March 1993 to disclose the magnitude of "loans to failed borrowers," which we label *BAD1*, and "loans to borrowers who can not pay within six months of due date," which we label *BAD2*. First and second regional banks, which are on average smaller than large banks, were also forced to disclose *BAD1*, but they were not required to disclose *BAD2*.

Banks sometimes engaged in "evergreening" of loans, namely renegotiating loan interest rates and due dates in order to avoid default.

This practice left disclosure of *BAD1* and *BAD2* poor indicators of a bank's true financial condition. In response, since September 1995 large banks have also been required to disclose the magnitude of "loans with interest rates lower than Bank of Japan's discount rates," which we label *BAD3*.

Regional banks were also obligated to begin disclosing *BAD2* and *BAD3* in March 1996. At that time large banks also began disclosing "the amounts of loans to borrowers whom banks supported," which we label *BAD4*.

Regulation forcing smaller regional financial institutions to disclose was slower in coming. Initially the MOF encouraged, but did not force, smaller financial institutions such as Shinkin banks and credit unions to disclose these figures. After the failure of several small financial institutions, however, the public demanded the disclosure of information concerning these small institutions' financial condition as well.

The MOF began releasing figures for problem loans of smaller institutions in September 1995. It initially only disclosed aggregate figures. The MOF defended its disclosure policy on the basis of concerns that adverse news about individual small banks might trigger runs. However, this policy was strongly criticized after many banks that reported adequate capital positions eventually failed. This led to a growing consensus that transparency in the Japanese financial sector would facilitate the revitalization of the sector.

Because of this external pressure, the National Association of Shinkin Banks (NASB) recommended that the Shinkin banks holding deposits equal to or larger than 100 billion yen disclose their *BAD1* positions at the end of March 1996 and that all Shinkin banks disclose their *BAD1* positions at the end of March 1997. However, as we demonstrate below, some Shinkin that fell within this criterion did not disclose their bad-loan figures at the end of March 1996. Indeed, a few did not even disclose their bad-loan figures by the end of March 1997. In March 1998 the NASB directed all Shinkin banks to disclose their *BAD1*, *BAD2*, *BAD3*, and *BAD4* positions. It follows that the disclosure of balance sheet positions was "voluntary" for Shinkin banks only in 1996 and 1997 (see table 4.2).

Because of the limited disclosure discretion faced by banks in the United States, evidence on voluntary bank disclosure among US banks is limited. There is nevertheless a large literature on voluntary disclosure across US corporations. Skinner (1994, 1997) posits that managers choose voluntary disclosure to limit exposure to stockholder litigation.

Table 4.2
"Bad-loan" disclosure requirements among Japanese financial institutions

	BAD1	BAD2	BAD3	BAD4
Large banks (city, long-term credit, and trust banks)	March 1993	March 1993	March 1996[a]	September 1996[b]
Regional banks	March 1993	March 1996	March 1997[c]	March 1997
Second regional banks	March 1993	March 1997[c]	March 1997[c]	March 1997
Shinkin banks	March 1996[d]	March 1998	March 1998	March 1998

Notes: This table is based on financial statement disclosure requirements. The total amount of bad loan that the entire deposit-taking financial institutions held has been disclosed since September 1995.
a. Voluntary disclosure has existed since September 1995. However, the figures were not included in the official financial statements for that year.
b. The figures have been voluntarily disclosed in annual report since March 1996.
c. The disclosure for March 1996 was voluntary and became required after March 1997. However, all banks actually voluntarily disclosed their figures in March 1996.
d. The National Association of Shinkin Banks recommended disclosure by Shinkin banks with deposits exceeding 100 billion yen. However, compliance was not universal.

Skinner (1994) finds that managers voluntarily disclose adverse earnings news "early," or before the mandated release date. Skinner (1997) also finds that early voluntary disclosure lowers expected legal costs. These results suggest that managers voluntarily disclose bad news more than good news.

Other research investigates whether voluntary disclosure reduces the cost of capital, as enhanced disclosure reduces information asymmetries. Botosan (1997) finds that greater disclosure is associated with a lower cost of equity capital for firms with low analyst followings. Information asymmetries would be greatest among these firms. Lang and Lundholm (2000) find that firms increase their disclosure activity prior to an equity offering announcement.[9] These results suggest that firms disclose favorable information to distinguish themselves from less successful firms.

Concerning the disclosure decisions of Japanese corporations, Cooke (1991, 1992, 1996) uses annual reports of Japanese corporations to measure the degree of voluntary disclosure. Cooke finds that size is the most important determinant of voluntary disclosure by Japanese firms. Singleton and Globerman (2002) also find that larger Japanese corporations tend to disclose more information.

In addition to size Cooke finds that firm voluntary disclosure decisions are affected by their equity listing characteristics, including whether and where a firm is listed (domestically or internationally).

He also finds that the degree of voluntary disclosure is affected by industry type, distinguishing between manufacturing and other industries, and by leverage.

Cooke (1996) examines the effect of Keiretsu membership on corporate disclosure. Within the Keiretsu, information may be more widely shared. As a result a firm in a Keiretsu may face less severe information asymmetry difficulties, as it primarily obtains its financing from its Keiretsu main bank partner. This would give firms within a Keiretsu less motivation to voluntarily disclose. However, after controlling for size, stock market listing status, leverage, and industry type, Cooke finds no evidence supporting the hypothesis that Keiretsu firms disclose less information than other firms.

4.4   Hypotheses Concerning Disclosure Levels

In this section we elaborate on the hypotheses we test in our study. As our sample consists of only Shinkin banks, there is no issue of listing status or industry type. Shinkin banks are all unlisted closed membership cooperatives.[10] Also, because of regulatory constraints, the basic activity of Shinkin banks are all identical. That is, they collect deposits from their member firms and local depositors and lend primarily to member firms.

4.4.1   Size

We expect size to have a positive effect on a firm's disclosure activity for a number of reasons: First, larger firms need to raise capital in the market more frequently and are under greater pressure from shareholders and market analysts for increased disclosure. While Shinkin banks raise little capital in the market, larger Shinkin banks may face greater disclosure pressure from their depositors because they usually operate in more financially-sophisticated environments than smaller Shinkin banks. Customers (both depositors and borrowers) of larger Shinkin banks are more often approached by commercial bank competitors, such as city banks and regional banks. In contrast, small Shinkin banks usually enjoy relatively isolated long-term relationships with their member firms, and are not as exposed to market pressures. For example, the largest Shinkin bank in Japan, Jonan Shinkin bank, is located in Tokyo, the second largest Shinkin bank, Okazaki Shinkin bank, is located in Aichi, and the third largest Shinkin bank,

Kyoto-Chuo Shinkin bank, is located in Kyoto. These are all major urban areas with sophisticated financial environments.

It has also been suggested that voluntary disclosure would be positively related to bank size due to economies of scale in the calculation of financial information. For example, Kyobashi Shinkin bank employed only twenty-three managers and workers as of March 1998. However, we doubt that this argument would apply to Shinkin banks for two reasons. First, the bad-loan amount we consider should be relatively easy for banks to calculate. Moreover, as the MOF has reported aggregate bad-loan figures for Shinkin banks since 1995, they must have received the disaggregated number from all of the Shinkin banks, including the smaller ones.[11] Finally, there may be regulatory reasons for larger banks to be more likely to voluntarily disclose. The National Association of Shinkin Banks recommended, but did not require, disclosure by Shinkin banks with deposits exceeding 100 billion yen. Therefore larger Shinkin banks were under more pressure from the NASB. On the other hand, bank regulation may induce a negative relationship between size and disclosure if larger Shinkin banks are considered too big to fail. We doubt this possibility as several banks that were larger than the largest Shinkin banks had failed by the time of our sample.

4.4.2   Leverage

Leverage has also been identified as an important determinant of voluntary disclosure. Firms with higher leverage ratios will incur higher monitoring costs, which can be reduced through disclosure (e.g., Cooke 1996). In addition leverage levels affect depositors' interpretation of the severity of bad-loan difficulties. Disclosure of bad-loan levels may be positive if the news indicates that management intends to address a bank's bad-loan problem. This would, of course, depend on a bank's capacity to address its difficulties, which would be greater at less leveraged banks, holding all else equal. This may leave managers of less leveraged banks more willing to disclose information on bad loans.

4.4.3   Adverse News

Whether disclosure revealed good or bad news concerning the bank's underlying financial position is obviously also relevant. As discussed above, however, the literature is mixed as to whether firms would be more willing to disclose good or bad information. Skinner (1994), among others, argued that managers had greater incentives to disclose adverse news due to the expected legal costs from failing to reveal such news, and to the potential enhancement of reputations from bad news disclosure. Darrough and Stroughton (1990) argue that managers are more likely to disclose bad news for entry deterrence reasons. Teoh and Hwang (1991) argue that the disclosure of adverse news reveals that a firm can handle the release of such news, and therefore serves as a positive signal of firm quality.

On the other hand, many studies predict that managers would be more willing to disclose good news in order to distinguish their firms from their competitors. For example, Lev and Panman (1990) documented that managers disclose good news forecasts more often than bad news forecasts. Scott (1994) examines Canadian firms' voluntary disclosure of defined benefit pension plan information and also finds that good news is more likely to be disclosed. Verrecchia (1983) finds that more favorable news is more likely to be disclosed, after controlling for disclosure costs.

Usually one has difficulty calculating the impact of news quality on the disclosure decision, as conditions faced by banks deciding not to disclose is unobservable. However, in the case of our sample all Shinkin banks faced compulsory disclosure in March 1998. Although there may be some disparities, we believe that the disclosure figures in March 1998 are good predictors of conditions that were not disclosed in 1996 and 1997.

We test this conjecture by looking at the correlation among banks that did choose to disclose during the voluntary periods with their figures in 1998. The correlation coefficient between $BAD1$ in March 1996 and that in March 1998 is 0.88 for Shinkin banks that disclosed both figures and the correlation coefficient between $BAD1$ in March 1997 and March 1998 is 0.94. These high correlation coefficients would appear to confirm our conjecture.

4.4.4 Market Structure

Shinkin banks generally operate within a prefecture or smaller region where their headquarters are located. Although these banks specialize in small-size business lending, they do face competition from the rest of the banking industry within their area. It is well known that the level of this competition varies greatly across the nation (Kano and Tsutui 2003).

We expect a bank that operated in a more competitive market to be more likely to pursue voluntary disclosure for a number of reasons: First, a bank in a more competitive market is likely to need to be more responsive to depositor demands for disclosure. Second, in a less competitive market, banks are less likely to voluntarily disclose information that is of potential use to rival banks.[12]

4.4.5 Data

Our dependent variable is binary, representing the discrete disclosure decision of a Shinkin bank concerning the relevant bad loan measure. Our data source is *Financial Statements of Shinkin Banks* (FSSB), which is published annually by the Kinyu Tosyo Consultant Sha. As this is the only available data source regarding Shinkin banks, if the relevant figures are not reported here, then we assume that the figures were not disclosed.[13]

The level of Shinkin bank disclosure in our sample is summarized in table 4.3. There were 416 Shinkin Banks at the end of March 1996, and 407 at the end of March 1997. At the end of March 1996, 305 of the 416 Shinkin banks disclosed *BAD1*. No banks disclosed *BAD2* or *BAD3*. We use a qualitative variable, *DISC96* as our dependent variable for the March 1996 sample. *DISC96* takes unit value if the Shinkin bank disclosed *BAD1* in March 1996 and zero value otherwise.

For March 1997 only 33 Shinkin banks, or 8 percent of the industry, pursued no voluntary disclosure. Of the 407 Shinkin banks, 139 disclosed *BAD1*, *BAD2*, and *BAD3*. While this represents an increase in disclosure levels, it still falls below the rest of the financial sector. Large banks had all disclosed *BAD1*, *BAD2*, and *BAD3* since September 1995, while regional banks had disclosed *BAD1*, *BAD2*, and *BAD3* since March 1996. For our March 1997 sample we use an ordered-dummy variable, *DISC97*, to indicate disclosure intensity. *DISC97* takes value zero if a Shinkin bank did not disclose *BAD1*, takes value one if it disclosed only *BAD1*, and takes value two if it disclosed both *BAD1* and *BAD2*. Similarly it takes value three if it disclosed *BAD1*, *BAD2*, and *BAD3*.[14]

Table 4.3 also displays the geographic distribution of Shinkin disclosure. It can be seen that the magnitude of disclosure by Shinkin banks

Table 4.3
Disclosure levels of Shinkin banks by region

	March 1996			March 1997				
Area	Noth-ing	BAD1	Total	Noth-ing	BAD1	BAD1+2	BAD1+2+3	Total
Hokkaido	13	19	32	1	19	0	12	32
Tohoku	21	18	39	2	15	3	12	35
Kanto (excluding Tokyo)	3	47	50	1	39	1	9	50
Tokyo	12	39	51	7	38	1	1	49
Koushinetsu	3	17	20	1	10	0	9	20
Hokuriku	8	17	25	1	4	0	20	25
Tokai	1	46	47	1	20	0	26	47
Kinki	9	44	53	6	32	0	15	53
Chugoku	18	20	38	2	25	0	7	36
Shikoku	2	12	14	1	3	0	10	14
Kyushu	21	26	47	2	25	0	18	46
Total	111	305	416	24	230	5	139	398

Notes: Indicators of disclosure levels are defined as follows: Nothing: No disclosure regarding any kind of bad loans. BAD1: Only loans to failed companies are disclosed. BAD1+2: Loans to failed companies and loans six month overdue are disclosed. BAD1+2+3: In addition to the two loans above, loans whose interest rates are lower than Bank of Japan's discount rates are disclosed.

is asymmetric by region. For example, 94 percent of Shinkin banks in Kanto (excluding Tokyo) disclosed *BAD1* at the end of March 1996, while only 46 percent of Shinkin banks in Tohoku disclosed *BAD1* in that year. This suggests that regional factors also affect the disclosure decision of Shinkin banks. We control for regional disparities in our robustness checks below.

Concerning the independent variables, we use assets as of March 1998 as a proxy for size (*LASSET*). We use the capital ratio as of March 1998 as a proxy of bank leverage (*CAPRATIO*). We use two measures of the severity of bad-loan news contained in the disclosure. *HATAN-RATIO* is defined as the ratio of *BAD1* to total loans on March 1998. *FURYORATIO* is defined as the ratio of *BAD2* and *BAD3* to total loans on March 1998.[15]

We also use two measures of market competitiveness. *LGDPBRANCH96* is defined as the log of gross prefectural product (for fiscal year 1995, ending at March 1996) divided by total bank branches and Shinkin banks in March 1996. *LGDPBRANCH97* is defined in the same manner and is used for the 1997 disclosure decision estimation. A low value of *LGDPBRANCH* would imply greater competition in that prefecture. The coefficient on *LGDPBRANCH* is therefore expected to be negative, since competition would induce more disclosure.

4.5   Results

4.5.1   Results for Failed Banks

Before formally investigating the determinants of Shinkin bank disclosure, we first check the disclosure patterns of the subset of Shinkin banks that failed after the end of March 1997. There was one Shinkin bank failure in 1999, seven in 2000, six in 2001, and thirteen in 2002. Disclosure decisions for these failed banks are compared to the rest of the sample in table 4.4. The twenty-seven failed Shinkin banks chose disclosure less frequently than the rest of the sample. Only 50 percent of Shinkin banks that failed between 1998 and 2001 disclosed *BAD1* in March 1996, while 75 percent of the surviving Shinkin banks reported *BAD1* in that year.

Table 4.4
Disclosure by failed Shinkin banks

	March 1996		March 1997			
Ex post solvency	Total	BAD1	Total	BAD1	BAD2	BAD3
Number						
Not failed	389	291	371	345	131	126
Failed in 1999, 2000, and 2001	14	7	14	10	2	2
Failed in 2002	13	8	13	10	2	1
Ratio						
Not failed	389	75%	371	93%	35%	34%
Failed in 1999, 2000, and 2001	14	50%	14	71%	14%	14%
Failed in 2002	13	62%	13	77%	15%	8%

Notes: Indicators of disclosure levels are defined as follows: Nothing: No disclosure regarding any kinds of bad loans. BAD1: Only loans to failed companies are disclosed. BAD1+2: Loans to failed companies and loans six month overdue are disclosed. BAD1+2+3: In addition to the two loans above, loans whose interest rates are lower than Bank of Japan's discount rates are disclosed. Failure dates are based on decisions by Deposit Insurance Corporation to inject funds to merging institutions.

It is also interesting to compare Shinkin banks that failed during 1998 to 2001 with those that failed in 2002. The former group, for whom failure was apparently more imminent in March 1997, was more reluctant to disclose bad-loan information than the latter group. This finding is consistent with the hypothesis that banks with solvency problems and adverse news disclosed less and that the magnitude of their difficulties affected their disclosure decision.

4.5.2   Disclosure Decisions in March 1996

As banks that did disclose in 1996 only disclosed *BAD1*, our dependent variable, is binary. We therefore report the results of both OLS and probit estimation for disclosure decisions in that year. Missing data reduced our sample size from 416 banks to 387 banks.[16]

Our results for 1996 are shown in table 4.5. The results for both OLS and probit estimation are essentially the same. First, our size variable, *LASSET*, is positive and significant as predicted and consistent with earlier studies.

Recall that the NASB recommended in this year that Shinkin banks holding larger than 100 billion yen deposits disclose their values of *BAD1*. To investigate whether this was a factor in the more frequent disclosure by larger Shinkin banks, we split the sample into two subsamples based on whether deposit amounts in March 1998 were larger or smaller than 100 billion yen. Out of the 245 Shinkin banks exceeding this deposit level in 1998, only 14 did not disclose their values of *BAD1* in March 1996. In contrast, out of the 142 Shinkin banks with less than 100 billion yen in assets, 65 did not disclose *BAD1*. Therefore we can conclude that the NASB's recommendation was a factor in the greater amount of disclosure among larger Shinkin banks.

The estimated coefficient on our leverage measure, *CAPRATIO*, is positive but insignificant, implying that leverage was not a very important factor in 1996 disclosure choices.

Turning to our bad-loan measures, the estimated coefficient for *HATANRATIO* is significantly negative at the 5 percent level for both specifications. This suggests that Shinkin banks that held more bad loans were less likely to disclose *BAD1* in March 1996. This implies that Shinkin banks were more likely to withhold bad information.

The estimated coefficient for *LGDPBRANCH96* is not significant and is unexpectedly positive. This suggests that disparities in market competition did not influence disclosure decisions in 1996.

Table 4.5
Estimation results for disclosure choices

Variable	March 1996		March 1997			
	OLS	Probit	OLS	Ordered probit	OLS binary disclosure	Probit binary disclosure
Constant	−1.908**	−11.758**	2.845**		1.102**	1.635
	(0.418)	(2.015)	(1.131)		(0.525)	(1.611)
LASSET	0.210**	1.045**	0.090	0.144**	0.026	0.084
	(0.022)	(0.129)	(0.059)	(0.072)	(0.027)	(0.083)
CAPRATIO	0.002	0.001	0.044**	0.050**	0.019**	0.045*
	(0.006)	(0.028)	(0.018)	(0.022)	(0.008)	(0.025)
HATANRATIO	−2.765**	−10.285**	−1.226	−0.597	−1.108	0.293
	(1.249)	(5.179)	(3.501)	(4.260)	(1.627)	(5.453)
FURYORATIO			−8.688**	−8.851**	−4.524**	−25.161**
			(2.331)	(2.853)	(1.083)	(5.236)
LGDPBRANCH96	0.034	0.084				
	(0.085)	(0.375)				
LGDPBRANCH97			−0.467**	−0.552*	−0.208*	−0.560*
			(0.237)	(0.291)	(0.110)	(0.340)
Number of observations	387	387	382	382	382	382
Adjusted R^2	0.246		0.121		0.139	
Loglikelihood	−160.603	−150.215	−527.081	−329.22	−234.28	−215.097
LR index (pseudo-R^2)				0.060		
MacFadden R^2		0.288				0.149
Percentage correct		80				67

Notes: See text for definitions of qualitative dependent variables. Figures in the parentheses are standard errors. ** Statistically significant at 5 percent confidence level; * statistically significant at 10 percent confidence level.

4.5.3   Disclosure Decisions in March 1997

As *DISC97* is also a qualitative dependent variable, we again report the results of both OLS and ordered probit estimation. Our specification now also includes the *FURYORATIO* variable. As shown in table 4.3, most Shinkin banks disclosed *BAD1* for March 1997. Therefore *HATANRATIO* was disclosed for most Shinkin banks, while *FURYORATIO* was still undisclosed for most banks.

The results are shown in table 4.5. The coefficient for *LASSET* is positive for both the OLS and ordered probit estimations. These results suggest that size was still an important determinant of Shinkin banks' disclosure decisions in 1997. The coefficient on our leverage variable, *CAPRATIO*, is now significant. This is quite distinct from our 1996 results and appears to be attributable to the decline in Japanese financial conditions between 1996 and 1997. With this decline in financial conditions, the value to sound banks of distinguishing themselves from the rest of the industry was increased.

Both *HATANRATIO* and *FURYORATIO* take their expected negative coefficients, as adverse news is less likely to be disclosed. However, the *HATANRATIO* coefficient is insignificant in both models, while the coefficient for *FURYORATIO* is highly significant in both models. This disparity appears to be attributable to the fact that by 1997 there was little variability across Shinkin banks in the disclosure of *BAD1*, as almost all banks disclosed this figure.

The coefficient for *LGDPBRANCH97* is now significantly negative at around 5 percent. This suggests that competition promotes bank disclosures, as predicted.

To check our robustness, we considered an alternative indicator of disclosure in 1997. We specify our dependent variable as a binary variable that takes value zero if there was no disclosure or if only *BAD1* was disclosed, and value one otherwise. Under this specification 238 Shinkin banks in the sample are given value zero, and 144 Shinkin banks are given value 1. The results are shown in table 4.5. The size variable, *LASSET*, is now insignificant, but the remaining results are all the same. The coefficients on *CAPRATIO*, *FURYORATIO*, and *LGDPBRANCH97* all enter significantly with their predicted signs. We therefore conclude that our results are fairly robust to using a binary dependent variable for the 1997 sample.

4.5.4 Regional Differences

Kano and Tsutsui (2003) find that Shinkin bank markets are segmented by region. There are also a number of reasons to expect that Shinkin bank disclosure decisions may differ across regions. Shinkin banks in regions where failures took place may find themselves under greater pressure from depositors to disclose. There are also regional disparities in economic conditions.[17] As such, one would want to condition on regional differences to evaluate the robustness of the results above.

We first examine the impact of regional failure histories. Prior to March 1997 there were only two Shinkin failures: Toyo Shinkin in

Osaka in 1992 and Kamaishi Shinkin in Iwate in 1993. However, local commercial bank failures may also have affected the disclosure pressure faced by Shinkin banks. There were four such bank failures before March 1997: Toho Sogo Bank in Ehime in 1992, Hyogo Bank in Hyogo in 1995, Taiheyo Bank in Tokyo in 1996, and Hanwa Bank in Wakayama in 1996. To accommodate regional differences that may have existed due to these failures, we introduce a *regional failure* indicator into our specification. This indicator takes value one if a Shinkin bank is located in one of the prefectures with failure histories mentioned above (i.e., if the bank is from Ehime, Hyogo, Tokyo, and Wakayama), and zero otherwise.

The results are shown in table 4.6. The *regional failure* indicator is universally insignificant and therefore leaves the original results largely intact. In particular, we retain the results that larger banks are more likely to disclose, as are banks in stronger financial positions. The most notable difference in our results is that the intensity of local competition no longer enters significantly, although it still takes on the appropriate negative sign.[18]

Finally, regional disparities may arise for a number of reasons, not limited to local failure histories. To more broadly entertain fixed regional disparities, we also ran our specification with separate dummies for all regions. We construct eight regional dummies: (1) *HOKATOHO*, which includes Hokkaido and Tohoku, (2) *KANTO*, which includes Tokyo, (3) *HOKURIKU*, (4) *CHUBU*, which includes Aichi, (5) *KINKI*, which includes Osaka and Hyogo, (6) *CHUGOKU*, (7) *SHIKOKU*, and (8) *KYUSHU*. The results are shown in table 4.7. Again, our results were largely robust to the inclusion of a full set of regional dummies except for the local competition variable.[19]

4.6   Conclusion

Disclosure is widely regarded as a necessary condition for market discipline in a modern financial sector. However, the determinants of disclosure decisions are still unknown, particularly among banks. To formulate optimal disclosure policy, it is necessary to know what factors affect disclosure decision of banks. In this chapter we investigated the determinants of Shinkin banks' bad-loan disclosure for March 1996 and 1997. This period is unique because disclosure was voluntary for Shinkin banks during this time. Voluntary disclosure information by financial institutions is very rare, primarily due to the fact that disclo-

Table 4.6
Estimation results for disclosure choices with *regional failure* dummy

Variable	March 1996 OLS	March 1996 Probit	March 1997 OLS	March 1997 Ordered probit	March 1997 OLS binary disclosure	March 1997 Probit binary disclosure
Constant	−2.146**	−12.466**	2.151*		0.842	1.113
	(0.456)	(2.149)	(1.219)		(0.567)	(1.684)
LASSET	0.211**	1.042**	0.096	0.152**	0.028	0.092
	(0.022)	(0.128)	(0.059)	(0.073)	(0.027)	(0.084)
CAPRATIO	0.002	0.001	0.042**	0.049**	0.018**	0.045*
	(0.006)	(0.028)	(0.018)	(0.022)	(0.008)	(0.025)
HATANRATIO	−2.679**	−10.132**	−0.958	−0.267	−1.008	0.268
	(1.250)	(5.168)	(3.499)	(4.275)	(1.628)	(5.464)
FURYORATIO			−8.696**	−8.913**	−4.527**	−24.622**
			(2.327)	(2.8861)	(1.083)	(5.254)
LGDPBRANCH96	0.080	0.236				
	(0.092)	(0.407)				
LGDPBRANCH97			−0.337	−0.388	−0.159	−0.471
			(0.251)	(0.310)	(0.117)	(0.351)
REGIONAL FAILURE	−0.066	−0.227	−0.203	−0.258	−0.076	
	(0.052)	(0.238)	(0.134)	(0.163)	(0.063)	
Number of observations	387	387	382	382	382	382
Adjusted R^2	0.247		0.124		0.140	
Loglikelihood	−159.763	−149.762	−525.92	−327.974	−233.526	−214.825
LR index (pseudo-R^2)				0.064		
MacFadden R^2		0.290				0.151
Percentage correct		80				67

Notes: See text for definitions of qualitative dependent variables. Figures in the parentheses are standard errors. ** Statistically significant at 5 percent confidence level; * statistically significant at 10 percent confidence level.

sure is mandatory among most institutions in most developed countries. As such, the differences in disclosure decisions across Shinkin banks should shed some light on the effectiveness of disclosure policies in enhancing financial transparency.

We obtained some interesting results. First, banks with more serious bad-loan problems were less likely to choose to voluntarily disclose. Second, larger Shinkin banks were more likely to disclose information, consistent with the corporate literature on disclosure. Finally, market forces, as measured by the intensity of local competition, did not force

Table 4.7
Estimation results for disclosure choices with regional dummies

Variable	March 1996 OLS	March 1996 Probit	March 1997 OLS	Ordered probit	OLS binary disclosure	Probit binary disclosure
Constant	−0.998	−9.602**	0.442		−0.097	−1.103
	(0.676)	(3.281)	(1.752)		(0.815)	(2.507)
LASSET	0.187**	1.052**	0.070	0.126	0.017	0.064
	(0.023)	(0.141)	(0.062)	(0.078)	(0.029)	(0.090)
CAPRATIO	0.004	0.007	0.037**	0.045**	0.015*	0.040
	(0.006)	(0.030)	(0.018)	(0.023)	(0.008)	(0.026)
HATANRATIO	−2.601**	−10.254*	−3.158	−2.911	−2.097	−3.386
	(1.259)	(5.699)	(3.528)	(4.451)	(1.641)	(5.764)
FURYORATIO			−6.978**	−7.449**	−3.636**	−22.282**
			(2.517)	(3.171)	(1.171)	(5.745)
LGDPBRANCH96	−0.074	−0.290				
	(0.122)	(0.576)				
LGDPBRANCH97			0.007	−0.077	0.025	−0.029
			(0.310)	(0.394)	(0.144)	(0.448)
Number of observations	387	387	382	382	382	382
Adjusted R^2	0.275		0.162		0.177	
Loglikelihood	−149.264	−137.44	−514.203	−317.827	−221.891	−205.923
LR index (pseudo-R^2)				0.093		
MacFadden R^2		0.349				0.186
Percentage correct		83				72

Notes: See text for definitions of qualitative dependent variables. Figures in the parentheses are standard errors. Specifications included regional dummies, which were not listed for space considerations. The estimations and standard errors of the dummy variables are available upon request. ** Statistically significant at 5 percent confidence level; * statistically significant at 10 percent confidence level.

banks to disclose more information in March 1996, but did in March 1997. This final result, however, was not robust to the inclusion of regional dummy indicators, leaving it difficult to conclude whether the observed regional differences were truly attributable to differences in local competition conditions, or to other factors such as disparities in local failure experiences.

There are several questions for future investigation. First, in this chapter we only investigated the decision to disclose bad-loan ratios. Some analysts contend that bad-loan disclosure is insufficient to evaluate banks' financial conditions. It is therefore important to examine the determinants of disclosure of other types of bank information. Second, the credibility of the disclosed information is also uncertain.[20] As Hutchison (1997) points out, the MOF several times changed financial disclosure and accounting rules to allow stock losses to be deferred and to delay the effect of real estate price declines on banks' reported capital. The quality of disclosed information could affect bank decisions as to whether or not to disclose. Third, our study demonstrates that weak banks are less likely to voluntarily disclose. There may therefore be a role for compulsory disclosure, since such a requirement may disproportionately fall on weaker banks. It would be interesting to evaluate the impact of such disclosure requirements on bank behavior.

Finally, the impact of disclosure on bank systematic risk is also of interest. Banks' assets are opaque, in the sense that it is hard for outsiders to evaluate bank loan quality due to information asymmetry. Furthermore banks rely heavily on short-term liabilities. Disclosure by individual banks may trigger marketwide actions by private stakeholders, leading to systemic risk (Federal Reserve System Study Group on Disclosure 2000).[21] Regarding US banks, Jordan et al. (2000) found that disclosure was not destabilizing. It would be interesting to examine if this was also the case for Japan.

Notes

This chapter was prepared for the CESifo workshop on Economic Stagnation in Japan, held in Venice, Italy. We thank Michael Hutchison and Frank Westermann for organizing an excellent conference. We thank all of the seminar participants for helpful comments, particularly Rob Dekle, Charles Horioka, Takeo Hoshi, and Takatoshi Ito. We also thank an anonymous referee. The views expressed in this paper are those of the authors and do not necessarily reflect those of the Board of Governors of the Federal Reserve or the Federal Reserve Bank of San Francisco.

1. Basel Committee on Banking Supervision (1999).

2. Singleton and Globerman (2002) find that voluntary disclosure by Japanese firms has increased significantly.

3. Yamori and Baba (2001) survey the international literature on disclosure standards.

4. Shinkin banks were regulated by the Ministry of Finance at the time of our study, and are now under the regulation of the Financial Services Agency (FSA). This is distinct from credit banks, which were under local regulatory control at the time of our study but are now also under the jurisdiction of the FSA.

5. See Spiegel (1999) for details on the Japanese convoy system.

6. Spiegel and Yamori (2004) find that the convoy system deteriorated over this period.

7. Darrough and Stroughton (1990) provide a theoretical model of this impact of market concentration on voluntary disclosure by firms.

8. Adachi Seiwa March 2003 (fiscal 2002) supplementary pamphlet (in Japanese). Available at ⟨http://www.adachishinkin.co.jp/01/Mreport/m5.pdf⟩.

9. Lang and Lundholm also find that firms that *substantially* increase their disclosure activity before the offering suffer much larger price declines at the announcement of their intent to issue equity. They interpret this fact as suggesting these firms use voluntary disclosure to "hype the stock."

10. Because Shinkin banks are unlisted, a number of the potential considerations for voluntary disclosure raised in the literature may not be relevant. For example, Healy and Palepu (2001) suggest that disclosure may reduce transactions costs in capital markets by lowering information asymmetries, affect corporate control contests, circumvent inside trade regulation when managers exercise stock options, or signal management talent. Some of these considerations may be irrelevant for unlisted Shinkin banks, while others may manifest themselves in different ways than they would under listed firms.

11. Chen et al. (2002) argue that disclosure costs are unimportant determinants of voluntary balance sheet disclosure decisions.

12. Chen et al. (2002) finds that investors demand greater disclosure when reported losses are higher. In response, managers disclose more when reported losses are large. However, as profits also increase a bank's ability to write off its bad loans, its net impact on willingness to disclose is ambiguous. To examine the impact of profitability, we added the natural log of business profits (Gyomu-rieki) as of March 1998 in our first-stage estimation as a proxy for expected future performance. The variable was insignificant. The results, with profits, are available from the authors on request.

13. A footnote in the FSSB notes that 18 Shinkin banks claimed that their figures were not available at the FSSB's publication deadline for the March 1996 version, but that they would be disclosed later. However, this claim appears to be dubious, as the publication deadline occurred after the June members' meeting, for which financial statements would have to calculated and approved by auditors. We therefore treat these 18 banks as failing to disclose. Information is unavailable as to whether or not they did eventually disclose their positions that year. We checked the robustness of our results below by re-running our specification with these 18 Shinkin banks excluded from our sample.

14. Scott (1994) uses a similar ordered-dummy variable method to indicate disclosure levels. In his study, firms can disclose both pension costs and interest assumptions, only pension costs, or neither.

15. We do not anticipate any causality problems with these variables. Bank bad-loan problems had been growing since the late 1980s, while Shinkin banks were not required to disclose their bad-loan amounts before the mid-1990s. See Core (2001) for further discussion.

16. Financial statements as of March 1998 for 29 Shinkin banks were not available because of mergers or failures.

17. There may also be regional disparities in regulatory treatment. While Shinkin banks from all regions were formally subject to the same regulatory restrictions, local regulator discretion could have resulted in heterogeneity in the enforcement of these restrictions.

18. It may be the case that smaller failures did not have as significant impact on their regions. To investigate this possibility, we also limited our *regional failure* dummy to those regions that had failures whose resolution costs to the Deposit Insurance Corporation exceeded 100 billion yen. These included Tokyo (Cosmo Credit Union, Taiheyo), Hyogo (Hyogo Bank), and Osaka (Kizu Credit Union). Our results with this alternative indicator were essentially the same and are available from the authors on request.

19. For space considerations, the dummy coefficients were not reported. These are available from the authors on request. To avoid multicollinearity, we dropped the *KANTO* dummy. As such, the constant coefficient should be interpreted as representing the *KANTO* region.

20. Although only limited information is available, there is some evidence that Japanese markets did discipline riskier banks (e.g., Genay 1999; Yamori 1999; Bremer and Pettway 2002). Therefore disclosure may enhance market discipline.

21. For example, Cordella and Yeyati (1998) construct a theoretical model to study the effect of disclosure on the probability of banking crises. They find that when banks do not control their risk exposure, disclosure may increase the probability of bank failures.

References

Balic, A., N. Bradley, and H. Kiguchi. 2002. Results of Japan transparency and disclosure Survey for S&P/TOPIX 150 Companies. Available at S&P Web site ⟨http://standardandpoors.com⟩.

Basel Committee on Banking Supervision. 1999. *New Capital Adequacy Framework*. Bank for International Settlement.

Botosan, C. A. 1997. Disclosure level and the cost of equity capital. *Accounting Review* 72 (3): 323–49.

Bremer, M., and R. H. Pettway. 2000. Information and the market's perceptions of Japanese bank risk: Regulation, environment, and disclosure. *Pacific-Basin Finance Journal* 10: 119–39.

Calomiris, C. W. 1999. Building an incentive compatible safety net. *Journal of Banking and Finance* 23 (10): 1499–1519.

Cargill, T., M. Hutchison, and T. Ito. 1997. *The Political Economy of Japanese Monetary Policy*. Cambridge: MIT Press.

Chen, S., M. L. DeFond, and C. W. Park. 2002. Voluntary disclosure of balance sheet information in quarterly earnings announcements. *Journal of Accounting and Economics* 33: 229–51.

Cordella, T., and E. Levy Yeyati. 1998. Public disclosure and bank failures. *IMF Staff Papers* 45 (1): 110–31.

Cooke, T. E. 1991. An assessment of voluntary disclosure in the annual reports of Japanese corporations. *International Journal of Accounting* 26: 174–89.

Cooke, T. E. 1992. The impact of size, stock market listing and industry type on disclosure in the annual reports of Japanese listed corporations. *Accounting and Business Research* 22: 229–37.

Cooke, T. E. 1996. The influence of the keiretsu on Japanese corporate disclosure. *Journal of International Financial Management and Accounting* 7 (3): 191–214.

Core, J. E. 2001. A review of the empirical disclosure literature: Discussion. *Journal of Accounting and Economics* 31: 441–56.

Darrough, M. H., and N. M. Stoughton. 1990. Financial disclosure policy in an entry game. *Journal of Accounting and Economics* 12: 219–43.

DeYoung, R., M. Flannery, M. Lang, and S. Sorescu. 2001. The information content of bank exam ratings and subordinated debt prices. *Journal of Money, Credit, and Banking* 33: 900–25.

Federal Reserve Study Group on Disclosure. 2000. Improving public disclosure in banking. *Board of Governors of the Federal Reserve System Staff Study* 173: 1–35.

Flannery, M. J., and S. M. Sorescu. 1996. Evidence of bank market discipline in subordinated debenture yields. *Journal of Finance* 51: 1347–77.

Fukuyama, H. 1996. Returns to scale and efficiency of credit associations in Japan: A nonparametric approach. *Japan and the World Economy* 8: 259–77.

Genay, H. 1999. Japanese banks and market discipline. *Chicago Fed Letter* 144: 1–3.

Gunther, J. W., and R. R. Moore. 2000. Financial statements and reality: Do troubled banks tell all? *Federal Reserve Bank of Dallas Economic and Financial Review* (3Q): 30–35.

Hancock, D., and M. L. Kwast. 2001. Using subordinated debt to monitor bank holding companies: Is it feasible? *Journal of Financial Services Research* 20 (2/3): 147–87.

Healy, P. M., and K. G. Palepu. 2001. Information asymmetry, corporate disclosure, and the capital markets: A review of the empirical disclosure literature. *Journal of Accounting and Economics* 31: 405–40.

Hsu, R. C. 1999. Shinkin banks. In his *The MIT Encyclopedia of the Japanese Economy*, 2nd ed. Cambridge: MIT Press, pp. 399–400.

Hutchison, M. 1997. Financial crises and bank supervision: New directions for Japan? *Federal Reserve Bank of San Francisco Economic Letter*: 97–37.

Jordan, J. S., J. Peek, and E. Rosengren. 2000. The impact of greater bank disclosure amidst a banking crisis. *Journal of Financial Intermediation* 9: 298–319.

Kano, M., and Y. Tsutui. 2003. Geographical segmentation in Japanese bank loan markets. *Regional Science and Urban Economics* 33: 157–74.

Kashyap, A. K. 2002. Sorting out Japan's financial crisis. *Federal Reserve Bank of Chicago Economic Perspectives* (4Q): 42–55.

Krainer, J., and J. A. Lopez. 2002. Incorporating equity market information into supervisory monitoring models. FRBSF Working Paper 2001-14.

Lang, M. H., and R. J. Lundholm. 2000. Voluntary disclosure and equity offerings: Reducing information asymmetry or hyping the stock? *Contemporary Accounting Research* 17 (4): 623–62.

Lev, B., and S. H. Penman. 1990. Voluntary forecast disclosures, nondisclosure, and stock prices. *Journal of Accounting Research* 28: 49–76.

Morgan, D. P., and K. J. Stiroh. 2001. Market discipline of banks: The asset test. *Journal of Financial Services Research* 20: 195–208.

Scott, T. W. 1994. Incentives and disincentives for financial disclosure: Voluntary disclosure of defined benefit pension plan information by Canadian firms. *Accounting Review* 69 (1): 26–43.

Singleton, W. R., and S. Globerman. 2002. The changing nature of financial disclosure in Japan. *International Journal of Accounting* 37: 95–111.

Skinner, D. J. 1994. Why firms voluntarily disclose bad news. *Journal of Accounting Research* 32: 38–60.

Skinner, D. J. 1997. Earnings disclosures and stockholder lawsuits. *Journal of Accounting and Economics* 23: 249–82.

Spiegel, M. 1999. Moral hazard under the Japanese "convoy" banking system. *Federal Reserve Bank of San Francisco Economic Review*: 3–13.

Spiegel, M., and N. Yamori. 2004. The evolution of bank resolution policies in Japan: Evidence from market equity values. *Journal of Financial Research* 27: 115–32.

Teoh, S. H., and C. Y. Hwang. 1991. Nondisclosure and adverse selection as signals of firm value. *Review of Financial Studies* 4: 283–313.

Verrecchia, R. E. 1983. Discretionary disclosure. *Journal of Accounting and Economics* 5: 179–94.

Yamori, N. 1999. Stock market reaction to the bank liquidation in Japan: A case for the informational effect hypothesis. *Journal of Financial Services Research* 15 (1): 57–68.

Yamori, N., and T. Baba. 2001. Japanese management views on overseas exchange listings survey results. *Journal of International Financial Management and Accounting* 12 (3): 286–316.

5   Secondary Bank Lending in Japan

Zekeriya Eser, Joe Peek, and
Eric S. Rosengren

5.1   Introduction

Japan has suffered from weak economic performance for more than a
decade. Many consider the poor health of the banking system as a key
contributing factor to the inability of the Japanese economy to return to
the robust health that characterized most of the postwar period prior to
the bursting of the stock market and real estate bubbles at the beginning of the 1990s. Because Japan is a bank-centered economy and bank
regulators have been unable to resolve the continuing banking crisis, it
is not surprising that banks are deemed to play a central role in the
extended malaise of the real economy.

Peek and Rosengren (2005) have shown that financially weakened
Japanese banks misallocated credit in the 1990s because of the perverse
incentives they faced to make additional loans to the weakest firms in
order to avoid having to declare the loans as nonperforming in order
to protect their own balance sheets. In this study we extend the analysis of Peek and Rosengren (2005) to investigate the role played by secondary (non–main) banks in this misallocation of credit. While much
attention has been focused on the special role of main banks in the Japanese system, secondary banks also play an important role, accounting
for about 75 percent of bank loans to firms listed on the first and second sections of the Tokyo stock exchange, and face many of the same
incentives and pressures as main banks, such as government pressure
to keep zombie firms operating and incentives to "evergreen" loans to
protect the bank's own balance sheet.

While secondary banks do not have the superior information about
firms to guide their lending decisions that comes with a main bank affiliation, many secondary banks still have keiretsu affiliations with the
firm or the firm's main bank, or both, that likely influence their lending

behavior. Furthermore, although secondary banks do not have direct access to the superior information from a main bank affiliation, they can still indirectly exploit such superior information by using main bank lending behavior as a signal of firm health, insofar as the main bank serves as the delegated monitor for other lenders to the firm.

However, such a leader–follower relationship becomes problematic when main banks face perverse incentives to evergreen loans to sick firms. On the one hand, close relationships between main banks and their borrowers should be particularly important during periods when the agency problem is most acute, such as occurred in the 1990s when the Japanese economy grew very slowly and stock and land prices were less than half the level they had been a decade earlier. If the main bank system improves information flows and causes Japanese banks to allocate credit more efficiently, main bank lending may be a good leading indicator of firms' future performance. On the other hand, the perverse incentives faced by unhealthy main banks to ever-green loans to the weakest firms in order to avoid having to declare the loans as nonperforming reduces the value of the signal provided to secondary banks not privy to the superior information about potential borrowers.

This study utilizes a detailed micro panel data set that identifies loans by individual Japanese banks to individual Japanese firms to investigate the behavior of secondary banks in Japan during the 1990s. We first document that these banks tended to evergreen loans, with the probability of the bank increasing loans to a firm increasing the weaker is the firm, the weaker is the bank, the greater is the exposure of the bank to the firm, and if the bank has a keiretsu affiliation with either the firm or the firm's main bank. We then investigate the extent to which these secondary banks tend to increase loans to a firm when the firm's main bank does so. We find that secondary banks are less likely to follow the lead of the main bank when the main bank has a particularly strong incentive to evergreen loans to a firm, as indicated by the main bank's poor health and by the main bank having a large exposure to the firm.

Section 5.2 of the chapter discusses the role of main bank and keiretsu affiliations in Japan. Section 5.3 describes the perverse incentives faced by Japanese banks during the 1990s and how these incentives distort the signal provided by a main bank increasing loans to a firm. Section 5.4 describes the data. Section 5.5 contains the primary hypotheses to be tested and the empirical specification used for the hypothesis tests. Section 5.6 provides the empirical results, and section 5.7 concludes.

5.2 Keiretsu and Main Bank Affiliations in Japan

Keiretsu and main bank affiliations have received a great deal of attention in descriptions of the Japanese economy and have played a key role in many explanations of Japanese economic performance, both during the Japanese "miracle" characterized by rapid growth following World War II and during the "lost decade" of the 1990s. During the 1980s and early 1990s most studies of Japanese corporate affiliations found significant benefits. These studies emphasized the unique features of Japanese corporate affiliations that reduced agency costs (Hoshi, Kashyap, and Scharfstein 1993; Hoshi, Kashyap, and Scharfstein 1990). Firms with intertwined business relationships, shareholding relationships, board of directors relationships, and financing relationships with other firms should have substantially more information about that firm than do external monitors, especially during times of economic distress when asymmetric information problems worsen. Furthermore, to the extent that a firm's main bank or members of its keiretsu would be willing to provide backup financing should the firm become financially troubled, firms were able to maintain a higher ratio of bank debt relative to their total assets.[1]

More recently studies have been more critical of Japanese corporate affiliations, viewing such affiliations as a problem that has contributed to a decade of subpar economic growth, rather than as an alternative market model (Kang and Stultz 2000; Morck and Nakamura 1999; Peek and Rosengren 2005). If the primary role of corporate affiliations is to insulate management from market forces by enabling firms to avoid the discipline that can be provided by external creditors and investors, this limiting of outside corporate governance would manifest itself in a misallocation of credit. Strong corporate affiliations would allow weak firms to sustain their operations relatively unchanged, rather than being forced by external creditors and shareholders to make the tough restructuring choices necessary to recover.

5.3 The Ambiguity of Signals from Main Bank Lending

A natural role for main banks is to serve as the delegated monitor for secondary banks not privy to such "inside" information. To the extent that the main bank system, as well as keiretsu relationships, improves information flows so that Japanese banks can allocate credit more efficiently, the superior information available to a firm's main bank may make main bank lending a good indicator of the future performance of firms that can be observed by other potential lenders. Having the most extensive, and likely the most timely, information about the firm, the main bank would take the lead, which would then be followed by the firm's other lenders.

While this may be a good description of main bank interactions with firms and secondary banks during good economic times, the combination of the severe problems at many individual firms and the crisis in the banking system during the 1990s changed the incentives faced by banks in Japan. In particular, Peek and Rosengren (2005) find that during the troubled 1990s banks misallocated credit as a consequence of the perverse incentives they faced associated with a weak bank supervision system and government pressures to aid unhealthy firms. In particular, they found that increased loans to a firm were associated with the firm's equity return underperforming the market during the following year. Their finding that financially troubled banks were more likely to increase loans the weaker was the firm's health and the stronger was the bank's affiliation with the firm suggests that an increase in loans to a firm by its main bank may not provide an unambiguous signal of the firm's prospects.

The conflicts arose because capital-constrained banks, faced with the necessity to shrink domestic lending, were forced to make choices about which firms would continue to receive scarce loans. How were banks to trade off their responsibilities to finance firms with strong main bank and keiretsu ties, even though many of these firms had poor prospects, with the need to make sound business decisions that would direct credit to the most creditworthy borrowers, even if they were not closely affiliated with the bank? At the same time banks faced growing pressure from government entities to continue lending to troubled firms in order to avoid a credit crunch and sharp increases in the unemployment rate and the number of firm bankruptcies.

Given the impaired health of most Japanese banks in combination with the perverse incentives arising from the unwillingness of bank supervisors to force recognition of asset quality problems, it was in the self-interest of banks to follow a policy of forbearance with their problem borrowers in order to avoid having to report impaired loans as nonperforming. A bank can avoid a mandatory increase in its reported nonperforming loans as long as it makes sufficient credit available to the firm to enable it to make interest payments on the outstanding loans from the bank and to avoid declaring bankruptcy.[2]

Furthermore, given the significant cross-share holdings of Japanese banks generally, and main banks in particular, banks have the added incentive to prevent firm bankruptcies to the extent that they hold equity positions in the firm. Consequently a bank may continue lending to troubled firms to provide sufficient financing to keep otherwise economically bankrupt firms afloat. This "evergreening" of loans benefits the firm because it can avoid (or at least delay) bankruptcy. It also enables the bank to avoid (or delay) a further increase in its reported nonperforming loans so that the bank does not have to make additional loan charge offs and loan loss provisions, which would reduce the bank's earnings, and thus capital. Such practices, particularly during a time of reduced bank lending, would appear as increases in loans to the most troubled firms. And, given the low interest rate environment in Japan, it does not require substantial amounts of new credit to enable troubled firms to make their interest payments.

Japanese banks also likely were responding to significant government pressure to avoid a credit crunch or a precipitous decline in economic conditions that might occur if they were to reduce credit to troubled firms. The government, faced with a growing budget deficit and a voting public weary of funding bank bailouts, preferred banks to continue their policies of forbearance in order to avoid the alternative scenario of massive firm, and perhaps bank, failures and, in particular, the associated costs, both financial and political.[3] The lack of transparency and the use of accounting gimmicks allowed bank supervisors to implement forbearance policies that allowed banks to understate their problem loans and overstate their capital so that they appeared to be sufficiently capitalized.[4]

Thus an increase in loans to a firm by its main bank cannot be viewed as an unambiguous vote of confidence in the firm's prospects. While the main bank may be exploiting its superior information about affiliated firms to provide credit to those firms with the most promising investments, it may instead be responding to its perceived obligation to aid the affiliated firm and/or the perverse incentives to evergreen loans to nonviable firms to protect its own balance sheet.

5.4   Data

We use a rich panel data set to examine bank lending patterns in order to determine how the secondary banks of Japanese firms reacted to their own problems, as well as to the problems faced by firms and the firm's main banks, in the 1990s, and how these reactions affected credit availability to Japanese firms. By using Japanese firm-level data, we are able to link individual Japanese firms to their individual lenders. This linking of individual lenders to individual borrowers is critical for understanding how bank lending behavior is affected by the financial health of individual firms and banks, as well as by the incentives faced by the banks. Such a link cannot be made clearly in many other countries, such as the United States, where bank–borrower relationships are considered private information.

For our tests we use annual data for 1992 through 1999. Because we utilize lagged values of data in our specifications, the starting date of our regression sample, 1993, corresponds to when the Basle Accord risk-based capital requirements were fully implemented in Japan. We then focus on the rest of the decade as banks came under increasing pressure to maintain capital ratios above minimum capital requirements. To investigate the factors that impact how banks allocate credit across firms, we examine the pattern of loans obtained by all firms included in the Pacific-Basin Capital Market Databases (PACAP), which includes all first- and second-section firms that are traded on the Tokyo stock exchange. The PACAP database includes the balance sheet and income statements of firms based on their fiscal year-end reports. The data for loans outstanding to individual firms from each lender are obtained from the Nikkei Needs Bank Loan database, with loan reporting based on the firm's fiscal year.

To avoid timing problems, we limit our sample to those firms with a fiscal year that ends in March, which is by far the date most commonly used by Japanese firms. We identify each firm's main bank as the bank with the largest volume of loans outstanding to the firm in the prior year.[5] Keiretsu membership is obtained from *Industrial Groupings in Japan: The Anatomy of the Keiretsu* by Dodwell Marketing Consultants.

The five major bank categories in Japan are city banks, trust banks, long-term credit banks, first-tier regional banks, and second-tier regional banks. For our sample of firms and banks, table 5.1 provides

Table 5.1
Shares of loans for publicly traded banks

	Main banks	Second-ary banks	City banks	Trust banks	Long-term credit	First regional banks	Second regional banks
1992	20.04	79.96	45.28	22.57	19.67	11.40	1.08
1993	20.84	79.16	45.74	22.14	19.25	11.78	1.09
1994	21.01	78.99	46.03	21.70	19.35	11.83	1.09
1995	21.45	78.55	45.61	21.84	19.19	12.12	1.23
1996	21.74	78.26	45.84	21.60	19.05	12.07	1.44
1997	22.98	77.02	46.57	21.09	19.01	11.75	1.58
1998	26.49	75.31	46.65	21.14	18.16	12.50	1.55
1999	25.60	74.40	46.61	21.59	17.67	12.54	1.58

information on the shares of loans provided to firms by each category of banks, as well as the shares of loans provided by banks in their role as main banks and as secondary banks. During the 1990s, main banks have provided a growing share of the loans to first- and second-section Tokyo stock exchange firms. Almost one-half of bank loans are provided by city banks, with the share rising slightly during our sample period. Trust banks have the next largest share, followed by long-term credit banks, although the shares of both of these categories have been declining. In contrast, the two categories of regional banks have increased their shares of total bank loans to these firms, although their shares remain much smaller than those for the other bank categories. The growth rates shown in table 5.2 are consistent with the pattern of loan shares exhibited in table 5.1.

Table 5.3 contains similar information for the set of city banks. Over our sample period, an increasing share of the loans from city banks have gone to firms with which the banks have a main bank relationship, rising from under 29 percent to nearly 36 percent. The last two columns show the corresponding growth rates of the loans of city banks in their roles as main banks and as secondary banks. It appears that city banks have increasingly focused their lending to those firms with which they have a main bank relationship at the expense of other borrowers, especially during the last half of the decade. This suggests that main bank relationships may have become an increasingly important source of credit for firms as the economic malaise in Japan continued.

Table 5.2
Growth of loans for publicly traded banks

	Private banks	Main banks	Second-ary banks	City banks	Trust banks	Long-term credit	First regional banks	Second regional banks
1993	0.41	4.38	−0.59	1.42	−1.47	−1.76	3.76	1.20
1994	1.69	2.50	1.46	2.31	−0.40	2.22	2.09	1.74
1995	−0.74	1.38	−1.30	−1.63	−0.08	−1.53	1.75	11.76
1996	−0.47	0.91	−0.84	0.04	−1.55	−1.20	−0.88	16.00
1997	−0.04	5.63	−1.62	1.56	−2.38	−0.26	−2.74	9.83
1998	−4.89	2.25	−7.00	−4.67	−4.62	−9.05	1.30	−6.19
1999	−0.47	3.17	−1.67	−0.54	1.69	−3.18	−0.11	1.39

Table 5.3
Shares and growth of loans for city banks

	Share of loans		Growth of loans	
	Main banks	Secondary banks	Main banks	Secondary banks
1992	28.43	71.57		
1993	29.62	70.38	5.66	−0.29
1994	29.95	70.05	3.40	1.82
1995	31.02	68.98	1.92	−3.14
1996	30.04	69.96	−3.11	1.48
1997	30.69	69.31	3.74	0.60
1998	33.70	66.30	4.75	−8.83
1999	35.84	64.16	5.82	−3.81

5.5 Hypotheses and Empirical Specification

We investigate two major hypotheses about the lending behavior of
secondary banks in Japan during the 1990s when the financial health
of both firms and banks had deteriorated substantially. The first
hypothesis is that secondary banks evergreened loans to the weakest
Japanese firms. This could be a consequence of a variety of pressures
and incentives, including pressure on banks generally by the government to aid troubled firms, pressure from a troubled firm's main bank
for secondary lenders to the firm to participate in the bailout of the
firm, obligations felt by the bank due to its being in the same keiretsu
as the firm or the firm's main bank, or as a consequence of the second-

ary bank's own weak health and the magnitude of its own exposure to the firm.

The evergreening hypothesis has at least two components. First, secondary banks acted in their own self-interest by making additional loans to weak firms to avoid having to declare existing loans as nonperforming. This hypothesis would be supported by evidence that weaker firms were more likely to obtain additional loans. It would also be supported by finding that the weaker was secondary bank health and the larger was the bank's exposure to the firm, the greater the likelihood that the secondary bank would increase loans to the firm. Finally, corporate affiliations, in the form of same-keiretsu ties with either the firm or the firm's main bank, would increase the likelihood that a secondary bank would increase loans to the firm.

The second major hypothesis concerns the extent to which secondary banks "follow the lead" of the firm's main bank. In particular, we hypothesize that secondary banks do not necessarily blindly follow the lead of the main bank by increasing loans to the firm when the main bank does so. Instead, when the firm's main bank increases loans to the firm, the probability of a secondary bank subsequently increasing loans to that firm will be lower the weaker is the main bank's health and the larger is the main bank's exposure to the firm—that is, the greater the likelihood that the increase in main bank loans to the firm reflects evergreening behavior rather than being a vote of confidence in the future prospects of the firm.

The basic equation for the hypothesis tests provides estimates for the contributions to the probability that a secondary bank increases credit to a firm based on firm health, secondary bank health and exposure to the firm, main bank health and exposure to the firm, and whether the main bank has increased loans to the firm, controlling for other firm and bank characteristics. The logit equation takes the following general form:

$$Pr(LOAN_{i,j,t}) = a_0 + a_1 FIRM_{i,j,t-1} + a_2 SECONDBANK_{i,j,t-1}$$

$$+ a_3 MAINBANK_{i,j,t-1} + a_4 TIME_{i,j,t} + u_{i,j,t}. \qquad (1)$$

The dependent variable has a value of one if loans to firm i by secondary bank j increased from year $t-1$ to year t, and zero if the bank's loans to firm i were unchanged or decreased from year $t-1$ to year t. Thus for a given firm i, the regression sample will contain in each year t one observation for each secondary bank j from which the firm borrows in that year. We focus on increases in loans, since that requires the lender to take action. The reasons underlying a decline in loans out-standing to a firm are much more heterogeneous, since such an out-come could result passively from the amortization of an outstanding loan or the loan maturing, as well as from the lender making the deci-sion to call a loan, to refuse to renew a loan, or even to forgive a loan.

FIRM is a vector of variables intended to capture firm health and other characteristics of the firm, including controlling for loan demand. The variables considered include the firm's percentage return on assets (FROA) during the prior year, the firm's liquid assets as a percent of its total assets (FLIQA) for the prior year, and the percent change in the firm's sales (FSALES) over the prior year. We also measure firm health based on the relative performance of its stock price. We first calculate the percentage return on each firm's equity, including dividend pay-ments, over the prior year.[6] We then create two (0, 1) dummy vari-ables: FRETLO, which takes on a value of one if the firm's stock price return is in the lowest one-third among all firms in our sample in that year, and zero otherwise; and FRETHI, which takes on a value of one if the firm's stock price return is in the highest one-third, and zero other-wise. Thus the estimated coefficients on these two measures will reflect differential effects relative to the firm being in the middle one-third in firm stock price performance during the prior year.

We also control for other firm characteristics by including the logarithm of the firm's total real assets (FASSET), a set of (0, 1) dummy variables indicating whether a firm just entered the bond market (FEN-TERBOND), is in the bond market (FINBOND), or just left the bond market (FEXITBOND), and a set of nine industry dummy variables.[7] While the set of industry dummy variables should help control for shifts in loan demand at a more aggregated level, the set of dummy variables for a firm entering, exiting, or being in the bond market should help control for shifts in loan demand at the individual firm level. In addition it is likely that the estimated coefficient on FSALES may reflect changes in loan demand as well as firm health.

SECONDBANK is a vector of variables intended to capture the health, the exposure to the firm, and the corporate affiliations of sec-ondary banks. For bank health we again use a relative measure based on each bank's stock price performance. We first calculate the percent-age return on each bank's equity over the prior year, including divi-dend payments. We then create two (0, 1) dummy variables: BRETLO, which takes on a value of one if the bank's stock price return is in the lowest one-third among all banks in our sample in that year, and zero otherwise; and BRETHI, which takes on a value of one if the bank's stock price return is in the highest one-third, and zero otherwise. Thus the estimated coefficients on these two measures will reflect differential effects relative to the bank being in the middle one-third in stock price performance during the prior year.

BEXPOSE measures the bank's exposure to the firm in the prior year. It is calculated as bank j's loans to firm i as a percent of total loans to firm i by all banks. BAFFIL is a (0, 1) dummy variable that has a value of one if the bank is in the same keiretsu with either the firm or the firm's main bank, and zero otherwise. The eight bank-centered financial (horizontal) keiretsus are Mitsubishi, Mitsui, Sumitomo, Fuyo, Dai-Ichi Kangyo, Sanwa, IBJ, and Sakura. Finally, we control for bank type with a set of (0, 1) dummy variables. LTCREDIT takes on a value of one if the bank is a long-term credit bank, and zero otherwise. REGION I takes on a value of one if the bank is a first tier regional bank, and zero otherwise. REGION II takes on a value of one if the bank is a second tier regional bank, and zero otherwise. Thus the estimated coefficients will reflect differential effects relative to the base group composed of city banks and trust banks.[8]

MAINBANK is a vector of variables measuring the health of the firm's main bank, the main bank's exposure to the firm, and whether the main bank increased loans to the firm in the prior year. As with firms and secondary banks, the measure of relative main bank health is based on the percentage return on the bank's equity, including dividend payments, during the prior year using two variables: MBRETLO and MBRETHI. MBRETLO takes on a value of one if the stock price return of the firm's main bank is in the lowest one-third among all banks in our sample in that year, and zero otherwise. MBRETHI takes on a value of one if the stock price return of the firm's main bank is in the highest one-third, and zero otherwise. Thus the estimated coefficients on these two measures will reflect differential effects relative to the main bank being in the middle one-third in stock price performance among all banks in our sample during the prior year.

MBEXPOSE measures the exposure of the main bank to the firm in the prior year. It is calculated as the main bank's loans to firm i as a percent of total loans to firm i by all banks. MBLUPLAG is a (0, 1) dummy variable that takes on a value of one if the main bank increased its loans to firm i during the prior year. Because the frequency of our observations is annual, in later specifications we also consider the contemporaneous effect, MBLUP, since a secondary bank's subsequent response to the main bank increasing loans to the firm might occur within the same year. We also include a set of annual time dummy variables to capture the effects of the macroeconomy. These annual dummy variables will capture the average effect of economic conditions in each year. Table 5.4 lists and describes the set of explanatory variables used in the empirical analysis.

5.6 Empirical Results

Table 5.5 contains the results for the basic logit specification. The sample is all Japanese firms listed on the first and second sections of the Tokyo stock exchange. For each of these firms, the dataset contains one observation per year for each secondary bank with loans outstanding to that firm in that year. Thus each firm will have multiple observations in each year. Recall that the dependent variable is a $(0, 1)$ dummy variable which takes on a value of one if the secondary bank increased loans to the firm from period t to period $t - 1$, and zero otherwise. Each estimated equation in this and subsequent tables includes a constant term, a set of annual time dummy variables, and a set of industry dummy variables, although the estimated coefficients are not reported for brevity. Coefficient standard errors are reported in the column to the right of the estimated coefficients.

   The first set of explanatory variables shown in the table is associated with firm characteristics. While some of these variables are intended to control for loan demand, the key variables reflect firm health. For the base specification shown in column 1, the variables associated with the financial health of the firm tend to have estimated coefficients with perverse signs, suggesting that the weaker is a firm's health, the greater is the likelihood that the bank will increase loans to the firm. The estimated coefficient on FROA is negative and statistically significant, as is the estimated coefficient on FLIQA. Thus firms with a lower accounting return on assets and firms with a lower liquid assets ratio are more likely to have their loans increased by a secondary bank, other things equal. Consistent with evidence reported in Peek and Rosengren (2005), these results are consistent with the evergreening hypothesis that secondary banks made loans to the weakest firms in order to protect their own balance sheets.

   The stock market's evaluation of a firm's health serves to supplement measures such as FROA and FLIQA that are constructed from

Table 5.4
Description of explanatory variables

Explanatory variables	Descriptions
Firm variables	
FASSET	Log real assets: calculated as total assets deflated by the consumer price index, which includes imputed rent.
FROA	Return on assets: calculated as operating income as a percentage of total assets at the beginning of the fiscal year.
FLIQA	Liquid asset ratio: calculated as total liquid assets as a percentage of total assets at the beginning of the fiscal year. These assets include cash, marketable securities, accounts and notes receivable, inventories and other current assets.
FSALES	Sales growth: calculated as the percentage growth rate of sales over the fiscal year.
FRET	Stock return: calculated as the annual percentage return of the firm's equity over the fiscal year. The stock return is comprised of price changes and all distributions, including cash dividends. In order to minimize the effect of single day stock price movements, we follow the following procedure. First, we create a daily stock price adjusted for any distributions. Then, we calculate volume-weighted averages of these daily distribution-adjusted prices for each month. The stock return variable is then calculated as the annual percentage change in these monthly weighted averages.
FRETLO	Takes the value of one if the firm's stock return is among the lowest one-third of the stock returns for all nonfinancial firms in our sample in that year, and zero otherwise.
FRETLO1	Takes the value of one if the firm's stock return is among the lowest one-ninth of the stock returns for all nonfinancial firms in our sample in that year, and zero otherwise.
FRETLO2	Takes the value of one if the firm's stock return is among the second lowest one-ninth of the stock returns for all nonfinancial firms in our sample in that year, and zero otherwise.
FRETLO3	Takes the value of one if the firm's stock return is among the third lowest one-ninth of the stock returns for all nonfinancial firms in our sample in that year, and zero otherwise.
FRETHI	Takes the value of one if the firm's stock return is among the highest one-third of the stock returns for all nonfinancial firms in our sample in that year, and zero otherwise.
FRETHI1	Takes the value of one if the firm's stock return is among the third highest one-ninth of the stock returns for all nonfinancial firms in our sample in that year, and zero otherwise.
FRETHI2	Takes the value of one if the firm's stock return is among the second highest one-ninth of the stock returns for all nonfinancial firms in our sample in that year, and zero otherwise.
FRETHI3	Takes the value of one if the firm's stock return is among the highest one-ninth of the stock returns for all nonfinancial firms in our sample in that year, and zero otherwise.

Table 5.4
(continued)

Explanatory variables	Descriptions
FENTERBOND	Firm entering bond market: takes on the value of one if the firm has no outstanding debentures at the beginning of the fiscal year and has positive debentures at the end of the fiscal year, and zero otherwise.
FINBOND	Firm in the bond market: takes on the value of one if the firm has outstanding debentures at the end of the fiscal year (and did not enter the bond market in that year), and zero otherwise.
FEXITBOND	Firm exiting bond market: takes on the value of one if the firm has positive outstanding debentures at the beginning of the fiscal year and has no outstanding debentures at the end of the fiscal year, and zero otherwise.
Bank variables	
BEXPOSE	Bank exposure: the share of loans from a bank to a firm measured as a percentage of all loans from private banks to that firm.
BRET	Bank's stock return: calculated in the same fashion as the firm's stock return.
BRETLO	Takes the value of one, if the bank's stock return is among the lowest one-third of the stock returns for all banks in our sample in that fiscal year, and zero otherwise.
BRETHI	Takes the value of one, if the bank's stock return is among the highest one-third of the stock returns for all banks in our sample in that fiscal year, and zero otherwise.
BAFFIL	Bank affiliation: takes the value of one if a bank is in the same keiretsu as the firm or as the firm's main bank, or both, and zero otherwise.
Main bank variables	
MB	Main bank: defined as the private bank that has the largest volume of loans to the firm at the end of the fiscal year. In case of a tie, the first bank listed as the reference bank in the Japan Company Handbook is taken to be the main bank. In order to provide some degree of continuity, a firm's main bank is changed only if the volume of loans from the candidate main bank to the firm is at least 10 percent larger than the loans from the currently designated main bank. If there are no private bank loans to the firm at the beginning of its Nikkei Needs observations (going as far back as 1977), then the main bank is undefined until there is a fiscal year with some positive private bank loans. After that point we keep the same main bank even if there are no private bank loans for subsequent observations.
MBLUP	Main bank loans up: takes on the value of one if loans from the firm's main bank increased during the *current* fiscal year, and zero otherwise.

Table 5.4
(continued)

Explanatory variables	Descriptions
MBLUPLAG	Main bank loans up, lagged: takes on the value of one if loans from the firm's main bank increased during the prior fiscal year, and zero otherwise.
MBRETLO	Takes the value of one if the stock return of the firm's main bank is in the lowest one-third of all bank stock returns for that fiscal year, and zero otherwise.
MBRETHI	Takes the value of one if the stock return of the firm's main bank is in the highest one-third of all bank stock returns for that fiscal year, and zero otherwise.
MBEXPOSE	Main bank's exposure to the firm: defined the same as for a bank's exposure.

Sources: All firm variables are from PACAP. The loan data are from the Nikkei Needs Bank Loan Database. Reference bank data (as needed) are from the Japan Company Handbook. Keiretsu affiliations are obtained from various issues of Dodwell's Industrial Groupings in Japan.
Note: All variables are measured over the prior fiscal year of the firm unless otherwise noted.

accounting ratios, especially since such accounting ratios may have questionable reliability to the extent that they are subject to manipulation by firm managers. The estimated coefficient on FRETHI is negative and significant, indicating that the strongest firms are less likely to obtain additional loans from a secondary bank, other things equal. Again, this suggests that secondary banks may not be allocating credit to the healthiest firms. While FRETLO also has a negative estimated coefficient, it is not statistically significant.

However, in column 2, when FRETLO, indicating that a firm is in the bottom one-third of firms ranked by the prior year's stock price performance, is further divided into thirds (FRETLO1, FRETLO2, and FRETLO3), again using (0, 1) dummy variables, we do obtain statistically significant estimated coefficients. FRETLO1 and FRETLO2 each have negative estimated effects, with that on FRETLO1 being statistically significant, indicating that firms with the very worst stock price returns among all firms are less likely to obtain increased loans from secondary banks, measured relative to the middle one-third of the sample of all firms. Interestingly, the third lowest ninth of firms ranked by their prior year's stock price returns has an estimated coefficient that is positive and statistically significant, indicating that they are

Table 5.5
Baseline specifications

	(1)		(2)	
	Coefficient	Standard error	Coefficient	Standard error
FROA	−0.048**	0.003	−0.049**	0.003
FLIQA	−0.003**	0.001	−0.003**	0.001
FRETLO	−0.027	0.018		
FRETLO1			−0.157**	0.027
FRETLO2			−0.026	0.026
FRETLO3			0.081**	0.025
FRETHI	−0.074**	0.018		
FRETHI1			−0.135**	0.026
FRETHI2			0.021	0.026
FRETHI3			−0.110**	0.027
FSALES	0.007**	0.001	0.007**	0.001
FENTERBOND	−0.103*	0.051	−0.107*	0.051
FINBOND	0.160**	0.020	0.159**	0.020
FEXITBOND	0.434**	0.035	0.440**	0.035
FASSET	−0.060**	0.007	−0.062**	0.007
BRETLO	−0.170**	0.019	−0.171**	0.019
BRETHI	−0.121**	0.020	−0.121**	0.020
BEXPOSE	0.043**	0.001	0.043**	0.001
BAFFIL	0.195**	0.030	0.195**	0.030
LTCREDIT	0.130**	0.026	0.130**	0.026
REGION I	−0.146**	0.018	−0.145**	0.018
REGION II	−0.335**	0.041	−0.329**	0.041
MBRETLO	0.012	0.022	0.016	0.022
MBRETHI	−0.097**	0.022	−0.096**	0.022
MBEXPOSE	−0.006**	0.001	−0.006**	0.001
MBLUPLAG	0.512**	0.015	0.515**	0.015
Number of observations	105,600		105,600	
Loglikelihood	−55,207		−55,165	
Pseudo-R^2 (%)	4.135		4.214	

Notes: The reported regressions also include a constant, a set of year dummy variables, and a set of industry dummy variables. For brevity, the estimated coefficients and standard errors of these variables are not reported. * Significant at 5 percent level; ** significant at 1 percent level.

more likely to receive an increase in loans from their secondary banks. Thus, while it appears that secondary banks evergreen loans to unhealthy firms, they apparently draw the line at bailing out the very sickest firms. Similarly, when the healthiest third of firms are divided into thirds (FRETHI1, FRETHI2, and FRETHI3), two of the three subgroups of firms are less likely to obtain increased loans from their secondary banks. These coefficient estimates are consistent with a significant misallocation of credit by secondary banks in favor of sicker firms and against the healthiest firms.

The estimated coefficient on FSALES is positive and statistically significant, suggesting that higher sales growth may be associated with higher loan demand. With respect to the other control variables for firm characteristics, the estimated coefficient on FASSET is negative and significant, indicating that larger firms are less likely to obtain increased loans from their secondary banks, other things equal. This may be due to the nature of loan demand by the largest firms, insofar as the largest firms are more likely to rely on their main banks for bank loans, and also are more likely to rely on the bond market for financing. In fact, at the time that firms enter the bond market, secondary banks are less likely to increase loans to the firm, as indicated by the significant negative estimated coefficient on FENTERBOND. Presumably firms that enter the bond market have decreased loan demand as they replace loans from secondary banks with newly issued bonds. On the other hand, the estimated coefficient on FINBOND is positive and significant, indicating that firms with bonds outstanding are more likely to obtain increased loans from their secondary banks, perhaps because these banks use the fact that such firms are able to pass the market test as a signal of their relatively good prospects. The significant positive coefficient on FEXITBOND indicates that those firms exiting the bond market have increased loan demand and rely to some extent on an increase in loans from their secondary banks in order to replace maturing bonds.

The next set of explanatory variables includes measures of secondary bank health, exposure to the firms, and affiliations with the firms, as well as general control variables for bank type. The estimated coefficient on BRETLO is negative and significant, indicating that secondary banks in the lowest one-third of the distribution of bank stock price returns are less likely to increase loans to firms relative to the middle one-third of secondary banks. The estimated coefficient on BRETHI also is negative and significant, indicating that secondary banks in the healthiest one-third of the sample of banks are less likely to increase loans to firms in their role as secondary banks. A possible explanation for the nonmonotonic pattern of estimated coefficients is that the weakest secondary banks may be less likely to increase lending to firms in their role as secondary banks because they have obligations of their own to aid the set of unhealthy firms for which they serve as a main bank. The coefficient estimates suggest that healthier banks also are less likely to increase loans to firms in their role as a secondary bank, perhaps because they have less of an incentive to evergreen loans to firms in order to protect their own balance sheets.

The estimated coefficient on BEXPOSE is positive and significant, indicating that secondary banks are more likely to increase loans to firms the greater the bank's exposure to the firm. This is consistent with the evergreening hypothesis, since the greater is the bank's exposure to the firm, the more the bank has to lose if the firm is unable to make timely interest payments or if the firm declares bankruptcy. Same-keiretsu affiliations also play a role in secondary bank lending. If the secondary bank has a keiretsu affiliation with either the firm or the firm's main bank, or both, the secondary bank is more likely to increase loans to the firm, other things equal. Finally, long-term credit banks, in their role as secondary banks, are more likely to increase loans to firms compared to the base group of city and trust banks, while the regional banks, especially second tier regional banks, are less likely to increase loans to firms.

The final set of explanatory variables describes the health and exposure of the firm's main bank, as well as whether the main bank increased loans to the firm during the prior year. The estimated coefficient on MBRETLO is positive, but statistically insignificant, while that on MBRETHI is negative and significant. These coefficient estimates indicate that secondary banks are more likely to increase loans to firms with a main bank among the weakest one-third in terms of stock price returns and are less likely to increase loans to firms with the healthiest main banks. This is consistent with secondary banks being less likely to come to the aid of those firms with relatively healthy main banks that are the most able to provide aid to the firms.

The negative and significant estimated coefficient on MBEXPOSE indicates that secondary banks are less likely to increase loans to a firm the greater is the exposure of the firm's main bank. This is consistent with main banks having a greater incentive to bail out a weak firm the greater is its exposure to that firm, since the main bank would be hurt more by the firm not being able to make its interest payments. Given this incentive for main banks to shoulder much of the responsibility to aid the firm, secondary banks might then be under less pressure and have less incentive to aid the firm by increasing loans, other things equal. Furthermore secondary banks are likely aware of the lemons problem associated with the increased incentive of main banks to avoid exposing problems at those firms to which they have the greatest exposure.

The significant positive estimated coefficient on MBUPLAG indicates that secondary banks are more likely to increase loans to a firm if the firm's main bank has increased loans to the firm in the prior year. However, it is not clear whether the secondary banks are reacting to a signal from main banks indicating confidence in the firm's prospects, or if it is simply the case that all (or most) lenders to the firm are taking on their proportionate share of any increase in loans to the firm.

Table 5.6 presents the results from an expanded specification that further investigates the nature of the signal given by main banks when they increase loans to a firm (column 1) and the interaction of bank health with bank exposure to the firm for secondary banks (column 2). Because the signs and significance of the estimated coefficients for the explanatory variables included in table 5.5 are quite similar, the discussion here will focus on the new variables added to the table 5.5 specification. Column 1 adds two new variables: MBUPLAG interacted with MBRETLO and with MBRETHI. The estimated coefficients suggest that secondary banks do not blindly follow the lead of main banks. Instead, they recognize the perverse incentives faced by the main banks to evergreen loans to weak firms. The significant negative estimated coefficient on MBUPLAG interacted with MBRETLO indicates that secondary banks are less likely to follow the main bank in increasing loans to a firm if the main bank is among the least healthy one-third of all banks, and thus has a strong incentive to bail out a sick firm to protect its own balance sheet. On the other hand, the positive (but insignificant) estimated coefficient on MBUPLAG interacted with MBRETHI suggests secondary banks are more likely to follow the lead of the main bank to increase loans to the firm if the main bank is among the healthier banks.

Column 2 adds two additional explanatory variables, BEXPOSE interacted with BRETLO and with BRETHI, in order to further investigate the extent to which secondary banks are likely to evergreen loans to firms. The evidence is consistent with the evergreening hypothesis,

Table 5.6
Bank health interactions

	(1)		(2)	
	Coefficient	Standard error	Coefficient	Standard error
FROA	−0.049**	0.003	−0.049**	0.003
FLIQA	−0.003**	0.001	−0.003**	0.001
FRETLO1	−0.155**	0.027	−0.154**	0.027
FRETLO2	−0.024	0.026	−0.024	0.026
FRETLO3	0.081**	0.025	0.082**	0.025
FRETHI1	−0.136**	0.026	−0.136**	0.026
FRETHI2	0.025	0.026	0.025	0.026
FRETHI3	−0.109**	0.027	−0.108**	0.027
FSALES	0.007**	0.001	0.007**	0.001
FENTERBOND	−0.111*	0.051	−0.110*	0.051
FINBOND	0.159**	0.020	0.159**	0.020
FEXITBOND	0.450**	0.035	0.450**	0.036
BRETLO	−0.172**	0.019	−0.236**	0.024
BRETHI	−0.121**	0.020	−0.134**	0.025
BEXPOSE	0.043**	0.001	0.037**	0.002
BEXPOSE*BRETLO			0.012**	0.003
BEXPOSE*BRETHI			0.003	0.003
BAFFIL	0.195**	0.030	0.191**	0.030
MBRETLO	0.122**	0.029	0.122**	0.029
MBRETHI	−0.107**	0.031	−0.107**	0.031
MBLUPLAG	0.597**	0.029	0.596**	0.029
MBLUPLAG*MBRETLO	−0.202**	0.037	−0.200**	0.037
MBLUPLAG*MBRETHI	0.012	0.040	0.011	0.040
MBEXPOSE	−0.006**	0.001	−0.006**	0.001
Number of observations	105,600		105,600	
Loglikelihood	−55,142		−55,129	
Pseudo-R^2 (%)	4.258		4.282	

Notes: The reported regressions also include a constant, a set of year dummy variables, a set of industry dummy variables, FASSET, LTCREDIT, REGION I, and REGION II. For brevity, the estimated coefficients and standard errors of these variables are not reported.
* Significant at 5 percent level; ** significant at 1 percent level.

since the weakest secondary banks are more likely to increase loans to a firm the greater is the bank's exposure to the firm, and thus the more the bank has to lose if the firm is unable to make its interest payments or declares bankruptcy. On the other hand, for secondary banks among the healthiest one-third of all banks, the small positive estimated coefficient is not statistically significant.

Column 1 of table 5.7 contains an expanded specification that further investigates the role played by same-keiretsu affiliations of the secondary bank with either the firm or the firm's main bank. The results of tables 5.5 and 5.6 indicate that secondary banks with same-keiretsu affiliations with either the firm or the main bank of the firm are more likely to increase loans to the firm. An interesting question is then whether the effect of keiretsu affiliations has other dimensions. For this purpose AFFIL is interacted with the FEXITBOND dummy variable to see if firms that exit the bond market are more likely to replace the lost funding with loans from affiliated secondary banks. AFFIL is also interacted with MBUPLAG and with MBUPLAG interacted with the main bank stock return indicators to investigate the extent to which secondary banks are more likely to follow the lead of a main bank in increasing loans to a firm when the secondary bank has a same-keiretsu affiliation with the firm or the firm's main bank.

The estimated coefficient on the interaction of AFFIL and FEXIT-BOND is positive, but not statistically significant. Similarly it does not appear that same-keiretsu affiliations play a role in affecting the response of secondary bank lending to an increase in loans by the firm's main bank. None of the three MBUPLAG variables interacted with AFFIL is statistically significant.

Until now, only prior year values of the explanatory variables were used in the reported regressions, including the dummy variable indicating an increase in main bank loans to the firm. However, since the estimation relies on annual data, the length of the period is so long that it is possible that some of the secondary bank response to an increase in main bank loans to the firm is missed, insofar as secondary banks respond within the current fiscal year. To investigate this possibility, column 2 contains a specification that adds the block of measures associated with the main bank increasing loans to the firm using contemporaneous values. The addition of these variables almost triples the pseudo R^2 of the equation.

While this specification reduces somewhat the estimated effects of MBUPLAG and MBUPLAG $*$ MBRETLO, both measures retain their

Table 5.7
Keiretsu affiliation interactions

	(1)		(2)	
	Coefficient	Standard error	Coefficient	Standard error
FROA	−0.049**	0.003	−0.033**	0.003
FLIQA	−0.003**	0.001	−0.003**	0.001
FRETLO1	−0.154**	0.027	−0.247**	0.028
FRETLO2	−0.024	0.026	−0.054*	0.027
FRETLO3	0.082**	0.025	0.078**	0.026
FRETHI1	−0.136**	0.026	−0.117**	0.028
FRETHI2	0.024	0.026	0.048	0.027
FRETHI3	−0.109**	0.027	−0.027	0.029
FSALES	0.007**	0.001	0.007**	0.001
FENTERBOND	−0.110*	0.051	−0.050	0.054
FINBOND	0.159**	0.020	0.103**	0.021
FEXITBOND	0.447**	0.037	0.278**	0.038
FEXITBOND*AFFIL	0.053	0.133	0.113	0.145
BRETLO	−0.236**	0.024	−0.248**	0.025
BRETHI	−0.134**	0.025	−0.140**	0.026
BEXPOSE	0.037**	0.002	0.043**	0.002
BEXPOSE*BRETLO	0.013**	0.003	0.011**	0.003
BEXPOSE*BRETHI	0.003	0.003	0.003	0.003
BAFFIL	0.205**	0.041	−0.003	0.056
MBRETLO	0.122**	0.029	0.187**	0.038
MBRETHI	−0.107**	0.031	0.040	0.039
MBEXPOSE	−0.006**	0.001	−0.003**	0.001
MBLUP			1.531**	0.033
MBLUP*MBRETLO			−0.098*	0.041
MBLUP*MBRETHI			−0.090*	0.044
MBLUP*AFFIL			0.392**	0.101
MBLUP*MBRETLO*AFFIL			0.014	0.123
MBLUP*MBRETHI*AFFIL			0.072	0.131
MBLUPLAG	0.597**	0.030	0.395**	0.032
MBLUPLAG*MBRETLO	−0.194**	0.037	−0.132**	0.040
MBLUPLAG*MBRETHI	0.008	0.040	0.001	0.043
MBLUPLAG*AFFIL	−0.011	0.090	0.029	0.109
MBLUPLAG*MBRETLO*AFFIL	−0.110	0.107	−0.189	0.140
MBLUPLAG*MBRETHI*AFFIL	0.046	0.106	−0.007	0.141
Number of observations	105,600		105,600	
Loglikelihood	−55,128		−50,649	
Pseudo-R^2 (%)	4.284		12.706	

Notes: The reported regressions also include a constant, a set of year dummy variables, a set of industry dummy variables, FASSET, LTCREDIT, REGION I, and REGION II. For brevity, the estimated coefficients and standard errors of these variables are not reported. * Significant at 5 percent level; ** significant at 1 percent level.

statistical significance. The estimated coefficient on MBLUP is about four times the size of the estimated coefficient of MBLUPLAG (and about two and one-half times the size of the estimated coefficient in column 1). This finding has one caveat though: there may be an upward bias in the estimate of the coefficient on MBLUP due to potential simultaneity bias. The estimated coefficient on the interaction of MBLUP with MBRETLO also is statistically significant, and is of approximately the same magnitude as that for MBUPLAG * MBRETHI. One difference in the results between the contemporaneous effects and the lagged effects occurs for the same-keiretsu affiliation measure. MPLUP * AFFIL has a positive and significant estimated coefficient, indicating that secondary banks with a same-keiretsu affiliation are more likely to increase loans to a firm when the firm's main bank increases loans to the firm. This evidence is consistent with keiretsu affiliations contributing to a sharing of the responsibility (and costs) of aiding a troubled firm among its keiretsu members. And, as one might expect, that sharing of the costs by secondary banks occurs more or less contemporaneously with the increase in loans from the main bank.

   Finally, table 5.8 provides information about the extent to which our estimates indicate meaningful differences in the probabilities of secondary banks increasing loans to firms across the various dimensions that we have investigated. Based on the coefficient estimates for the specification shown in column 1 of table 5.7, some of these differences are substantial. For example, the first row in the table shows that the probability of a loan increase rises from less than 23 percent for a bank with a low exposure to a firm with a high ROA to almost 34 percent for a bank with a high exposure to a firm with a low ROA when the firm's main bank had a low exposure to the firm and increased loans to the firm in the prior year. In general, the lower is the firm's ROA, the higher is the bank's exposure to the firm, the lower is the main bank's exposure to the firm, and the higher is the main bank's stock return, the higher the probability that a secondary bank will increase loans to the firm.

5.7   Conclusions

We investigated two main hypotheses about the lending behavior of secondary banks in Japan during the troubled 1990s. First, we found strong evidence consistent with the evergreening hypothesis. Secondary banks were more likely to increase loans to a firm the weaker was

Table 5.8
Estimated probability of loan increase

Bank's exposure			Low		High	
Firm's ROA			Low	High	Low	High
	Main bank exposure	Main bank stock return				
Main bank	Low	Low	25.48	22.77	33.93	30.69
loans increased		High	28.00	25.11	36.87	33.49
in prior year	High	Low	23.62	21.05	31.72	28.59
		High	26.02	23.27	34.57	31.29
Main bank	Low	Low	20.50	18.19	27.92	25.03
loans did		High	17.02	15.02	23.55	20.98
not increase	High	Low	18.91	16.74	25.94	23.19
in prior year		High	15.65	13.78	21.79	19.36

Notes: The calculated probabilities are based on the coefficient estimates for the specification in column 1 of table 5.7, where the representative firm is a manufacturing firm not in the bond market, with fiscal year ending in March 1999. The representative bank has a keiretsu affiliation with either the firm or the firm's main bank, and has a stock return in the lower one-third of all banks during the prior year. Continuous variables are measured at the median value of all manufacturing firms in 1999. Probabilities are expressed as percentages. Low main bank stock return indicates that the stock return of the firm's main bank is in the lower one-third of all banks in the prior year, and high indicates that it was in the upper one-third. Low main bank exposure indicates that the main bank's share of all private bank loans to the firm in the prior year was at the 25th percentile of the MBEXPOSE variable for manufacturing firms in 1999, and high indicates that it was at the 75th percentile. Low bank exposure indicates that the share of loans of the representative bank among all private bank loans to the representative firm was at the 25th percentile of the BEXPOSE variable for manufacturing firms in 1999, and high indicates that it was at the 75th percentile. Low ROA indicates that the representative firm has an ROA at the 25th percentile of the ROA variable for manufacturing firms in 1999, and high indicates a value at the 75th percentile.

the firm's health. Furthermore secondary banks were more likely to increase loans to a firm the greater the bank's exposure to the firm, and this likelihood was greater if the bank's health was relatively poor. Same-keiretsu affiliations also played a role in secondary bank lending, with secondary banks in the same keiretsu as the firm or the firm's main bank more likely to increase loans to the firm.

The evidence supports the hypothesis that secondary banks "follow the lead" of a firm's main bank. However, secondary banks do not do so blindly. Rather, they take into account the incentives the main bank has to evergreen loans to a firm. Thus, secondary banks are less likely to increase loans to a firm whose main bank has increased loans if the main bank is in relatively poor health. However, if the secondary bank is in the same keiretsu as the firm or the firm's main bank, the secondary bank is more likely to follow the lead of the main bank increasing loans to the firm. Furthermore much of the response of secondary banks appears to occur contemporaneously with the increase in main bank loans to the firm.

Notes

We would like to thank Steven Fay for invaluable research assistance and Thomas Cargill for helpful comments. This study is based on work supported by the National Science Foundation under Grant SES-0213967. Any opinions, findings, and conclusions or recommendations expressed in this study are those of the authors and do not necessarily reflect the views of the National Science Foundation, the Federal Reserve Bank of Boston, or the Federal Reserve System.

1. However, the benefits of close firm–main bank ties may be limited. For example, although Weinstein and Yafeh (1998) find that a close relationship with a firm's bank increases the availability of credit, this does not lead to higher profitability or growth for the firm, perhaps because the bank discourages the firm from investing in high risk, high expected return projects, or because the bank extracts all the rents.

2. A bank must classify a loan as nonperforming when the borrower has failed to make interest payments for more than three months, the loan is restructured, or the firm declares bankruptcy.

3. For example, it appears that almost half of the public funds injected into the banking system in 1998 and 1999 was used to provide debt forgiveness to construction companies (Tett and Ibison 2001). Such pressures have come out into the open recently with reports that Shinsei Bank, perhaps the only bank in Japan that has seriously applied credit risk analysis in its lending decisions, has been pressured by the FSA to continue lending to severely troubled firms, with FSA Commissioner Shoji Mori quoted as saying, "Shinsei should behave in line with other Japanese banks" (Singer and Dvorak 2001).

4. For example, a study by the *Nikkei* newspaper found that nearly 75 percent of loans to Japanese firms that declared bankruptcy in 2000 had been classified as sound or merely in need of monitoring (*The Economist* 2001). And there is much evidence of government complicity with banks in the understatement of problem loans. For example, the put options granted to Shinsei and Aozora associated with the purchases of supposedly cleaned up banks were awarded to the buyers of the failed banks because the government prevented the bidders from inspecting the banks' books so that the exposures of other banks with loans to the same firms would not be exposed (*The Economist* 2002).

5. In case of ties in terms of the volume of loans to the firm in a given year, we select as the main bank the first listed reference bank in the *Japan Company Handbook*. To avoid erratic switching between banks in a few instances, perhaps related to the relative timing of loan maturation or of the issuance of new loans, we impose a rule that in order to switch the designated main bank, the loans from the candidate main bank to the firm must exceed the volume of loans from the current designated main bank by at least 10 percent.

6. We calculate the annual return using the average dividend-adjusted price for the last month of the current fiscal year and the average dividend-adjusted price for the last month of the prior fiscal year, rather than the prices on the last day of the current and prior fiscal years, in order to avoid excessive noise in the series.

7. A firm is deemed to enter the bond market in the year in which its amount of bonds outstanding changes from zero to a positive value. A firm is in the bond market in any year in which it has outstanding bonds, other than the year in which it enters the bond market. A firm is deemed to exit the bond market in the year in which its bonds outstanding become zero after having had a positive value in the prior year.

8. We combined city banks and trust banks into a single group because our sample contained very few trust banks, and the differential effect of trust banks relative to city banks was never significant.

References

Hoshi, T., and A. Kashyap. 1999. The Japanese banking crisis: Where did it come from and how will it end? In B. Bernanke and J. Rotemberg, eds., *NBER Macroeconomics Annual 1999*. Cambridge: MIT Press.

Hoshi, T., and A. Kashyap. 2001. *Corporate Financing and Governance in Japan*. Cambridge: MIT Press.

Hoshi, T., A. Kashyap, and D. Scharfstein. 1990. The role of banks in reducing the costs of financial distress in Japan. *Journal of Financial Economics* 27: 67–88.

Hoshi, T., A. Kashyap, and D. Scharfstein. 1991. Corporate structure, liquidity, and investment: Evidence from Japanese industrial groups. *Quarterly Journal of Economics* 106: 33–60.

Hoshi, T., A. Kashyap, and D. Scharfstein. 1993. The choice between public and private debt: An analysis of post-deregulation corporate financing in Japan. Unpublished manuscript.

Kang, J.-K., and R. M. Stultz. 2000. Do banking shocks affect borrowing firm performance? An analysis of the Japanese experience. *Journal of Business* 73: 1–23.

Kang, J.-K., and A. Shivdasani. 1995. Firm performance, corporate governance, and top executive turnover in Japan. *Journal of Financial Economics* 38: 29–58.

Kaplan, S. N., and B. Minton. 1994. Appointments of outsiders to Japanese corporate boards: Determinants and implications for managers. *Journal of Financial Economics* 36: 225–58.

Morck, R., and M. Nakamura. 1999. Banks and corporate control in Japan. *Journal of Finance* 54: 319–39.

Morck, R., M. Nakamura, and A. Shivdasani. 2000. Banks, ownership structure and firm value in Japan. *Journal of Business* 73: 539–67.

Peek, J., and E. S. Rosengren. 2005. Unnatural selection: Perverse incentives and the misallocation of credit in Japan. *American Economic Review* 95 (4): 1144–66.

Singer, J., and P. Dvorak. 2001. Shinsei bank pressured to keep shaky loans. *Wall Street Journal*, September 26, p. C1.

Tett, G., and D. Ibison. 2001. Tokyo "May Have to Support Banks." *Financial Times,* September 14.

The Economist. 2001. Mere fiddling. June 30, p. 69.

The Economist. 2002. Nationalized once, nationalized again? July 6, p. 71.

Weinstein, D. E., and Y. Yafeh. 1998. On the costs of a bank-centered financial system: Evidence from the changing main bank relations in Japan. *Journal of Finance* 53: 635–72.

6   Monetary Policy in the Great Stagnation

Yoichi Arai and Takeo Hoshi

6.1   Introduction

Since the early 1990s Japan has been experiencing the longest stagnation and recession that a developed economy has ever seen in the postwar period. Over this time the price level measured by the GDP deflator declined by 3.2 percent. The deflation rate over the past five years has been especially serious at 8.6 percent, rising about 1.8 percent per year. As the economy stopped growing, the unemployment rate more than doubled from 2.2 percent (early 1990) to around 5 percent (2004). Although the economy has shown some signs of a hesitant recovery, it is too early to tell if the Japanese economy is finally coming out of the more than decade-long recession. The GDP deflator in 2004 still continued to fall by 2.6 percent from the previous year.

In this chapter we review the monetary policy during this Great Stagnation in Japan. We focus especially on the conduct of monetary policy after February 1999, when the Bank of Japan (BOJ) introduced the ZIRP (zero interest rate policy). Governor Masaru Hayami characterized this policy "super-superexpansionary" during the press conference when the BOJ lifted the ZIRP on August 11, 2000.[1] We ask the following questions. Has the monetary policy been really superexpansionary? If so, why did it fail (at least so far) to stop the deflation and recession? If the policy is found not that expansionary, what more (than the BOJ has already done) can the BOJ do?

The chapter starts with a brief overview of the Japanese monetary policy since the early 1990s in section 6.2. In section 6.3 we examine whether the monetary policy has been superexpansionary by looking at several measures of the monetary policy stance. From the nominal interest rates we see the monetary policy in the late 1990s was indeed expansionary. Other measures such as growth rates of monetary aggregates suggest, however, the monetary policy in the late 1990s was not superexpansionary compared with some past episodes of monetary expansion. In section 6.4 we discuss the "quantitative easing" of the BOJ, which was started in 2001, and we examine the effectiveness of such monetary policy both theoretically and empirically. In section 6.5 we draw some conclusions.

6.2 Chronology

In our chronology, shown in table 6.1, we give the major events since the Bank of Japan was granted independence from the Ministry of Finance. In particular, the Bank of Japan Act of 1942, which made the BOJ formally dependent on the government, was repealed by the New Bank of Japan Act of 1998, and the BOJ gained formal independence.

Although interest rates were lowered following the New Bank of Japan Act, the BOJ has also claimed that nonmonetary structural factors were at work in slowing the economy. In the statement released immediately after the monetary policy meeting in September 1998, the BOJ cited the possibility of deflation as an important factor that influenced their decision to lower rates. The BOJ stated "the monetary policy objective of the Bank of Japan is to pursue price stability, avoiding both inflation and deflation."[2] At the end of the statement, however, the BOJ added:

At present, recovery of business conditions and revitalization of the financial system are the imminent issues in the Japanese economy. The Bank of Japan strongly hopes that the decision to make money market operations more accommodative will facilitate the resolution of these issues and that all parties concerned will make their utmost efforts in surmounting the economic difficulties they face. ("Change of the Guideline for Money Market Operations," September 9, 1998)

Essentially the statement shows that the BOJ viewed the recession as a structural problem that calls for structural reform in order for Japan to recover from the recession. This view continued to influence the monetary policy formulation at the BOJ during the period examined in this chapter. Numerous speeches and press releases emphasized the structural nature of the recession and problems in the financial system. For example, when the BOJ started the zero interest rate policy (ZIRP) in February 1999, the press release at the time stated:

Table 6.1
Major changes in the monetary policy stance of the BOJ, 1998 to 2005

April 1, 1998	• BOJ gained independence • Masaru Hayami becomes the 28th BOJ governor • Continue to encourage the uncollateralized overnight call rate to remain on average slightly below the official discount rate (0.50%)
September 9, 1998	• Encourage the uncollateralized overnight call rate to move on average around 0.25%
February 12, 1999	• Encourage the uncollateralized overnight call rate to move as low as possible (start of the ZIRP)
August 11, 2000	• Encourage the uncollateralized overnight call rate to move on average around 0.25%
February 9, 2001	• Reduce the official discount rate by 15 basis points to 0.35% • Introduce a standby lending facility at the official discount rate ("Lombard-type" lending facility) • Increase outright operations of short-term government securities
February 28, 2001	• Encourage the uncollateralized overnight call rate to move on average around 0.15% • Reduce the official discount rate to 0.25%
March 19, 2001	• Change the main operating target from the uncollateralized overnight call rate to the outstanding balance of the current accounts at the BOJ • The new procedure continue to be in place until the consumer price index (excluding perishables, on a nationwide statistics) registers stably a 0% or an increase year on year • Target the current-account balance at the BOJ to be around ¥5 trillion • Expect the uncollateralized overnight call rate to be close to zero
August 14, 2001	• Raise the target balance of current accounts held at the BOJ to ¥6 trillion • Increase outright purchase of long-term government bonds to ¥600 billion per month
September 18, 2001	• For the time being, provide ample liquidity to the money market by aiming at maintaining the outstanding balance of current accounts held at the BOJ above ¥6 trillion • Reduce the official discount rate by 15 basis points to 0.10% • Increase the maximum number of business days for using the Lombard-type lending facility (from 5 to 10 days)
December 19, 2001	• Raise the target outstanding balance of the current accounts at the BOJ to around ¥10 trillion to ¥15 trillion • Increase outright purchase of long-term government bonds to ¥800 billion per month
February 28, 2002	• For the time being, provide more liquidity to meet a surge in demand irrespective of the target of current account balances • Increase outright purchase of long-term government bonds to ¥1 trillion per month

Table 6.1
(continued)

September 18, 2002	• Announce the plan to purchase stocks from banks
October 11, 2002	• Set the limit of stock purchase from banks at ¥2 trillion by the end of September 2004
October 30, 2002	• Raise the target outstanding balance of the current accounts at the BOJ to around ¥15 trillion to ¥20 trillion • Increase outright purchase of long-term government bonds to ¥1.2 trillion per month
March 20, 2003	• Toshihiko Fukui becomes the 29th BOJ governor
March 25, 2003	• From April 1, raise the target range to ¥17 trillion to ¥22 trillion (due to the establishment of the Japan Post) • For the time being, provide more liquidity irrespective of the target when necessary to secure financial market stability • Raise the limit of stock purchase to ¥3 trillion by the end of September 2004
April 30, 2003	• Raise the target outstanding balance of the current accounts at the BOJ to around ¥22 trillion to ¥27 trillion • For the time being, provide more liquidity irrespective of the target when necessary to secure financial market stability
May 20, 2003	• Raise the target outstanding balance of the current accounts at the BOJ to around ¥27 trillion to ¥30 trillion • For the time being, provide more liquidity irrespective of the target when necessary to secure financial market stability
October 10, 2003	• Raise the upper bound for the target range for the outstanding balance of the current accounts at the BOJ to ¥32 trillion • Clarify the commitment to maintain the quantitative easing. To terminate the quantitative easing, it is necessary (1) for the core CPI inflation of 0% or above to continue for a few months, and (2) for the BOJ to be convinced the core CPI inflation will not be expected to register 0% or below in the near future.
January 20, 2004	• Raise the target outstanding balance of the current accounts at the BOJ to around ¥30 trillion to ¥35 trillion
May 20, 2005	• Announce that the balance of current accounts may fall short of the target when liquidity demand is judged exceptionally weak

Source: Bank of Japan Web site "Monetary Policy" section ⟨http://www.boj.or.jp/en/seisaku/05/seisak_f.htm⟩.

In order to bring Japanese economy back to a solid recovery path, it is important not only to provide support from monetary and fiscal sides but also to steadily promote financial system revitalization and structural reforms. ("Change of the Guideline for Money Market Operations," February 12, 1999)

Resolution of the nonperforming loan problem, however, did not move as swiftly as the BOJ hoped. The Financial Services Agency (FSA) carried out the "special inspection" of major banks, focusing on the loans to their largest borrowers. The result of the inspection, which was published in April of 2002, concluded that all the major banks were well capitalized and would not need recapitalization.

The reluctance of the FSA to admit the seriousness of the nonperforming loan problem and to consider the use of public funds to recapitalize the banks eventually prompted the Prime Minister Koizumi to change the head of the FSA on October 1. With the new FSA Minister Heizo Takenaka, the government reformulated the antideflationary package and published "Comprehensive Measures to Accelerate Reforms" on October 30.[3]

Earlier on the same day the BOJ announced a change in the monetary policy whereby it increased the targeted level of current accounts held at the Bank. In the same press release the BOJ re-iterated the importance of structural reform in the financial system to revive the Japanese economy:

In order to ensure the abundant liquidity provision by the Bank leading to the revitalization of the economy, improvement in credit allocation function of capital markets is important in addition to the strengthening of the financial intermediary function of banks. In this regard, the Bank will closely monitor the impact of expected government measures to accelerate the resolution of the NPL problem on corporate financing and explore possible measures to secure the smooth working of corporate financing. ("Change in the Guideline for Money Market Operations," October 30, 2002)

In subsequent months the BOJ raised the target on current accounts several times. On January 20, 2004, the BOJ raised the target range for the outstanding balance of current accounts surprising many observers who thought the economy was recovering. The BOJ explained this by pointing to the continuing deflation and to the Bank's commitment to quantitative easing. The indication is that BOJ would continue the quantitative easing until it is certain that the deflation has ended. As the economy continued to recover in 2005, however, the BOJ started discussing the "exit strategy" from the quantitative easing, even though deflation had not completely ended.

6.3   Has the Monetary Policy Been Super Expansionary?

The BOJ continued to cut the interest rate in an attempt to boost the economy for most of the 1990s. By February 1999 the target overnight call rate reached effectively zero, which was "unprecedentedly low in the history of central banking at home and abroad."[4] The ZIRP was suspended in August 2000 but then restored in March 2001. Since 2001

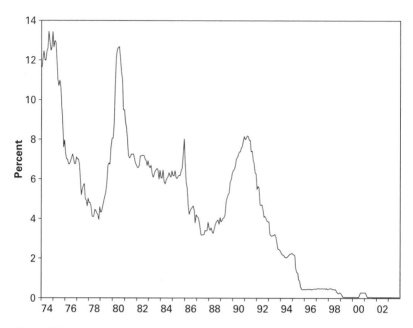

Figure 6.1
Overnight call rate (collateralized), 1974:01 to 2003:12.

the BOJ has been targeting the amount of current accounts held at the Bank instead of the interest rate. In this section we examine how expansionary those monetary policy measures have really been. We will show that until late 2001 the monetary policy of the BOJ has not been as expansionary as it was claimed to be.

Figure 6.1, which shows the overnight call rate from January 1974 to December 2003, is consistent with the BOJ's claim that the monetary policy since the late 1990s has been superexpansionary.[5] The call rate fell substantially in the 1990s and eventually reached the level where it could not go lower.

When we look at the ex post real call rate, subtracting the CPI inflation rate, the picture becomes less clear (figure 6.2).[6] The real rate also came down during the 1990s, but the real rate stayed often substantially above zero because of deflation. As a result the real call rate in the late 1990s and the early 2000s did not go as low as it did in the inflationary 1970s.

As the nominal interest rate plummeted to zero, many economists in Japan and elsewhere, academic and nonacademic, started to discuss the possibility of effective monetary expansion when the zero interest

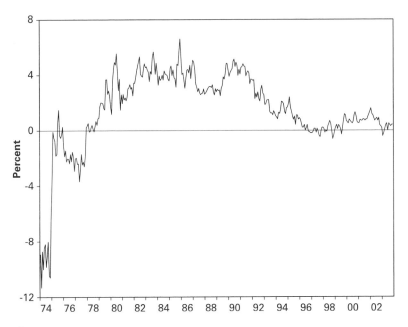

Figure 6.2
Real call rate (call rate minus CPI inflation rate), 1974:01 to 2003:12.

rate constraint is binding. Many suggested aggressive expansion of monetary aggregates. That is to say, if the central bank prints and injects more money into the economy, the nominal aggregate demand eventually increases. This point is most simply illustrated by the quantity equation, $MV = PY$, where M is money, P is the price level, Y is real aggregate demand, and V is the income velocity of money. As M increases, PY must increase in the limit unless V declines at the same speed (or faster). Even if the increase in the nominal aggregate demand does not immediately show up as an increase in output, the increase in the monetary aggregates will raise the price level and create inflation, thereby allowing the real interest rate to fall below zero, which will help the economy. Bernanke (2000) explains this point quite clearly:

The monetary authorities can issue as much money as they like. Hence, if the price level were truly independent of money issuance, then the monetary authorities could use the money they create to acquire indefinite quantities of goods and assets. This is manifestly impossible in equilibrium. Therefore money issuance must ultimately raise the price level, even if nominal interest rates are bounded at zero. (Bernanke 2000, p. 158)

Figure 6.3
Growth rate of M2 + CD (year on year), 1974:01 to 2003:12.

In the Japanese recession the BOJ has not explicitly targeted growth of monetary aggregates. Provision of "ample funds" to the financial market under the "unprecedented accommodative monetary policy," however, could have led to a substantial quantitative easing. It is possible that such a strategy could have worked after March 2001, when the BOJ started explicitly targeting the balance of current accounts held at BOJ, which is an important component of the monetary base.

In figures 6.3 and 6.4 we plot the year on year growth rates of monetary aggregates to see whether one can observe such quantitative easing in Japan. The growth rate of M2 + CD (figure 6.3) increased from 1993 to 1995 but stabilized after 1995 at around 3 percent per annum.[7] If we compare monetary growth in recent years to that in the 1970s and the 1980s, we find the recent growth rate to be low.

Figure 6.4 shows the growth rates of adjusted monetary base (monetary base adjusted for the changes in the reserve requirement). Again, the monetary growth rates in the late 1990s are slightly higher than those in the early 1990s, but the rates are fairly low compared with the growth rates in the 1970s and the 1980s. The exceptions are the spikes of growth in December 1999 and January 2000, when the BOJ increased

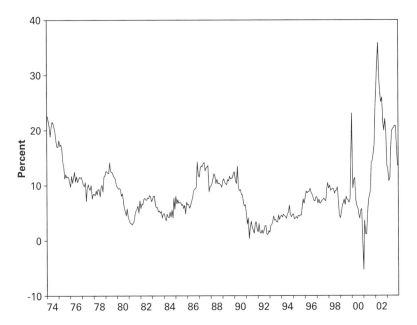

Figure 6.4
Growth rate of adjusted monetary base (year on year), 1974:01 to 2003:12.

liquidity to deal with potential Y2K problems, and the spike of monetary growth from September 2001 on. Nevertheless, the growth rates
due to these two episodes are roughly comparable to the growth
observed in the mid-1970s.

Thus, judging from the growth rate of monetary aggregates, we cannot observe clear evidence for "superexpansionary" monetary policy.
The growth rate of M2 + CD has been low throughout the 1990s and
early 2000s. Even the monetary base, which should be easier to control,
did not show dramatically high growth rates before the September
2001. Thus it seems reasonable to conclude that the quantitative easing
was not attempted in Japan until late 2001.

One could argue that nominal growth rates of monetary aggregates
are not good measures of monetary policy stance. For example, a 2
percent monetary growth may represent a tight monetary policy when
the inflation rate is in double digits, but the same 2 percent monetary
growth may be somewhat expansionary under deflation. We address
this concern in figures 6.5 and 6.6, which show the growth rates of real
balances, which are defined to be the level of monetary aggregates
divided by the CPI. Compared with earlier figures, figures 6.5 and 6.6

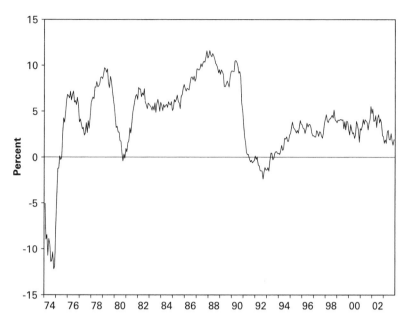

Figure 6.5
Growth rate of M2 + CD minus CPI inflation rate, 1974:01 to 2003:12.

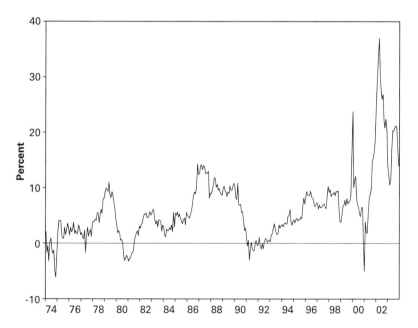

Figure 6.6
Growth rate of adjusted monetary base minus CPI inflation rate, 1974:01 to 2003:12.

make the monetary policy in the high inflation 1970s look less expansionary. The main result, however, does not change. The growth rates of M2 + CD in the 1990s and the 2000s were not very high. The growth rates of monetary base were not high, either, until late 2001.

6.4 Effects of Quantitative Monetary Easing

Under what the BOJ called "unprecedented accommodative monetary policy," the overnight call rate dipped as close to zero as it can get. The monetary policy in Japan appears to have been extremely expansionary. The real rate, however, stayed positive for most of the period, because of deflation. Moreover the low growth of monetary aggregates (M2 + CD and adjusted monetary base before the late 2001) suggests that the BOJ did not concede to substantial quantitative monetary easing as many economists advocated. In this sense the monetary policy during the Great Stagnation was not superexpansionary.

Since around September 2001 the growth rate of monetary base has been high, although the growth of M2 + CD has been modest. Has such quantitative monetary easing had expansionary effects on the economy? If the BOJ continues the policy of quantitative monetary easing, will it eventually stop the deflation and put the Japanese economy on a recovery path? These are the questions we address in this section.

The theoretical basis for quantitative monetary easing has been provided by many researchers. For example, Bernanke (2000) forcefully argues that monetary policy can be used to increase the aggregate demand even with zero nominal interest rate, as we noted above. He lists four kinds of actions that a central bank can undertake to stimulate aggregate demand, all of which are accompanied by some form of quantitative easing. Bernanke's list serves as a useful summary of the theoretical arguments on quantitative monetary easing advanced by many economists.

First, the central bank can continue to set the interest rate at the lowest level (zero) with an explicit inflation target. This is an idea that was initially advanced by Krugman (1998, 2000). If the central bank commits to continue the accommodative interest rate policy until the inflation rate reaches some positive level (e.g., 3 to 4 percent), it can raise the people's inflation expectation and hence push the real interest rate below zero. To change the inflation expectation, the central bank may have to show its commitment by taking an action that will eventually lead to inflation, such as printing more money.

It is important to note that quantitative monetary easing in this case works by changing people's expectations.[8] Eggertsson and Woodford (2003) show that simply increasing the quantity of money when the short-term interest rate is already at zero does not have any impact on the economy unless such an action changes the expectation about future interest rate policy or the future government liabilities. If the quantitative monetary easing successfully signals more expansionary policy will be in place when the zero interest rate constraint is no longer binding, then it can stimulate the economy now.

Eggertsson and Woodford (2003) also find that the optimal interest rate policy is to continue the zero interest rate for a while even after the economy comes out of the zero interest rate trap, consistent with the result obtained by Jung, Teranishi, and Watanabe (2001). They show that the optimal policy can be implemented as relatively simple price-level targeting (with time-varying target levels as the zero interest rate continues). They argue that quantitative monetary easing can be useful in communicating the central bank's intent on following the price-level targeting when the zero interest rate constraint is binding. Even if the central bank is not able to meet its target when the interest rate is at zero, by supplying the amount of money that would be demanded if the price level were at the target level, the bank can signal that it is serious about reaching the target.

Auerbach and Obstfeld (2003) present another extension of the Krugman (1998) model where quantitative monetary easing works by changing the expectations regarding the future monetary policy when the zero interest rate constraint is not binding. According to their model, as long as there is nonzero probability that the economy escapes the zero nominal interest rate bound some time in the future, the central bank can change the price level of that period by *permanently* increasing the level of money supply today.

The second policy Bernanke (2000) discusses is depreciation of the home currency. Yen depreciation, for example, could stimulate aggregate demand by increasing the demand for Japanese exports, by stopping the import-price deflation, and by influencing the future expected inflation. Such policy would call for large sales of yen and hence could raise monetary growth. Many economists, among them Meltzer (2001), McCallum (2000), and Svensson (2000), have advocated quantitative easing that allows for yen depreciation.

The third on the Bernanke's list is money-financed transfers to households. This is the equivalent of a helicopter drop of new money.

Theoretically, as is obvious, such policy should eventually raise the price level and thus help the economic recovery. Otherwise, the Japanese households could just continue to accumulate the financial assets (new money) without bound, which is implausible.

Eggertsson and Woodford (2003) argue that money-financed fiscal transfers can also give the central bank an incentive to commit to the optimal policy. In their model the optimal policy involves maintaining zero interest rate and allowing higher inflation rate when the economy comes out of the zero nominal rate trap. Expansion of the government debt and/or central bank liabilities during the zero interest rate periods can give the central bank another incentive to inflate, thereby sticking to the commitment.

Finally, Bernanke (2000) adds nonstandard market operations to the list. The central bank buys nonperforming loans in the banking sector or long-term government bonds (instead of short-term government bonds), thereby expanding the monetary base. He argues that this will eventually increase the aggregate demand. Purchase of real assets can serve as another commitment device because it also increases the incentive for the central bank and the government to inflate (Eggertsson and Woodford 2003).

The theoretical arguments show that quantitative easing must eventually raise the nominal aggregate demand through some mechanism even when the short-term interest rate is zero. The empirical evidence, however, is limited, partly because the interest rate in major countries did not hit zero until it did in Japan and partly because the BOJ did not really try a substantial quantitative easing until recently.

Hsieh and Shimizutani (2001) is one of the few exceptions. They examine the effects of ¥620 billion consumption vouchers that were distributed to households with children or elderly in April 1999. This is something of a small-scale helicopter drop of money, a form of quantitative monetary easing with fiscal transfers. They find the consumption vouchers increased the consumption by 10 percent (of the amount of vouchers) in the long run in a typical household with children. Data constraint prevented them from estimating the impact of the program on households with elderies. Thus their study suggests that the consumption vouchers experiment increased the aggregate consumption by at least ¥62 billion (about 0.012 percent of GDP).

Miyao (2000) estimates a VAR (vector autoregressive) model of monetary base, call rate, exchange rate, and industrial production. He finds that the effect of monetary base expansion on industrial production ceased in the mid-1990s (1993 to 1998). Using data from more recent period, Kimura et al. (2002) obtain similar results. For quarterly data on inflation rate, output gap, the overnight call rate, and the growth rate of monetary base, they estimated a VAR with time-varying parameters for two sample periods (1971Q2–1985Q2 and 1985Q3–2002Q1), and they compared the estimated impulse response function at 1985Q2 to that at 2002Q1. The positive effect of monetary growth on inflation and output existed at 1985Q2 but disappeared by 2002Q1.

Kuttner and Posen (2001) estimate a VEC (vector error correction) model of M2, real GDP, and the GDP deflator. They find that a permanent increase in M2 in fact raises the price level. The relation seems to have gotten weaker in the 1990s, but still exists. They failed to find a similar relation between monetary base and the price level, however, mainly because of the lack of observed permanent shocks to monetary base in Japan between 1969 and 2000.[9] They nevertheless observed that an increase in the monetary base leads to a temporary (two- to three-year) increase in the price level.

Okina and Shiratsuka (2003) examine the impact of the BOJ's monetary policy on expectations of the future interest policy by following the behavior of the yield curve. They find both ZIRP and quantitative easing to have been effective in increasing the expected duration of zero interest rates in the future. They caution, however, that the clear expansionary effects observed in the yield curves "failed to be transmitted outside the financial system" (p. 18).

In the rest of this section we reexamine the issue of effectiveness of monetary expansion in Japan especially under the zero short-term nominal interest rates. Our approach is similar to that employed by Kuttner and Posen (2001), Miyao (2000), and Kimura et al. (2002) in that we study the time series property of monetary aggregates (M2 + CD), price (GDP deflator), and output (GDP). This chapter's exercise is distinguished from the others in its focus on the long-run relation (cointegration) of the variables and on the possibility that the long-run relation may have changed over time, especially under the zero interest rates. In terms of the quantity equation there will be such a change, for example, when the mean level of velocity shifts permanently. In this case we may fail to find the cointegration of money, price, and output for the whole sample period even when a different cointegration relation exists for the period before the change and the period after the change. Thus the failure to find the cointegration for the whole sample does not necessarily imply the absence of a long-run relation between money and output. It still may be the case that the monetary aggregate can influence the output, although the magnitude of such influence changed over time.

To examine the cointegration between money and output with possible structural changes, we apply two different but complementary tests of cointegration for the system of real GDP and real M2 + CD (calculated by dividing M2 + CD with the GDP deflator).[10] The first is the test developed by Gregory and Hansen (1996). Their tests are designed to test the null hypothesis of no cointegration against the alternative hypothesis of cointegration with a possible change in the cointegrating relation. Thus we first apply Gregory and Hansen test to see if the variables are likely to be cointegrated, with or without regime changes. Gregory and Hensen test is designed to detect a structural change at unknown point within the middle 70 percent of the time series observations. In other words, the test cannot detect the regime shift if it happened in the first 15 percent or the last 15 percent of the observations.

If we find an evidence for cointegration using Gregory and Hansen test, we apply the test developed by Seo (1998) to see if there was a regime shift. Seo (1998) extended the work by Andrews (1993) and Andrews and Ploberger (1994), which developed the tests for structural changes in stationary variables, to the case of testing a change in cointegrating vectors. Seo's tests test the null of cointegration without regime shift against the alternative of cointegration with a regime shift. We use the version that examines the supremum LM (sup-LM) statistic. If the null hypothesis of cointegration with no regime shifts is rejected, we identify the date when the supremum is obtained as the most likely break point. Seo (1998) plots the asymptotic critical values of the statistic for several alternative ranges of the possible structural break. In this chapter we allow the structural break to take place in the middle 90 percent of the observations. This is the maximum range that Seo (1998) considers. Since we are especially interested in the possibility of a structural change in the zero interest rate period, this test, which allows us to test the existence of a structural change near the end of the sample, seems reasonable to use.

Table 6.2 reports the results for augmented Dickey-Fuller tests for the variables we use for our anlaysis: GDP, GDP deflator (PGDP), M2 + CD, and adjusted monetary base (M0). The last column shows the test result for real money, which is defined to be (M2 + CD)/ PGDP. The sample period is from the first quarter of 1980 to the fourth

Table 6.2
Phillips-Perron test for unit root

	GDP	GDP deflator	M2 + CD	Monetary base	Real money
$Z(t)$ Statistic	−0.5025	−2.6756	−0.6632	−0.8167	−1.6703

Notes: Sample period is from 1980Q1 to 2003Q4. Real money is calculated by dividing M2 + CD by the GDP deflator. The tests allow both drift and trend in the process. The null hypothesis is presence of a unit root in the univariate process. The critical values of $Z(t)$ statistics are −4.0570 (1 percent level), −3.4571 (5 percent level), and −3.1542 (10 percent level).

Table 6.3
Gregory and Hansen test for cointegration: Real GDP and real M2 + CD

Sample period	1980Q1–2003Q4
$Z(t)$ Statistic	−6.7403

Notes: The null hypothesis is absence of cointegration. The critical value at 5 percent level is −4.95.

quarter of 2003. For all variables we cannot reject the hypotheses that they have unit roots.

The result for Gregory Hansen test for cointegration between real GDP and real M2 + CD is reported in table 6.3. Because we are primarily interested in the possibility of a change in the slope of the cointegrating vector, we use the test that allows both the intercept and the slope of the cointegrating relation to change. The test rejects the null hypothesis of no cointegration, and suggests that the two series are cointegrated with possible breaks in the cointegrating vector. From this test alone, however, we cannot tell if there was a regime shift in the relation during our sample period.

To test for regime shifts, we apply Seo's test. The result is reported in table 6.4. The test rejects the null hypothesis of cointegration without structural breaks, and suggests a structural break at the fourth quarter of 1995.

In table 6.5 we estimate the cointegrating vector for the two sub-period (1980Q1–1995Q3 and 1995Q4–2003Q4) using Johansen (1988, 1991) approach. For both subperiods the null hypothesis of zero cointegrating relation is rejected at 5 percent statistical significance but the null of only one cointegrating relation is not rejected. Thus we can conclude that there was a stable long-run relation between real money and real GDP both before and after 1995Q3.

Table 6.4
Seo test for structural change: Real GDP and real M2 + CD

Sample period	1980Q1–2003Q4
Sup-LM	12.17
Most likely break point	1995Q4
Number of lags	2

Notes: The lag length for each system was chosen to minimize Schwartz's criterion. The null hypothesis is cointegration without structural breaks. The critical value for Sup-LM at 5 percent level is 10.04. The test tests for a structural change in the middle 90 percent range of the sample.

Table 6.5
Test for cointegration in subperiods: Real GDP and real M2 + CD

Sample period	1980Q1–1995Q3	1995Q4–2003Q4
H_0: no cointegration	27.7035	22.6419
H_0: at most one cointegration	8.6024	8.4459
Normalized cointegrating vector (GDP, M2 + CD)	$(1, -0.6220)$	$(1, -0.4139)$
Number of lags	4	4

Notes: The lag length for the system was chosen to minimize Schwartz's criterion. The first test tests the null of no cointegration against the alternative of at least one cointegration. The critical value for the test statistic is 19.96 (5 percent level). The second test tests the null of at most one cointegration against the alternative of at least two cointegrations. The critical value for the test statistic is 9.24 (5 percent level) in this case. The critical values are taken from the tables in Osterwald-Lenum (1992).

The estimated (normalized) cointegrating vectors suggest that the cointegration was stronger before the break in the following sense. The estimated cointegration vector suggests that a 1 percent increase in the (log) real money balances led to 0.62 percent increase in the (log) real GDP in the long run before 1995. After 1995 the estimates suggest that an increase in the real money still increases the real GDP in the long run, but the magnitude is somewhat smaller: 1 percent increase in real balances leads to 0.41 percent growth of real GDP.

Overall the examinations of long-run relation between real GDP and real M2 + CD suggest a structural break in the late 1995. The timing of the structural break coincides with the reduction of the BOJ discount rate from 1.00 to 0.50 percent (September 1995), which started the period of extreme low interest rates. After the break, the long run relation between real GDP and real M2 + CD has become weaker in the sense that the magnitude of the long-run impact of an increase in the real

Table 6.6
Gregory and Hansen test for cointegration: M2 + CD and monetary base

Sample period	1980Q1–2003Q4
$Z(t)$ Statistic	−2.6016

Notes: The null hypothesis is absence of cointegration. The critical value at 5 percent level is −4.95.

Table 6.7
Seo test for structural change: M2 + CD and monetary base

Sample period	1980Q1–2003Q4
Sup-LM	2.9773
Most likely break point	NA
Number of lags	2

Notes: The lag length for each system was chosen to minimize Schwartz's criterion. The null hypothesis is cointegration without structural breaks. The critical value for Sup-LM at 5 percent level is 10.04. The test tests for a structural change in the middle 90 percent range of the sample.

money on the real GDP has become smaller. Even in the period after the break, which includes the periods of ZIRP, however, the estimated long-run relation between real GDP and real M2 + CD is positive, suggesting that a permanent increase in M2 + CD increases the real GDP in the long run.

Although the results so far suggest a long-run relation between real M2 + CD and real GDP existed even under low interest rate regime, the BOJ and many observers pointed out the difficulty of increasing the growth rate of M2 + CD in the low interest rates environment, especially with ZIRP. Even if the BOJ massively increase the monetary base, the argument went, it does not add to M2 because the banks cannot find worthy borrowers and just hoard the new money in the form of reserves. Kuttner and Posen (2001) and Hutchison (2004) also find the M2 multiplier (M2 divided by the monetary base) declined substantially over the 1990s.

Tables 6.6 through 6.10 examine the long-run relation between M2 + CD and the monetary base.[11] Table 6.6 reports the result of the Gregory and Hansen test. The result suggests that the null of no cointegration cannot be rejected. The result of Seo's test reported in table 6.7 suggests that the null of cointegration without structural breaks cannot be rejected either. Two results are inconsistent because if the two series

Table 6.8
Gregory and Hansen test for cointegration using monthly data: M2 + CD and monetary base

Sample period	1970:1–2003:12
$Z(t)$ Statistic	−2.1354

Notes: The null hypothesis is absence of cointegration. The critical value at 5 percent level is −4.95.

Table 6.9
Seo test for structural change using monthly data: M2 + CD and monetary base

Sample period	1970:1–2003:12
Sup-LM	44.0295
Most likely break point	1998:10
Number of lags	2

Notes: The lag length for each system was chosen to minimize Schwartz's criterion. The null hypothesis is cointegration without structural breaks. The critical value for Sup-LM at 5 percent level is 10.04. The test tests for a structural change in the middle 90 percent range of the sample.

Table 6.10
Test for cointegration in subperiods: M2 + CD and monetary base

Sample period	1970:1–1998:9	1998:10–2003:12
H_0: no cointegration	53.2856	33.5735
H_0: at most one cointegration	7.9763	9.0980
Normalized cointegrating vector (M2 + CD, monetary base)	(1, −4.4150)	(1, −0.5034)
Number of lags	4	2

Notes: The lag length for the system was chosen to minimize Schwartz's criterion. The first test tests the null of no cointegration against the alternative of at least one cointegration. The critical value for the test statistic is 19.96 (5 percent level). The second test tests the null of at most one cointegration against the alternative of at least two cointegrations. The critical value for the test statistic is 9.24 (5 percent level) in this case. The critical values are taken from the tables in Osterwald-Lenum (1992).

are not cointegrated as the Gregory and Hansen test suggests, Seo's test should detect that and reject the null of cointegration (without breaks). Thus the results from tables 6.6 and 6.7 are inconclusive on the long-run relation between M2 + CD and the monetary base.

For M2 + CD and the monetary base the data are available at higher frequencies than quarterly. To check the possibility that the use of quarterly data in tables 6.6 and 6.7 reduced the power of these tests, we apply the same tests using monthly data. We also extended the sample period to start in 1970.[12] The results are reported in tables 6.8 and 6.9. Again, the Gregory and Hansen test fails to reject the null of no cointegration (table 6.8). Seo's test, however, rejects the null of cointegration without a structural change and suggests a break at October 1998. Strictly speaking, we again have an inconclusive result because October 1998 is within the middle 70 percent range of the sample where we allow the Gregory and Hansen test to detect the break. This observation, however, is almost at the very end of the range, and the power of the Gregory and Hansen test is known to decline as the break point approaches the boundary of the range. If we discount the result of the Gregory and Hansen test on this ground and focus on the Seo's test, we can conclude that the result from monthly data suggests a cointegrating relation between M2 + CD and the monetary base with a structural break at October 1998. The examination of quarterly data failed to detect this probably because of the lack of the power.

We proceed and test for cointegration for two subperiods suggested by the result of Seo's test. Table 6.10 shows the result. The Johansen (1988, 1991) test of cointegration rejects the null of no cointegration for both subperiods. Thus we find a cointegrating relation between M2 + CD and the monetary base in each subperiods. The examination of the estimates of cointegrating vectors for the two periods suggests that the size of monetary base that corresponds to a certain level of M2 + CD increased over time. Before October 1998, to increase M2 + CD by 1 percent, the BOJ needed to increase the monetary base by 0.23 percent. After October 1998 the BOJ needed to raise the monetary base by 1.99 percent to increase M2 + CD by 1 percent.

The finding here is overall consistent with the finding by Hutchison (2004) on the change in the money multiplier over time. Using the recursive residual test, he finds a structural break in money multiplier in late 1997. We also find a similar structural break in the long-run equilibrium money multiplier.

Both our result and that of Hutchison (2004) suggest that the relation between M2 + CD and the monetary base has become weaker in the late 1990s. The positive relation between monetary base and M2 + CD, however, still existed even after the structural break. Thus it was still possible to increase M2 + CD by expanding the monetary base. It just took a larger amount of monetary base to increase M2 + CD by a certain proportion.

6.5 Conclusion

In this chapter we reviewed the conduct of monetary policy in Japan during the Great Stagnation. We paid special attention to the period when the ZIRP (zero interest rate policy) was in place. The nominal call rate reached as close to zero as it could get under the ZIRP. The real call rate, however, stayed above zero because of deflation. Growth rates of monetary aggregates under the ZIRP were not particularly high until the BOJ expanded their efforts of quantitative monetary easing in late 2001.

Our empirical analysis shows there was a long-run relation between the real M2 + CD and the real GDP throughout our sample period (1980–2003), although the slope of the cointegrating vector changed around late 1995. Thus monetary policy did not lose its long-run effectiveness. The central bank, however, cannot directly control M2 + CD. The cointegrating relation between M2 + CD and the monetary base is less clear-cut when we use the quarterly data. Using monthly data, however, we find a cointegrating relation between M2 + CD and the monetary base with a structural break around October 1998. In both before and after the regime shift, the long-run relation between M2 + CD and the monetary base is positive, suggesting an increase in the monetary base leads to an increase in M2 + CD in the long run. Over time the relation has become weaker in the sense that it takes a larger increase in the monetary base to generate a reasonable growth in M2 + CD. Even after the regime change, however, the relation between M2 + CD and the monetary base has been still positive, suggesting that an increase in the monetary base still leads to an increase in M2 + CD. Thus our results suggest that a massive quantitative monetary easing increases M2 + CD, and eventually increase the output as well.

Our results do not refute the BOJ's view that the Japanese economic problems are mostly structural and there is little monetary policy can do. Indeed, the structural break that we find in the long-run relation between the monetary base and M2 + CD is consistent with the view that the structural problem substantially weakened an important part of the monetary transmission mechanism. As Hutchison (2004) and others argue, the reduction of money multiplier may have been caused by the problems in the Japanese financial system.[13] We stress the finding, however, that the long-run relation between the monetary base and M2 + CD has been still positive even after the structural break in the late 1990s. Thus the monetary policy could have been more expansionary.

Since the late 2001 the BOJ has been increasing the monetary base. Consistent with our result, M2 + CD also has been increasing albeit slowly. Mr. Toshihiko Fukui stressed that the quantitative monetary easing would not be terminated until Japan is out of deflation. The economy also started to recover in late 2003. Whether the recovery will finally pull Japan out of the Great Stagnation and how much credit monetary policy can claim for the recovery remain to be seen.

Notes

Earlier versions of this chapter were presented at the Workshop on Japanese Monetary Issues, March 20 and 22, 2002, at Economic and Social Research Institute, Tokyo, and CESifo Summer Institute Workshop on Economic Stagnation in Japan, July 25–26, 2003, Venice. We thank anonymous referees, Reuven Glick, Michael Hutchison, Tsutomu Watanabe, and other participants of the conferences for comments.

1. A transcript of the press conference is found at ⟨http://www.boj.or.jp/press/kisha064.htm⟩. The BOJ re-instated the ZIRP in March 2001, seven months after the original ZIRP was lifted.

2. *Change of the Guideline for Money Market Operations*, September 9, 1998; available at ⟨http://www.boj.or.jp/en/seisaku/98/pb/k980909c.htm⟩.

3. The policy announcement is available at the Web site of the prime minister's office ⟨www.kantei.go.jp/foreign/policy/2002/021030sougou_e.html⟩.

4. Bank of Japan, *New Procedures for Money Market Operations and Monetary Easing*, March 19, 2001; available at ⟨http://www.boj.or.jp/en/seisaku/01/pb/k010319a.htm⟩.

5. The figure shows the monthly averages for collateralized overnight rates. The uncollateralized overnight rate series, used as the target rate by the BOJ, is available only after July 1985. The difference between the two rates is miniscule, which was especially the case in the 1990s. The data on the call rate and other financial variables used in this section were obtained from the Web site of Bank of Japan ⟨www.boj.or.jp/en/stat/dlong_f.htm⟩ unless noted otherwise.

6. We use the general CPI index published by the Statistics Bureau of Ministry of Public Management, Home Affairs, Posts and Telecommunications. The data are available at

their Web site ⟨www.stat.go.jp/english/data/cpi/index.htm⟩. We adjust the CPI to remove the effects of the introduction of the consumption tax in 1989 and its rate hike in 1997. To do this, we first estimate an ARMA model of the CPI in level with two dummy variables: one that takes 1 only before the tax change in 1989 and the other that takes 1 only before the tax change in 1997. Using the coefficient estimates on these dummies, we adjust the values of CPI before the tax changes so that they are comparable to the series after the changes.

7. The coverage of M2 + CD published by the Bank of Japan has changed from April 1998 to include the deposits at branches of foreign banks and the Central Shinkin Bank. Thus the M2 + CD series before and after April 1998 are not strictly comparable. We link the two series to get the M2 + CD series that we use for the analyses in this chapter in the following way: First, we calculate the difference between the two definitions as of April 1998. We can do this because the Bank of Japan continued to publish the M2 + CD with the old definition till March 1999. We find the new definition was larger than the old definition by 0.48 percent in April 1998. We assume the gap between the old definition and the new definition was negligible in January 1975 and grew linearly over time. This allows us to convert the M2 + CD series with the old definition to something comparable to that with the new series.

8. As Blanchard (2000) pointed out, this is not "exotic." "[O]ne can argue that monetary policy works mostly—entirely?—through its effects on expectations. If, when the federal funds rate changed in the United States, financial markets did not expect this change to last for some time, the change would barely affect the term structure of interest rates. It is only because financial markets expect the change in the federal funds rate to last for some time... that the term structure is so strongly affected by monetary policy." (Blanchard, 2000, pp. 191–92).

9. Their augmented Dickey-Fuller test rejects the null hypothesis that the monetary base has a unit root.

10. We adjust the GDP deflator to correct for the effects of consumption tax changes using the method described in the note 7.

11. Both series are seasonally adjusted. We further adjust the adjusted monetary base to remove the effects in December 1999 and January 2000. To do this, we first estimate an ARMA model of the (monthly) M0 with dummy variables for December 1999 and January 2000. We estimate the M0 for those observations in the absence of Y2K effects using the estimates when the dummies are set to zero. The quarterly data for M0 are obtained by averaging the monthly data for each quarter.

12. We could just extend the sample period without increasing the frequency of the data. In this case, however, the result is qualitatively the same with the result for quarterly data from 1980Q1 to 2003Q4.

13. See Hoshi and Kashyap (2004) for more on the problems of the Japanese financial system.

References

Andrews, D. W. K. 1993. Tests for parameter instability and structural change with unknown change point. *Econometrica* 61: 821–56.

Andrews, D. W. K., and W. Ploberger. 1994. Optimal tests when a nuisance parameter is present only under the alternative. *Econometrica* 62: 1383–1414.

Auerbach, A. J., and M. Obstfeld. 2003. The case for open-market purchases in a liquidity trap. Unpublished manuscript. University of California, Berkeley.

Bernanke, B. S. 2000. Japanese monetary policy: A case of self-induced paralysis? In R. Mikitani and A. S. Posen, eds., *Japan's Financial Crisis and Its Parallels to U.S. Experience.* Washington, DC: Institute for International Economics, pp. 149–66.

Blanchard, O. 2000. Bubbles, liquidity traps, and monetary policy. In R. Mikitani and A. S. Posen, eds., *Japan's Financial Crisis and Its Parallels to U.S. Experience.* Washington, DC: Institute for International Economics, pp. 185–93.

Eggertsson, G., and M. Woodford. 2003. The zero bound on interest rates and optimal monetary policy. *Brookings Papers on Economic Activity* 2: 139–233.

Engle, R., and C. Granger. 1987. Co-integration and error correction: Representation, estimation and testing. *Econometrica* 35: 251–76.

Gregory, A. W., and B. E. Hansen. 1996. Residual-based tests for cointegration in models with regime shifts. *Journal of Econometrics* 70: 99–126.

Hoshi, T., and A. Kashyap. 2004. Japan's financial crisis and economic stagnation. *Journal of Economic Perspectives* 18: 3–26.

Hsieh, C.-T., and S. Shimizutani. 2001. Helicopter drops of money: Assessing an unusual experiment in Japanese fiscal policy. Unpublished manuscript. Princeton University.

Hutchison, M. 2004. Deflation and stagnation in Japan: Collapse of the monetary transmission mechanism and echo from the 1930s. In R. Burdekin and P. Siklos, eds., *Deflation: Current and Historical Perspectives.* Cambridge; Cambridge University Press.

Johansen, S. 1988. Statistical analysis of cointegrating vectors. *Journal of Economic Dynamics and Control* 12: 231–54.

Johansen, S. 1991. Estimation and hypothesis testing of cointegration vectors in Gaussian vector autoregressive models. *Econometrica* 59: 1551–80.

Jung, T., Y. Teranishi, and T. Watanabe. 2001. Zero bound on nominal interest rates and optimal monetary policy. KIER Discussion Paper 525.

Kimura, T., H. Kobayashi, J. Muranaga, and H. Ugai. 2002. The effect of the increase in monetary base on Japan's economy at zero interest rates: An empirical analysis. Bank of Japan IMES Discussion Paper 2002-E-22.

Krugman, P. 1998. It's baaack: Japan's slump and the return of the liquidity trap. *Brookings Papers on Economic Activity* 2: 137–205.

Krugman, P. 2000. Thinking about the liquidity trap. *Journal of the Japanese and International Economies* 14: 221–37.

Kuttner, K. N., and A. S. Posen. 2001. The great recession: Lessons for macroeconomic policy from Japan. *Brookings Papers on Economic Activity* 2: 93–185.

Meltzer, A. H. 2001. Monetary transmission at low inflation: Some clues from Japan in the 1990s. *Bank of Japan Monetary and Economic Studies*: 13–34.

McCallum, B. S. 2000. Theoretical analysis regarding a zero lower bound on nominal interest rates. *Journal of Money, Credit, and Banking* 32: 870–904.

Miyao, R. 2000. The role of monetary policy in Japan: A break in the 1990s? *Journal of the Japanese and International Economies* 14: 366–84.

Okina, K., and S. Shiratsuka. 2003. Policy commitment and expectation formations: Japan's experience under zero interest rate. Bank of Japan IMES Discussion Paper 2003-E-5.

Osterwald-Lenum, M. 1992. Note with quantiles of the asymptotic distribution of the maximum likelihood cointegration rank test statistics. *Oxford Bulleting of Economics and Statistics* 54: 461–72.

Phillips, P. C. B., and P. Perron. 1988. Testing for a unit root in time series regression. *Biometrika* 75: 335–46.

Posen, A. S. 1998. *Restoring Japan's Economic Growth.* Washington, DC: Institute of International Economics.

Seo, B. 1998. Tests for structural change in cointegrated systems. *Econometric Theory* 14: 222–59.

Shiratsuka, S. 1999. Measurement errors in the Japanese consumer price index. *Bank of Japan Monetary and Economic Studies* 17: 69–102.

Svensson, L. E. O. 2001. The zero bound in an open economy: A foolproof way of escaping from a liquidity trap. *Bank of Japan Monetary and Economic Studies*: 277–322.

7

The Policy Duration Effect under Zero Interest Rates: An Application of Wavelet Analysis

Kunio Okina and Shigenori Shiratsuka

7.1 Introduction

In this chapter we analyze a yield curve to examine the effectiveness and limitations of monetary policy commitment in Japan's recent deflationary economic environment. Specifically, we apply "wavelet analysis" by which we examine the nature of the term structure of interest rates in Japan.[1] Theoretically, even when short-term interest rates decline to virtually zero, a central bank can produce a further easing effect by its policy commitment.[2] Moreover a central bank can influence market expectations by making an explicit commitment to the duration for which it will hold short-term interest rates at virtually zero. If the bank succeeds in credibly extending its commitment duration, it can reduce long-term interest rates. We call this mechanism the "policy duration effect," after Fujiki, Okina, and Shiratsuka (2000) and Fujiki and Shiratsuka (2002).

Insight into the policy duration effect may be gleaned by analyzing the behavior of yield curves under the past zero interest rate policy as well as under the current quantitative monetary easing. In Okina and Shiratsuka (2003) we take a two-step approach. The first step is to employ a curve-fitting method to estimate a forward rate curve by using a set of spot rates with different times to maturity per day, and to compile indicators for the policy duration effect.[3] The second step is to examine the changes in the shape of yield curves and the indicators over time, thereby assessing the policy duration effect.

This chapter extends our earlier work by applying wavelet analysis to develop an alternative indicator of policy duration.[4] A wavelet is a small wave, and wavelet analysis expresses a time series as a sum of localized small and temporary waves. This technique enables us to decompose a time series into both frequency domain and time domain simultaneously. As a result it has an advantage in analyzing data that show irregular fluctuations as well as time-varying frequency characteristics.

Recent monetary policy in Japan has been characterized by heavy reliance on the policy duration effect. Under the zero interest rate policy, the Bank of Japan (BOJ) committed to a zero interest rate until deflationary concerns were dispelled, and under the quantitative monetary easing, the BOJ has committed to providing ample liquidity that easily exceeds the required reserve until CPI inflation stabilizes at or above zero percent. These policy frameworks employ a policy commitment to compensate for a central bank's inability to lower rates below zero and thus alter the expected course of its monetary policy actions.

In February 1999 the BOJ began to lower gradually the overnight call rate to 0.02 percent. In April of that year, Bank of Japan's Governor Masaru Hayami announced the BOJ's commitment to a zero interest rate until deflationary concerns were dispelled. Then, in August 2000, in view of clear signs of a sustained recovery in the economy, the BOJ terminated its zero interest rate policy and raised the overnight call rate to 0.25 percent.

However, in late 2000, the economy once again slowed, reflecting adjustments in the area of global information technology related to investments and exports. As a result deflationary concerns were once again aroused. The BOJ reacted by lowering the policy interest rate to 0.15 percent in mid-February 2001, and at the end of March it adopted a policy of "quantitative monetary easing." In an effort to stabilize CPI inflation at or above zero percent, the BOJ then committed itself to targeting the current account balance. This led the overnight call rate to decline initially to 0.01 percent, below the 0.02 percent low experienced under the BOJ's zero interest rate policy. Then, in September 2001, the rate further declined to 0.001 percent due to the reduction of the interest rate unit for call market transactions from 1/100 percent to 1/1000 percent.

The chapter is organized as follows: Section 7.2 summarizes an analytical framework employed for estimating the policy duration effect, based on information contained in the yield curve. Section 7.3 provides an overview of data and estimation results, including an assessment on the effectiveness of the policy duration effect. Section 7.4 reports the results of wavelet analysis to the four indicators for policy duration effect. Section 7.5 offers a concluding discussion. Further appendix A provides numerical examples of how changes in the parameter values of our yield curve model affect the shape of the instantaneous forward rate curve, and appendix B summarizes the basic framework of wavelet analysis.

7.2   Analytical Framework

In this section we briefly review the basic framework for our analysis of the policy duration effect. We first define the policy duration effect, and then examine how to assess such effects. In addition we explain the extended versions of Nelson and Siegel's (1987) model to estimate the shape of the yield curve over time. We then introduce indicators for policy duration effect, based on the estimates of the extended Nelson-Siegel model.

7.2.1   The Policy Duration Effect

The policy duration effect arises from expectations over how long into the future a current abundant provision of funds (quantitative monetary easing) will last.

The BOJ's commitment to sustaining zero interest rates to ease deflationary concerns, and a similar commitment later to quantitative monetary easing proved highly effective in stabilizing market expectations for the path of short-term interest rates. Guiding the overnight rate to virtually zero for a considerable period of time served to anchor medium- to long-term interest rates. As a result the yield curve flattened and stabilized at very low levels.

The policy duration effect mechanism mentioned above is underpinned by the expectations hypothesis on the term structure of interest rates. The pure expectations theory of the term structure of interest rates tells us that long-term interest rates today should reflect the future course of short-term interest rates.[5] For example, a one-year interest rate is determined by market expectations for overnight interest rates during the subsequent twelve-month period. Based on a more practical and general formula, long-term interest rates are the sum of market expectations for the path of short-term interest rates and a term premium (based on risks posed by uncertainties or preferences of market participants). With premiums being constant, fluctuations of interest rates on term instruments reflect changes in such expectations.[6]

In this regard it should be noted that there exists a two-way causality between a policy action and the economy's performance in interpreting the behavior of the yield curve. This is because the BOJ's policy commitments are conditional to the economic environments: during the ZIRP, the BOJ committed itself to maintaining zero interest rates until deflationary concerns were dispelled, and under the current QME the BOJ also has committed itself to maintaining QME until the core CPI inflation becomes stably positive. This implies that if the economy is on a downward trend, market participants believe termination of the policy should be put off, thus bringing longer term interest rates down to flatten the yield curve. Conversely, if the economy is on an upward trend, market participants believe the termination should get closer, thus raising longer term interest rates to twist the yield curve, acting as a brake on the easing effect.

7.2.2 *The Extended Model of Nelson and Siegel (1987)*

An estimation of the yield curve is typically conducted by looking at the instantaneous forward (IFR) rate curve. Here we employ an extended version of Nelson and Siegel's (1987) model, proposed by Söderlind and Svensson (1997).[7]

Our specification of the IFR for a settlement at period m, denoted by $r(m)$, is

$$r(m) = \beta_0 + \beta_1 \cdot \exp\left(-\frac{m}{\tau_1}\right) + \beta_2 \cdot \left(\frac{m}{\tau_1}\right) \cdot \exp\left(-\frac{m}{\tau_1}\right)$$

$$+ \beta_3 \cdot \left(\frac{m}{\tau_2}\right) \cdot \exp\left(-\frac{m}{\tau_2}\right), \tag{1}$$

where β_0, β_1, β_2, β_3, τ_1, and τ_2 are parameters to be estimated from the data. We expect β_0, τ_1, and τ_2 to be positive.

The IFR curve, generated by equation (1), includes four terms. The first term is a constant β_0. The second term is an exponential function $\beta_1 * \exp(-m/\tau_1)$. When β_1 takes a negative (positive) value, this term produces an upward-trending (downward-trending) shape in the short end of the IFR curve. A large (small) value of τ_1 means that this exponential effect decays more slowly (quickly). The third term is $\beta_2 * (m/\tau_1) * \exp(-m/\tau_1)$, producing a U-shape (hump shape) when β_2 takes a negative (positive) value. The fourth term produces a U-shape (hump shape) when β_3 takes a negative (positive) value. τ_2 controls the rate of convergence of the fourth term, as does τ_1 for the second and third terms.

The specification for the spot rate at maturity m, denoted $R(m)$, can in turn be derived by integrating the equation (1) from zero to m and dividing by m. That is,

$$R(m) = \frac{1}{m} \int_{s=0}^{m} r(s)\,ds, \tag{2}$$

and the specific functional form employed in the estimation is as follows:

$$R(m) = \beta_0 + \beta_1 \cdot \left(\frac{\tau_1}{m}\right) \cdot \left(1 - \exp\left(-\frac{m}{\tau_1}\right)\right)$$

$$+ \beta_2 \cdot \left[\left(\frac{\tau_1}{m}\right) \cdot \left(1 - \exp\left(-\frac{m}{\tau_1}\right)\right) - \exp\left(-\frac{m}{\tau_1}\right)\right]$$

$$+ \beta_3 \cdot \left[\left(\frac{\tau_2}{m}\right) \cdot \left(1 - \exp\left(-\frac{m}{\tau_2}\right)\right) - \exp\left(-\frac{m}{\tau_2}\right)\right]. \tag{3}$$

The important features of equations (1) and (3) are that the limits of forward and spot rates when maturity approaches zero and infinity, respectively, are equal to $\beta_0 + \beta_1$ and β_0.[8]

7.2.3 Indicators for the Policy Duration Effect

We next define indicators for the policy duration effect, using the parameters of the extended Nelson-Siegel model. In figure 7.1 we illustrate the indicators taking the following parameter values: $\beta_0 = 2.8$, $\beta_1 = -2.8$, $\beta_2 = 0.0$, $\beta_3 = -6.0$, $\tau_1 = 0.3$, and $\tau_2 = 1.0$. In this figure the upper and lower thin curving lines indicate the IFR curve, $r(m)$, and the spot rate curve, $R(m)$, respectively. $r(m)$ starts from zero at maturity zero, manifests a two-stage upward trend from the short end to midrange, and finally converges to a long-term forward rate of β_0, shown as a dashed horizontal line close to the top.

In order to capture market expectations on the duration of the policy commitment as well as the policy impacts, we define four indicators for the policy duration effect below. First, we define the policy duration, denoted by PD, at point τ_2, where $r(m)$ becomes increasingly upward-trending in the second stage increase, typically at the year-to-settlement of around one year or more. As mentioned earlier, the

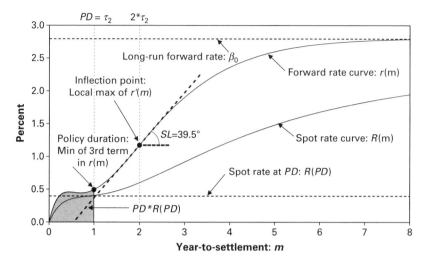

Figure 7.1
Indicators for the policy duration effect. Forward rate and spot rate curves are computed by equations (1) and (3), with parameter values $\beta_0 = 2.8$, $\beta_1 = 2.8$, $\beta_2 = 0.0$, $\tau_1 = 0.3$, and $\tau_2 = 1.0$.

fourth term in the right-hand side of equation (1) takes a minimum value at this point. All the downward factors are exhausted at this point, since τ_2 always take a larger value than τ_1. In the figure PD is one year, indicated by the first dashed vertical line to the left.[9]

Second, we use the estimated spot rate at PD, $R(PD)$, as a measure of market confidence in the BOJ's policy commitment to a zero interest rate.[10] This is because $R(PD)$ is equivalent to the lower area of the IFR curve from zero to PD (as shown in equation 2). That is,

$$R(PD) = \frac{1}{PD} \int_{s=0}^{PD} r(s)\, ds. \tag{4}$$

In other words, $R(PD)$ is the averaged IFR between zero and PD. A smaller $R(PD)$ implies that financial market participants expect a lower path of short-term interest rates and have greater confidence in the BOJ's commitment to zero interest rates. In the figure $R(PD)$ is approximately equal to 0.4 percent, shown as a dashed horizontal line close to the bottom. It is equivalent to the shaded area, or the integral of the IFR curve from zero to PD, divided by PD.

Third, we employ a slope of $r(m)$ at the inflection point as a proxy for the flatness of the whole shape of the curve. Due to the definition of the inflection point, this is the maximum grade of $r(m)$ in the second stage increase. $r(m)$ then gradually converges to the long-term forward rate, given by β_0. This slope is denoted SL. Given that the inflection point approximately corresponds to $2 * \tau_2$ in our specification, the slope at this point is

$$SL = \arctan r'(2 * \tau_2). \tag{5}$$

In the figure, $2 * \tau_2$ is 2.0 years, depicted by the second dashed vertical line from the left. SL is approximately 39.5 degrees.

Fourth, we use β_0, which corresponds to a long-term forward rate, or LFR, as a proxy for the summation of expected inflation and expected economic growth, or expected nominal economic growth.[11] More precisely the steady-state nominal interest rate i^* is equal to the sum of the steady state real interest rate r^* and the steady state rate of inflation π^* by Fisher's equation. Thus LFR can be written as

$$LFR = i^* + \rho = r^* + \pi^* + \rho, \tag{6}$$

where ρ is a risk premium. This is deemed to reflect market expectations for long-term economic performance.

Among the four indicators for the policy duration effect, it should be noted that the first two indicators look at the term structure of interest rates in the short term, tracing the expected initial impacts of policy actions. In contrast, the other two indicators focus on the term structure at the medium to long term to extract an indication of market expectations regarding future inflation and real interest rates, thereby indicating market assessments of those policy impacts.

7.3   Empirical Evidence on the Policy Duration Effect

We first present the data used to estimate the IFR curve over time and provide the estimated results of the extended Nelson-Siegel model. In addition we compute indicators for the policy duration effect, based on the estimation result for the IFR curve.

7.3.1   Data

We use data for euro-yen Tokyo interbank offered rates (TIBOR) as short-term interest rates, ranging from one- to twelve-month contracts, and yen swap rates as medium- to long-term interest rates from two- to twelve-year contracts.[12] As mentioned earlier, we also use the overnight uncollateralized call rate to impose the restriction that the overnight call rate be equal to $\beta_0 + \beta_1$. The sample period, which is determined by data availability, is every business day from March 2, 1998, to February 28, 2003.[13]

7.3.2 Estimated Results for the Nelson-Siegel Model

Figure 7.2 summarizes the estimated results of Okina and Shiratsuka (2003) for parameters β_0, β_1, β_2, β_3, τ_1, and τ_2 as indicated from the top to the bottom panels.[14] In each panel a solid line shows the estimated parameters. Shaded lines show the upper and lower bounds of the confidence interval for each parameter, obtained by adding and subtracting two times the standard errors of the estimated coefficient.

The magnitudes and signs of the estimated parameters are consistent with our assumptions for the typical shape of the IFR curve since 1998. For example, β_0 and β_1 typically range from 2 to 3, and -3 to -2, respectively, except for the periods of market boom of Japanese government bonds (JGB) in the fall of 1998 and in January 2003. β_2 deviates insignificantly from zero, except for the period when the IFR curve manifests a complex shape, such as the initial stage of the zero interest rate policy, and the end of a fiscal year or end of the reserve maintenance period when the overnight rate temporarily jumps. β_3 always takes a negative value, and has been stable, ranging from -6.0 to -3.5, except in 1999, when it often had values less than -7.0. τ_1 and τ_2 always take positive values and were stable until 2000, rising gradually from the beginning of 2001.

We examine the robustness of estimation results against the zero bound of nominal interest rates by using the trade date January 29, 2003, as an example, when β_0 or LFR take a minimum value in the sample period. In figure 7.3 we plot the observed spot rates and estimated spot and instantaneous forward rates. The circles are observed spot rates for the overnight call rate, 12 euro-yen TIBORs, and 13 yen swap rates. The thin and bold lines indicate the estimated spot and instantaneous forward rates, respectively. The shaded lines associated with these two lines indicate their confidence intervals, which we computed using the delta method.

We can see from the figure that the parameters for the extended Nelson-Siegel model are a fairly precise estimation, and that the confidence intervals for the spot and instantaneous forward rates are very narrow. The figure apparently indicates that restricting the shortest

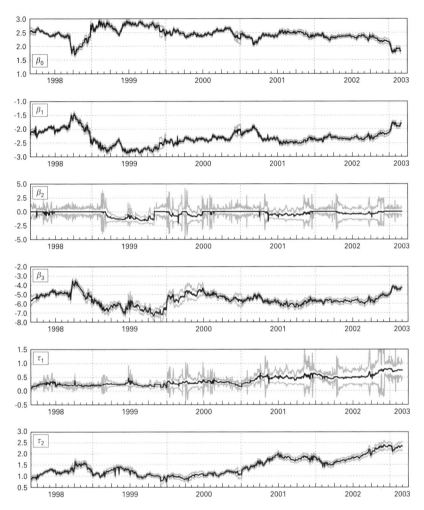

Figure 7.2
Estimated coefficients for NS model. Plots of estimated coefficients are in bold, and shaded for upper and lower bounds of the confidence interval (estimated coefficients $\pm 2^*$ standard errors). Year-end is indicated by dotted vertical lines.

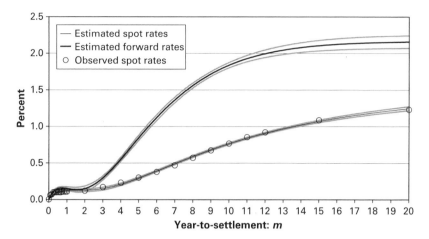

Figure 7.3
Estimated results for January 29, 2003. Circles indicate spot rates for the overnight call, 12 euro-yen TIBORs, and 13 yen swap rates. Solid lines show estimated spot rates (thin line) and instantaneous forward rates (bold line). Proximate shaded lines show their confidence intervals. Estimates of parameter values are $\beta_0 = 1.787$ (s.e. = 0.036), $\beta_1 = -1.785$ (s.e. = 0.083), $\beta_2 = -0.000$ (s.e. = 0.170), $\beta_3 = -4.221$ (s.e. = 0.083), $\tau_1 = 0.720$ (s.e. = 0.079), and $\tau_2 = 2.266$ (s.e. = 0.073).

end to equivalency to the overnight uncollateralized call rate is sufficient to keep the zero-bound of nominal interest rates from influencing the estimates, even under the recent low and flat yield curve.

7.3.3 Estimated Indicators for the Policy Duration Effect

Given this background, we are now able to compute indicators for the policy duration effect, based on the estimated results in the previous section, and assess the policy duration effect under the zero interest rate policy as well as quantitative monetary easing.

Figure 7.4 displays the computed results of the aforementioned indicators over time shown in Okina and Shiratsuka (2003): panel a represents the policy duration $(PD = \tau_2)$, panel b represents the estimated spot rate at PD $(R(PD))$, panel c represents the slope of the IFR curve at the inflection point $(SL = \arctan r'(2 * \tau_2))$, and panel d represents the long-term forward rate $(LFR = \beta_0)$. The figure also shows the confidence intervals for each indicator by shaded lines, obtained by adding and subtracting two times the standard errors for each indicator.[15] The confidence intervals for each indicator are tight except for the

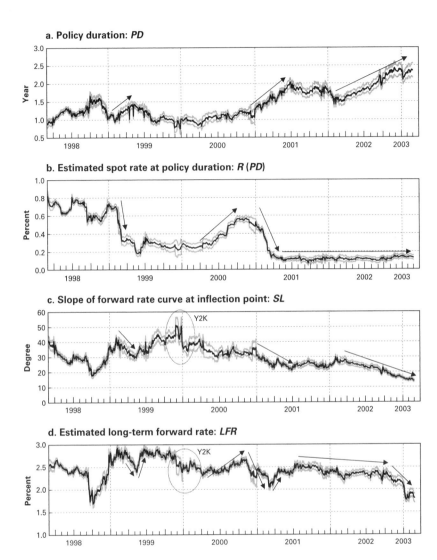

Figure 7.4
Estimated indicators for the policy duration effects.

volatile period of Y2K, suggesting that all the indicators are precisely estimated.

Among the four indicators, *PD* and *R(PD)* represent the term structure of interest rates in the short horizon, tracing the expected initial impacts of policy actions. *SL* and *LFR* represent the term structure for the medium to long term to extract an indication of market expectations regarding future inflation and real interest rates, thereby deriving market assessments of those policy impacts.

Panel a of figure 7.4 shows that *PD* has three upward trend phases: (1) the period soon after the launch of the zero interest rate policy, (2) the period from January 2001 to June 2001, and (3) the period from April 2002 to December 2002. Among the three phases, the last phase exhibits more persistent but less rapid increases than do the previous two.

Panel b covers two major declines for *R(PD)*: one for February to March 1999, and the other for early 2001. Both cases show significant declines of approximately 40 bp in a month. The first decline is soon after the launch of the zero interest rate policy, while the second one is shortly before the launch of quantitative monetary easing, not after. In the latter case a large part of the commitment effect appears in advance to making an explicit commitment.

Panel c shows that *SL* declines significantly three times, each corresponding to the three rising phases of *PD*. The first decline, after the launch of the zero interest rate policy, led to a subsequent rebound as business conditions recovered, especially in the spring of 2000. In contrast, the second decline did not appear to be accompanied by a significant rebound, and the third decline persists as of February 2003, which is the end of the sample period for our estimations.

Panel d demonstrates that *LFR* has a general downward trend since 2000, with some cyclical ups and downs within this downward trend. Declines grow with passing time, while rebounds become weaker. Moreover a major decline is observed following the beginning of 2003, reflecting prolonged deflationary expectations in the financial markets.

To sum up our empirical observations on the policy duration indicators in Okina and Shiratsuka (2003), *PD* generally increases over time while the other three indicators, *R(PD)*, *SL*, and *LFR*, decline. Increased *PD* and declined *R(PD)* indicate that the IFR curve in the short end becomes flatter, and declined *SL* and *LFR* imply that the IFR curve in the longer end levels off as well.[16]

The observation above suggests two points. First, quantitative monetary easing within the sample period strengthened the policy duration effect, enhancing market credibility to the BOJ's commitment to zero interest rates. Second, despite such a policy duration effect, which was fairly strong, the policy duration effect alone failed to reverse market expectations that deflation and low economic growth would persist well into the future. The policy duration effect confined market expectations of prolonged deflation, thereby leading market participants to adjust to such a state of the economy and further hampering the BOJ's effort to reverse the deflationary expectations.

If the policy duration effect is strong enough to alter market expectations regarding the future course of the economy in a positive direction, the slope of the IFR curve in the midrange as well as the long-term forward rate are expected to increase. In addition such positive expectations shorten the expected duration of the policy commitment to a zero interest rate or quantitative monetary easing. Conversely, if the policy duration effect is not sufficiently effective and expectations of deflation and low economic growth remain, the slope of the IFR curve in the midrange and the long-term forward rate are unlikely to increase.

Quantitative monetary easing also reduces the incentive for financial institutions to assume interest rate risks. As market expectations of a prolonged zero interest rate intensify, financial institutions are more likely to purchase JGBs with less concern for interest rate risks and potential capital losses. In fact they are less likely to hedge their interest rate risks from a massive purchase of JGBs by swapping fixed rates in exchange for floating rates. As a result the yen swap rate declined substantially from mid-1999, and the yen swap spread, defined as the difference between the yen swap rate and the JGB rate at the same maturity, has been reduced to below zero since the end of 2001, as shown in figure 7.5. This observation implies that interbank markets not only for short-term contracts but also for longer-term contracts have virtually ceased to function as a risk-sharing device among financial institutions and are insensitive to interest risks.

7.4 Wavelet Analysis on Indicators for Policy Duration Effect

In this section we apply the wavelet analysis to indicators of the policy duration effect in order to examine the robustness of early work in this area.

bps

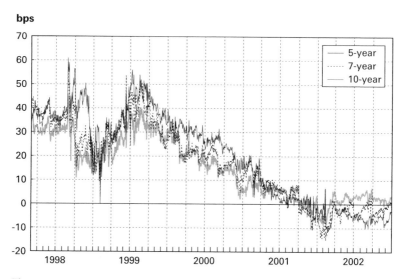

Figure 7.5
Yen swap spread. Source: Bloomberg data service.

7.4.1 Policy Duration Effect and Wavelet Analysis

A wavelet is a small wave, and wavelet analysis expresses a time series as a sum of localized small and temporary waves. This technique enables us to decompose a time series into both frequency and time domains simultaneously. It thus is useful in analyzing data that show irregular fluctuations as well as time-varying frequency characteristics.

Fourier analysis, which is often used in analyzing frequency characteristics of time series data, decomposes a time series into a sum of sine and cosine functions at different wavelengths. Fourier analysis, however, has a limitation in that it is unable to capture time-varying frequency characteristics, if any, because information on the time domain is lost.

It is important to note the time-varying nature of policy impacts under the zero interest rate policy and quantitative monetary easing. The time-varying nature of policy comes from two elements: one is the accumulation of experience on the part of market participants, and the other is a change in financial and macroeconomic environments. Therefore it seems reasonable to examine the policy duration effect from the viewpoint of how the frequency patterns of the indicators for the policy duration effect evolved. Such analysis extends our empirical results in Okina and Shiratsuka (2003).

7.4.2 Wavelet Analysis of Indicators for Policy Duration Effect

We apply wavelet analysis to the four indicators of the policy duration effect as shown in figure 7.6.[17] In the figure we take six components as indicators of the policy duration effect: one low-frequency component (wavelet smooth at level 5) and five higher frequency components (wavelet details at levels 1 to 5). In the top panel the smooth wavelet at level 5 captures the trend component from which we have removed cyclical components up to the frequency of 2^5, or one and half months. The wavelet details at levels 1 through 5, from the second top panel to the bottom panel, represent, respectively, stationary components with the frequencies of 2, 4, 8, 16, and 32 business days.

The period over which the wavelets were estimated is from March 24, 1998, to February 28, 2003. This is slightly shorter than the sample period of our data set because estimation of five levels of wavelets requires a sample size that is a multiple of $2^5 = 32$. We set the end of the estimation period as the end of our data set, and then decided the beginning of the estimation period retroactively so that the sample size would equal 1,216, which is the greatest multiple of 32 within our data set.

PD in panel a of the figure shows three phases of upward trending. During the first two phases, that is, soon after the launch of the zero interest rate policy and before and after the launch of quantitative monetary easing, volatility at levels 1 to 3 showed higher frequencies of increases. In the third phase, however, the frequency of fluctuations remained low and fairly stable. We can infer that market expectations with respect to the prolonged policy duration had smoothed by the third phase.

$R(PD)$ in panel b starts its decline in the whole range of cyclical components from levels 1 to 5 at the launch of the zero interest rate policy. This is what precisely occurred from late 2001 to early 2003. In addition the wavelet smooth in or at level 5 shows a marked decline. These findings correspond to the market credibility to the BOJ's commitment to a zero interest rate, which stabilized the market at a high level during the period of quantitative monetary easing.

a. Policy duration: *PD*

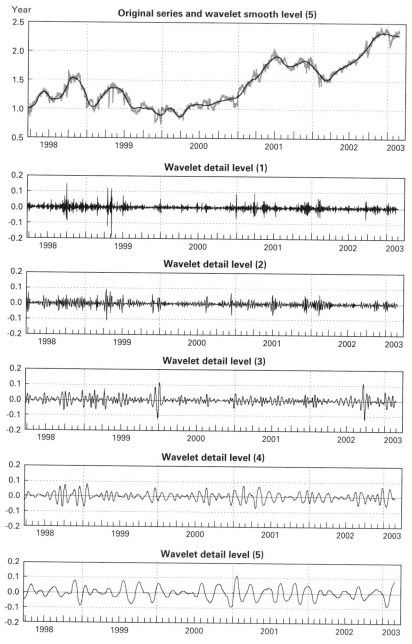

Figure 7.6
Wavelet transformation of indicators for the policy duration effect.

b. Estimated spot rate at policy duration: *R* (*PD*)

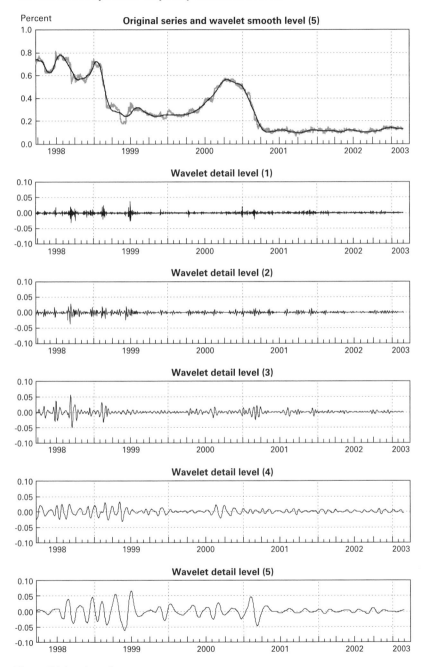

Figure 7.6 (continued)

c. Slope of forward rate curve at inflection point: *SL*

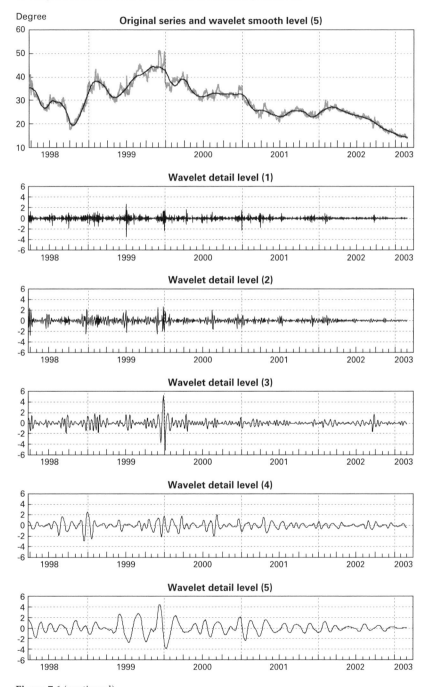

Figure 7.6 (continued)

d. Estimated long-term forward rate: LFR

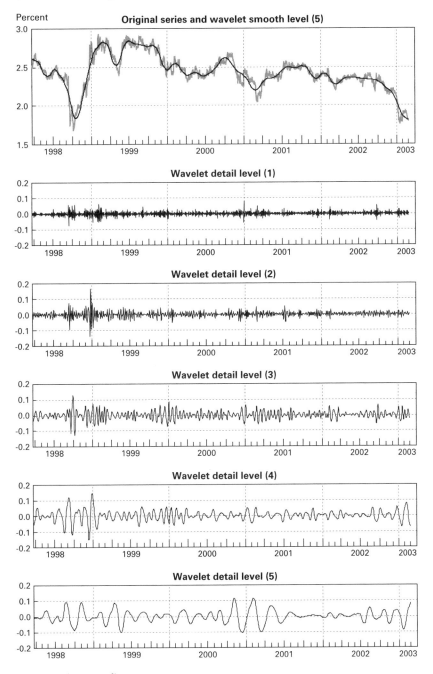

Figure 7.6 (continued)

SL in panel c reflects the stabilization of a whole range of cyclical components since 2002. As a result the yield curve in the midrange is fairly stable, and it is flattened in the aforementioned third phase of upward trending in the *PD*. In other words, the policy duration effect appeared to anchor the yield curve formation in the midrange.

LFR in panel d shows the stabilization of cyclical components at all levels in 2002. This suggests that market expectations on long-term interest rates were stably formed. The low volatility of the wavelet details at level 5 may be due to people's deflationary expectations becoming suppressed over time.

From the analysis above two conclusions can be drawn. First, quantitative monetary easing within the sample period reinforced the policy duration effect, adding market credibility to the BOJ's commitment to a zero interest rate. Second, despite such congruous effect, quantitative monetary easing failed to reverse market expectations that deflation and low economic growth would persist well into the future. The policy duration effect instead led market participants to adjust to the deflationary state of the economy. This in turn made it difficult for the BOJ to reverse the deflationary expectations.

7.5   Concluding Remarks

In this chapter we examined the policy commitment effect, or policy duration effect, of recent monetary policy in Japan, which has been characterized by the unusual environment of zero nominal short-term interest rates. To do so, we introduced wavelet analysis to four indicators of policy duration effects.

We observed two trends. First, the policy duration effect did stabilize market expectations for short-term interest rates, lowering longer term interest rates and flattening the yield curve. This policy even to a certain extent succeeded in bolstering Japan's economy, especially by helping to stabilize the financial system. Second, the lowered long-term interest rates signaled to the financial market that the deflation would be prolonged and persist for several years rather than rapidly reversing.

Appendix A: An Illustration of the Contributions of Each Component in the Nelson-Siegel Model

In this appendix we explain the estimates we used in our extended Nelson-Siegel model.

a. A typical shape under a zero interest rate policy and quantitative monetary easing

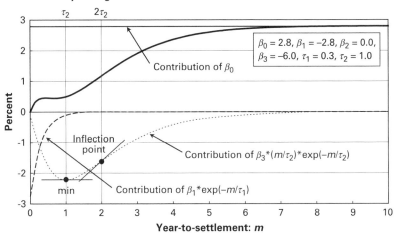

b. A complex shape in the case of liquidity events

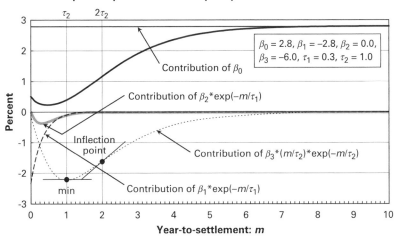

Figure 7.7
Illustrated IFR curve. The IFR curves are computed using equation (1) with the following parameter values: $\beta_0 = 2.8$, $\beta_1 = -2.8$, $\beta_2 = 0.0$, $\beta_3 = -6.0$, $\tau_1 = 0.3$, and $\tau_2 = 1.0$ for the upper panel, and $\beta_0 = 2.8$, $\beta_1 = -2.8$, $\beta_2 = 0.0$, $\beta_3 = -6.0$, $\tau_1 = 0.3$, and $\tau_2 = 1.0$ for the lower panel.

Figure 7.7 gives a hypothetical version of IFR curves used in the extended Nelson-Siegel model. The parameters are as follows: $\beta_0 = 2.8$, $\beta_1 = -2.8$, $\beta_2 = 0.0$, $\beta_3 = -6.0$, $\tau_1 = 0.3$, $\tau_2 = 1.0$ for the upper panel, and $\beta_0 = 2.8$, $\beta_1 = -2.3$, $\beta_2 = -1.0$, $\beta_3 = -6.0$, $\tau_1 = 0.3$, $\tau_2 = 1.0$ for the lower panel. The parameters are the same in the two panels except for β_1 and β_2. These parameters represent the shapes of the IFR curve under a zero interest rate policy and quantitative monetary easing. The upper panel illustrates the typical IFR curve. The lower panel corresponds to a situation where the overnight rate temporarily jumps at the end of the calendar year, the fiscal year, or the reserve maintenance period.[18]

This figure also shows the contributions of each term. The first and fourth terms occur in both panels because the same parameters, except for β_1 and β_2, are used. The first term, β_0, is constant over the whole range of the time to settlement. The second term $\beta_1 * \exp(-m/\tau_1)$ is an exponential function, exhibiting an upward trend at the short end of the IFR curve where β_1 is negative. Its impact decays gradually (quickly) as τ_1 becomes larger (smaller). The third term in the lower panel, $\beta_2 * (-m/\tau_1) * \exp(-m/\tau_1)$, takes a U-shape in the short-term because β_2 is negative.

The fourth term, $\beta_3 * (-m/\tau_2) * \exp(-m/\tau_2)$, also takes a U-shape because β_3 is negative (a hump shape when positive). This term allows a nonmonotonic increase in the IFR curve. In addition, the U-shape decays slower than that of the third term because τ_2 is larger than τ_1. A large (small) value of τ_2 means that the effects decay more slowly (quickly), and the IFR converges to the long-term forward rate more slowly (quickly).

Since β_3 is negative, the fourth term takes a U-shape, with a minimum at τ_2 and an inflection point at $2 * \tau_2$. The point $2 * \tau_2$ approximately corresponds to the inflection point for the overall IFR curve because the second and the fourth terms almost converge to zero at point $2 * \tau_2$. Therefore, at this point, $r'(m)$ is approximately locally maximized and $r''(m)$ is approximately zero.

Appendix B: A Basic Framework of Wavelet Analysis

In this appendix we offer a brief exposition of wavelet analysis by using the basic framework of discrete wavelet transform. See Ramsey (2002), for example, for more on wavelets for applications to economic analysis.

Wavelet Filter

Wavelet analysis can be viewed as a kind of linear filtering. Wavelet filter h is defined so as to satisfy the conditions below:

$$\sum_{k=1}^{L} h_k = 0, \quad \sum_{k=1}^{L} h_k^2 = 1, \quad \sum_{k=1}^{L} h_k h_{k+2n} = 0, \tag{A1}$$

where L denotes the length of filter or support and n is a nonzero integer. The first condition implies that the filter is a high-pass filter that captures cyclical fluctuations and extracts high-frequency components. The second condition is for standardization. The third condition means that filters are orthogonal to each other with respect to a shift of even numbers.

Scaling filter g, which is twin to the wavelet filter, is defined so as to satisfy the quadrature mirror relationship below:

$$g_i = (-1)^i h_{L-i+1} \Leftrightarrow h_i = (-1)^{i-1} g_{L-i+1} \qquad (i = 1, 2, \ldots, L). \qquad \text{(A2)}$$

Given the relationship above, a scaling filter is shown to meet the conditions below:

$$\sum_{k=1}^{L} g_k = \sqrt{2}, \quad \sum_{k=1}^{L} g_k^2 = 1, \quad \sum_{k=1}^{L} g_k g_{k+2n} = 0, \qquad \text{(A3)}$$

where n is a nonzero integer. The first condition implies that the scaling filter is a low-pass filter to extract low-frequency components. The second and third conditions are, respectively, for standardization and orthogonality, which are the same as for the wavelet filter. Then we have

$$\sum_{k=1}^{L} g_k h_{k+2n} = 0, \qquad \text{(A4)}$$

where n is a nonzero integer. Equation (A4) implies that the wavelet filter and scaling filter are orthogonal to each other with respect to a shift of even numbers.

The family of Daubechies wavelets is one of the often-used wavelets. Let $D(L)$ denote the Daubechies wavelet with support L (L is an even number), then $D(L)$ is defined so as to simultaneously satisfy the equation (A1) as well as the set of equations (A5) below:

$$\sum_{k=1}^{L} (k-1)^i h_k = 0, \qquad i = 1, 2, \ldots, \frac{L}{2} - 1. \qquad \text{(A5)}$$

For example, the Daubechies wavelet with the support of 10, or $D(10)$, is obtained from a set of equations (A5) by setting $i = 4$.

Wavelet Transform

The process of breaking up a time series into the time and frequency domains by using a wavelet filter is referred as wavelet transform. This process yields wavelet coefficients and scaling coefficients. Conversely, the process of reproducing the original time series from wavelet and scaling coefficients is referred to as inverse wavelet transform.

For example, let x be a sequence of the time series. Suppose that the length of the time series is N. Let w_i and v_i denote the wavelet coefficient and scaling coefficient at level i. In addition define the scaling coefficient at level 0 as equal to the time series data, and $v_0 = x$. Then apply the wavelet filter h with support

L to the scaling coefficient at level $i - 1$, v_{i-1}, to obtain the wavelet coefficient at level I, w_i, from the equation below:

$$w_{i,t} = \sum_{k=1}^{L} h_k v_{i-1,\{(2t-k) \bmod N/2^{i-1}\}+1}. \tag{A6}$$

Here $A \bmod B$ is the operator that divides A by B and returns only the remainder, thus producing an integer ranging from zero to $B - 1$. Similarly, when we apply the scaling filter g with support L to the scaling coefficient at level $i - 1$, $v_i - 1$, we obtain the scaling coefficient at level i, w_i, from the equation below:

$$v_{i,t} = \sum_{k=1}^{L} g_k v_{i-1,\{(2t-k) \bmod N/2^{i-1}\}+1}. \tag{A7}$$

What should be noted here is that the downsampling operation proceeds by every second data point. A process of filtering reduces computed wavelet and scaling coefficients by halves. However, the sum of the two coefficients is equal to the original time series, and no information is lost through filtering.

Since wavelet transform preserves all information contained by the original time series, the original series can be reproduced from the computed wavelet and scaling coefficients.

The process of reproducing the scaling coefficient at level i, v_i, from the wavelet coefficient at level $i + 1$, w_{i+1}, and the scaling coefficient at level $i + 1$, v_{i+1}, is given below.

First, upsampling is implemented to increase the reduced number of data at level $i + 1$ by downsampling and inserting zeros between the samples. More precisely, the upsampled sequences of wavelet and scaling coefficients at level $i + 1$ are $w_{i+1}^0 = (0, w_{i+1,1}, 0, w_{i+1,2}, \ldots, 0, w_{i+1,N/2^{i+1}})$ and $v_{i+1}^0 = (0, v_{i+1,1}, 0, v_{i+1,2}, \ldots, 0, v_{i+1,N/2^{i+1}})$.

Next the wavelet and scaling filters are applied to the upsampled wavelet and scaling coefficients. By summing up this result, the scaling coefficient at level i is obtained. That is,

$$v_{i,t} = \sum_{k=1}^{L} h_k w_{i+1,\{(t+k-2) \bmod N/2^i\}+1}^0 + \sum_{k=1}^{L} g_k v_{i+1,\{(t+k-2) \bmod N/2^i\}+1}^0. \tag{A8}$$

Multiresolution Analysis

Last we review multiresolution analysis. Wavelet detail and wavelet smooth are the basic concepts in this analysis. Wavelet detail and wavelet smooth at level i respectively capture cyclical components with the frequency of 2^i and trend components after removing the cyclical components up to the frequency of 2^i.

Suppose that the wavelet coefficients and scaling coefficients are obtained from the original time series by implementing wavelet transform. Then wavelet detail at level i, with the same length of time series as the original time series, is obtained by implementing an inverse wavelet transform while replacing all wavelet and scaling coefficients equal to zero except for the wavelet coefficient at level i w_i. Similarly, wavelet smooth at level i s_i is obtained by implementing inverse wavelet transform v_i.

When we define $s_0 = x$, the following equation holds:

$$s_{i-1} = d_i + s_i. \tag{A9}$$

When we define wavelet rough as $r_i = \sum_{k=1}^{i} d_k$, the following equation holds:

$$x = r_i + s_i. \tag{A10}$$

Notes

We appreciate helpful comments on our previous study from Bill Gavin, Michael Hutchison, Ken Kuttner, Makoto Saito, Pierre Siklos, and Tsutomu Watanabe; from the participants of the workshop at Claremont McKenna College, the seminar at the Board of Governors of Federal Reserve System, the Federal Reserve Bank of New York, and the International Monetary Fund, and CESifo Venice Summer Institute; from the panelists at the 2003 spring meeting of the Japan Society of Monetary Economics; from the staff of the Monetary Affairs Department, Financial Markets Department, Research and Statistics Department, and Institute for Monetary and Economic Studies of the Bank of Japan. We also thank Hiroyuki Oi and Masakazu Inada for their superb research assistance. The views expressed in the chapter are those of the authors and do not necessarily reflect those of the Bank of Japan or the Institute for Monetary and Economic Studies.

1. See, for example, Ramsey (2002) for the reviews of the recent developments in the application of wavelet analysis to economics and finance.

2. See Reifschneider and Williams (2000), Jung, Teranishi, and Watanabe (2005), and Eggertsson and Woodford (2003) for detailed discussions on the policy commitment effect when a central bank faces a zero boundary of nominal interest rates.

3. Assessment of the policy duration effect from observed interest rates can be based on two methods: a direct introduction of policy duration effect into a structural model for interest rate dynamics, or analysis of the time series movement of the shape of the yield curve. We take the latter approach, while Marumo et al. (2003) take the former.

4. We follow Okina and Shiratsuka (2003) to analyze the movements of nominal interest rates. Admittedly, one problem in interpreting the results by this methodology is that it is not possible to decompose movements of nominal yield curve into real interest rates and expected inflation components. However, given that market data on inflation index bonds are not available for the sample period we consider in this chapter, it is necessary to make ad hoc assumptions to make such decomposition in a daily frequency. The current Japan's problem of deflation is a combination of mild price decline and low trend growth, suggesting the importance of analyzing the nominal interest rates. Therefore we did not try to decompose the movements into real interest rates and expected inflation components.

5. See Goodfriend (1998) for an excellent discussion on the use of the term structure of interest rates in monetary policy analysis.

6. Given the possibility of time-varying risk premiums, we need to be cautious in interpreting time series movements of estimates.

7. The extended Nelson-Siegel model, shown in equation (1), adds a third term to allow up to two hump- or U-shapes in the IFR curve, while the original one has only one hump- or U-shape.

8. In our estimation we exploit the first feature to keep the very short end of the IFR curve from becoming negative, by imposing the restriction that the overnight uncollateralized call rate be equal to $\beta_0 + \beta_1$. This restriction is sufficient to prevent the zero-bound of nominal interest rates from influencing the estimates. We also use the second feature to compile an indicator for policy duration effect, since it corresponds to the restriction that forward rates for settlements very far into the future be constant.

9. An alternative definition of PD is possible, depending on how we define the end of the flattened zone before the second-stage increase. For example, it could also be defined as the point where the second derivative of $r(m)$, or acceleration of the speed of increase in $r(m)$, is locally maximized. Although the estimates based on our definition are somewhat greater than those based on the alternative definition, these two estimates show very similar movements over time, with a very high coefficient of correlation of 0.96. Our definition has the advantage of allowing one to easily compute standard errors for PD as well as $R(PD)$ based on the closed form solution for PD.

10. As shown by Fujiki and Shiratsuka (2002), $r(m)$ is also affected by the liquidity concerns of financial institutions, especially in times of large liquidity events such as the Y2K problem and the introduction of the real time gross settlement system.

11. In examining the time series movements of the long-term forward rate, we need to be careful to account for the possible effects of demand–supply conditions in financial markets with long-term maturity.

12. As pointed out in Shigemi et al. (2000) and Fukuta, Saito, and Takagi (2002), the pricing of JGBs referred in the text depends on their convenience, reflecting a difference in the characteristics of each issue, such as outstanding volume and coupon rate, as well as market liquidity. In particular, the pricing of JGBs in 1998 to 2000 was highly distorted by various problems in market liquidity, including the Y2K problem. It would thus be difficult to extract a unique yield curve as a benchmark from the market rates of JGBs, given the possible effects of the credit premium and other perturbing factors, such as macro-hedge accounting, on euro-yen TIBORs and swap rates.

13. Our sample period corresponds approximately to Governor Hayami's term of office (from March 20, 1998, to March 19, 2003). However, it should be noted that our sample period starts shortly before the launch of the ZIRP. Thus it is difficult to compare the yield curve behavior under the ZIRP and the QME with those under a normal policy regime in which nominal short-term interest rates are well above zero.

14. Our estimations use the CML procedure in GAUSS 3.5.

15. We apply the delta method to compute standard errors for $R(PD)$ and SL.

16. In Okina and Shiratsuka (2003) we also carry out case study analyses to detect the impact of changes in monetary policy in the short run, which are of interest but not shown here because of space constraints. These case study analyses show that positive and statistically significant impacts are observed in LFR soon after the two policy actions: one is Governor Hayami's announcement of committing to the ZIRP on April 13, 1999, and the other is the introduction of the QME on March 19, 2001.

17. We choose the Daubechies (10) wavelet, $D(10)$, by comparing wavelet filters with a certain length of support in order to extract trend fluctuations of policy duration indicators. See appendix B for a brief summary of wavelet analysis.

18. $r(0)$, which is equal to $\beta_0 + \beta_1$, is supposed to be zero under the zero interest rate policy as well as quantitative monetary easing, as shown in the upper panel, while $r(0)$ in the lower panel, which is also equal to $\beta_0 + \beta_1$, is significantly higher than zero. Since β_0 is equal to the limits of forward and spot rates when maturity approaches infinity, this parameter is common to both panels. Therefore the absolute value of β_1 must take a different value from that of β_0 when the overnight rate temporarily jumps.

References

Eggertsson, G. B., and M. Woodford. 2003. The zero interest-rate bound and optimal monetary policy. Mimeo.

Fujiki, H., K. Okina, and S. Shiratsuka. 2001. Monetary policy under zero interest rate—Viewpoints of central bank economists. *Monetary and Economic Studies* 19 (1): 89–130.

Fujiki, H., K. Okina, and S. Shiratsuka. 2002. Policy duration effect under the zero interest rate policy in 1999–2000: Evidence from Japan's money market data. *Monetary and Economic Studies* 20 (1): 1–31.

Fukuta, Y., M. Saito, and S. Takagi. 2002. Kokusai no Kakaku Keisei to Konbiniansu: 1990-nendai Kouhan no Nihon Kokusai no Keesu (Pricing of government bonds and their convenience: A case from the Japanese government bonds in the late 1990s). In M. Saito and N. Yanagawa, eds., *Ryudo-sei no Keizai-gaku* (Economics of Liquidity), pp. 209–24 (in Japanese).

Goodfriend, M. 1998. Using the term structure of interest rates for monetary policy. Federal Reserve Bank of Richmond, *Economic Quarterly* 84 (3): 13–30.

Jung, T., Y. Teranishi, and T. Watanabe. 2001. Zero interest rate policy as optimal central bank commitment. Mimeo.

Kimura, T., H. Kobayashi, J. Muranaga, and H. Ugai. 2002 The effect of the increase in monetary base on Japan's economy at zero interest rates: An empirical analysis. IMES Discussion Paper 2002-E-22. Institute for Monetary and Economic Studies, Bank of Japan.

Marumo, K., T. Nakayama, S. Nishioka, and T. Yoshida. 2003. Zero Kinri Seisaku-ka ni okeru Kinri no Kikan Kozo Moderu (A term structure model of interest rates under zero interest rate policy). Financial Markets Department Working Paper 2003-J-1. Financial Markets Department, Bank of Japan (in Japanese).

Nelson, C. R., and A. F. Siegel. 1987. Parsimonious modeling of yield curves. *Journal of Business* 60 (4): 473–89.

Okina, K., and S. Shiratsuka. 2003. Policy commitment and expectation formations: Japan's experience under zero interest rates. IMES Discussion Paper 2003-E-5. Institute for Monetary and Economic Studies, Bank of Japan.

Ramsey, J. B. 2002. Wavelets in economics and finance: Past and future. *Studies in Nonlinear Dynamics and Econometrics* 6(3), article 1 ⟨http://www.bcpress.com/snde/vol6/iss3/art1⟩.

Reifschneider, D., and J. C. Williams. 2000. Three lessons for monetary policy in a low-inflation era. *Journal of Money, Credit and Banking* 32 (4): 936–66.

Shigemi, Y., S. Kato, Y. Soejima, and T. Shimizu. 2002. Honpo Kokusai Shijo niokeru Shijo Sankasha Koudou to Kakaku Kettei Mekanizumu: 1998 nen-matsu kara 1999 nen-chu no Shijo no Ugoki wo Rikai Suru tameni (Market participants' behavior and pricing mechanism of Japanese government bond markets: An interpretation of the market behavior from the end-1998 to 1999). *Kin'yu Kenkyu* 19 (S-2): 145–84 (in Japanese).

Söderlind, P., and L. E. O. Svensson. 1997. New techniques to extract market expectations from financial instruments. *Journal of Monetary Economics* (40): 383–429.

8   Exchange Rate Pass-through in Deflationary Japan: How Effective Is the Yen's Depreciation for Fighting Deflation?

Eiji Fujii

8.1   Introduction

Deflation seems to be inexorable in the ailing Japanese economy. After years of stagnation the world's second largest economy appears to be trapped in a vicious cycle of output contraction and price decline. As the economy continues to languish, it is more urgent than ever before to create an upward pressure on prices to put an end to the on-going deflation. Economists, policy makers, and politicians have been debating on how to do it. Many agree on the devastating effect of the enduring deflation and the urgency of effective policy action to address the problem. Nevertheless, they disagree strongly with each other on what to be done in concrete terms. As the economic slump prolongs, a number of people have come forward to advocate for non-conventional measures such as adoption of inflation targeting by the Bank of Japan (BOJ). The call for aggressive measures, however, has been tenaciously disputed by those who opt for more conventional measures.

In the current debate over how to fight the deflation, there is an increasing endorsement for the yen's depreciation as a means to generate a significant inflationary pressure in the economy. News media report economists and policy makers in Japan endorsing *yenyasu-yudo*, meaning active inducement of the yen's depreciation, for the purpose of creating an upward price pressure via import inflation.[1] Calls for depreciating the currency come also from international economists, among policy recommendations on how to pull the economy out of a liquidity trap.[2] Given the persistence of the downward movements in the domestic prices, it is not surprising that an increasing amount of attention is directed to potential roles of a currency depreciation and import inflation as an instrument for alleviating the situation.

While the idea of spurring inflation via depreciation may sound straightforward, it implicitly assumes a condition that remains controversial in international economics.[3] Specifically, it is presupposed that foreign producers will stabilize the prices of their exports to Japan in their own currency terms, and hence pass the effects of the yen's depreciation substantially, if not fully, to the Japanese importers and consumers.[4]

In this chapter we examine the empirical validity of this assumption specifically in the recent Japanese environment where domestic prices exhibit a clear downward trend. We do so by estimating the exchange rate pass-through (ERPT) to the Japanese import prices and quantifying its effects on overall domestic inflation. The objective is to assess quantitatively the expected effectiveness of the proposed measure to tame the deflation by actively weakening the yen.[5]

Our investigation of ERPT specifically for the recent deflationary Japan is motivated primarily by a hypothesis put forward by Taylor (2000). In analyzing the relationship between firms' pricing behavior and inflation environment, Taylor (2000) contends that pass-through has declined substantially in many countries as a consequence of successful transitions to low-inflation regimes. If valid, Taylor's conjecture has an important implication for the current policy debate in Japan. Specifically, it implies that the yen's depreciation can be substantially less inflationary now than it was in the past. If so, the proposed measure of combating deflation via depreciation can be significantly less effective than what its advocates may have in mind. It is therefore important to carefully quantify the responsiveness of the Japanese import and overall prices to exchange rate fluctuations in the recent deflationary environment.

The remainder of this manuscript is organized in the following manner. Section 8.2 discusses Taylor's conjecture on ERPT and domestic inflation and how it relates to the current Japanese environment. Section 8.3 describes the data. An empirical model of ERPT is presented in section 8.4. In section 8.5 we estimate the ERPT to the Japanese imports using disaggregated price indexes. Then we examine whether or not the degrees of the pass-through in the recent deflationary period differ from those in prior periods. An empirical investigation is extended in section 8.6, where we adopt alternative data with a finer level of disaggregation by industry to obtain pass-through estimates for the most recent period. These pass-through estimates are used to quantify the expected inflationary effects of the yen's depreciation. The empirical results are further analyzed in section 8.7, where we explore the cross-product category differences in the rate of change in the pass-through over time, and also compare the Japanese experience to those of other industrialized nations. Finally, in section 8.8 we make some concluding observations.

8.2   Exchange Rate Pass-through and Domestic Inflation Environment

If the yen were depreciated against the currencies of major exporters to Japan, prices of the Japanese imports would rise in general, which in turn could spur overall inflation. However, the import price does not necessarily have to rise at the same rate as the yen depreciates. The degree of the yen price responsiveness can be anywhere from zero to 100 percent, depending on how much of the exchange rate change the exporting firms decide to absorb or shift to the Japanese importers and consumers.

To illustrate the point more precisely, consider an imperfectly competitive foreign firm exporting its product to the Japanese market while facing competition from the Japanese domestic producers. As a price setter the firm solves the following profit maximization problem:

$$\max_p \ \pi = s^{-1} p q(p, p^d, y) - C(q(.), w^*), \tag{1}$$

where s is the exchange rate measured by units of yen per unit of the exporter's currency, p is the import price of the product in yen, and $q(.)$ is the demand for the product, which depends not only on own price but also on the price of the domestic competing product p^d and the income level y. The production cost $C(.)$ is determined by the level of the demand for the product and the input price w^* measured in the exporter's currency units.

Solving (1) yields the following first-order condition:

$$p = s C_q \mu, \tag{2}$$

where $\mu \equiv \eta/(\eta - 1)$ and η is the demand elasticity of the product that depends on its relative price to the competing domestic product. With all terms converted into logarithms, the effect of exchange rate change on the import price (in yen) is

$$\frac{\partial p}{\partial s} = 1 + \frac{\partial C_q}{\partial s} + \frac{\partial \mu}{\partial s}. \tag{3}$$

Because the marginal cost C_q and the markup ratio μ depend on other factors besides the exchange rate, it is important to control for w^*, y, and p^d when estimating ERPT, $\partial p / \partial s$.

Equation (3) suggests that full pass-through is a special case where neither the marginal cost nor the markup is altered in the face of exchange rate fluctuations.[6] In general, the degree of ERPT depends on the behavior of the marginal cost and markup, which are likely to be specific to the exporting firm and/or industry. Consequently the literature has treated ERPT primarily as a microeconomic phenomenon.[7] Recently, however, Taylor (2000) has brought an explicit macroeconomic perspective to the issue using a staggered price-setting model. Specifically, the model posits that firms set prices of their products at different points in time and keep them unaltered for four periods. Thus, in deciding on their own prices, firms maximize their expected profits for the next four periods based on their expectations about future movements of other firms' prices, own production costs, and the market demand. In discussing how projected changes to these variables affect firms' decisions, Taylor points out that the price response will be greater if the changes are perceived to be more permanent. In relating the perceived persistence of changes to the competing product prices to the persistence of general inflation, he argues that the effective control over inflation established in recent years has resulted in a decline in the pricing power of firms in many countries.[8]

Taylor's conjecture has a significant ramification on the current policy debate over deflation in Japan. To describe the Japanese situation, Figure 8.1 depicts Japan's domestic and overall monthly wholesale price indexes in logarithms since 1973:3.[9] The price indexes exhibit a very steep upward trend through the 1970s. However, they more or less flatten out in the first half of the 1980s. In the second half of the 1980s, several factors, both external and domestic, induced a substantial fall of the wholesale price index. These factors included a decline of oil and primary product prices, appreciation of the yen, easing demand conditions, and stabilization of inflation expectations and wages. Entering the 1990s, the price indexes show a gradual but consistent decline, except for a few occasional and short-lived upward shifts. To portray the domestic inflation environment further, we provide some descriptive statistics for alternative sample periods in the upper panel of table 8.1. As seen in the first column, the average wholesale inflation in Japan, that reached 0.7 percent per month in the 1970s, turned nega-

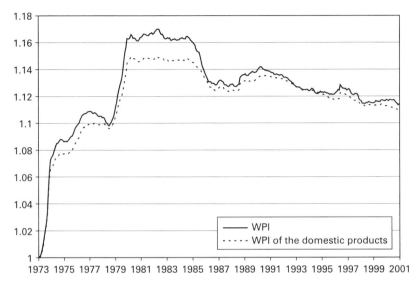

Figure 8.1
Wholesale price indexes. The overall wholesale price index (WPI) and the WPI for the domestic products in logarithms (normalized to be unity in 1973:3) are plotted.

tive in the second half of the 1980s and has remained so since then.[10] In a corresponding fashion, the inflation variability decreased substantially as the sample variances denote. Even more noteworthy is an unequivocal reduction of the inflation persistence reported in the last column. The reported persistence figures denote the estimated half-life in months of the wholesale inflation process using the first-order autoregressive coefficient.[11] The magnitude of the decline is astonishing. The inflation persistence has been reduced from 3.8 months in the 1970s to just 0.3 month by the second half of the 1990s. Overall, it is unambiguous that the Japanese inflation environment has experienced a substantial transformation, in particular, a remarkable reduction of its persistence.

The lower panel of table 8.1 summarizes similarly the descriptive statistics for monthly changes in the logged nominal effective exchange rate of the yen.[12] The consistently negative value of the average exchange rate change reflects the secular appreciation of the yen through the first half of the 1990s, which is shown in figure 8.2. A cross-panel comparison of the reported sample variances and coefficient of variations corroborate that the exchange rate change is much more volatile

Table 8.1
Descriptive statistics

Sample period	Mean	Variance	Coefficient of variation	Persistence
A. Wholesale inflation				
1973:4–2001:12	0.135	0.639	5.904	2.690
1973:4–1979:12	0.702	1.468	1.725	3.796
1980:1–1984:12	0.163	0.539	4.483	1.083
1985:1–1989:12	−0.185	0.309	2.993	1.381
1990:1–1994:12	−0.072	0.062	3.432	0.804
1995:1–2001:12	−0.053	0.129	6.762	0.321
1997:7–2001:12	−0.092	0.100	3.450	0.501
B. Exchange rate changes				
1973:4–2001:12	−0.325	6.073	7.562	0.631
1973:4–1979:12	−0.114	4.584	18.732	0.731
1980:1–1984:12	−0.374	5.764	6.419	0.499
1985:1–1989:12	−0.711	6.667	3.629	0.633
1990:1–1994:12	−0.644	4.862	3.419	0.431
1995:1–2001:12	0.007	8.123	369.635	0.692
1997:7–2001:12	−0.188	7.325	14.352	0.585

Notes: Panels A and B contain the descriptive statistics for the first difference series of the logged wholesale price index and the logged nominal effective exchange rate (both multiplied by 100), respectively. The exchange rate is measured in units of yen per foreign currency so that negative entries indicate appreciation of the yen. The persistence is measured by half-life estimates in months using the first-order autoregressive models.

than the inflation. However, it is important to note that unlike the inflation case, there is no indication for the volatility or the persistence of the yen's effective exchange rate to be shrinking over time.

The overview of the inflation and exchange rate data suggests that Japan's deflation is a good case to testify empirically whether or not the pass-through has declined as the inflationary environment shifted, as argued by Taylor (2000). For the current policy debate in Japan, empirical evidence on the issue will provide useful information regarding the effectiveness of the yen's depreciation as a means to generate inflationary pressure. If the import pass-through has indeed been declining, the inflation-spurring effect of the yen's depreciation is also likely to be weakening. Under the circumstances the efficacy of the *yenyasu-yudo* will be inhibited.

There are numerous previous studies on the Japanese ERPT and a closely related subject matter of pricing to market. Many of these

Figure 8.2
Nominal effective exchange rate. Yen's nominal effective exchange rate in logarithms measured in units of yen per unit of the foreign currency.

studies, however, investigate the responses of Japanese export prices, rather than import prices, to the exchange rate movements.[13] In contrast, there are relative few studies that focus on the relationship between the Japanese import price and exchange rate fluctuations. Sazanami, Kimura, and Kawai (1997) examine the movements of both import and export prices of numerous tradable goods, during the 1985 to 1995 period of the yen's steady appreciation. For a large number of products, these authors find that the import price did not decline as much as the yen appreciated. A recent paper by Otani, Shiratsuka, and Shirota (2003) examines stability of the Japanese import pass-through using disaggregated import price indexes for eight product categories for 1978 to 2002. These authors report that contrary to the finding of a cross-country analysis by Campa and Goldberg (2002), shifts in import composition over time are not a primary factor for instability of Japan's import pass-through.

Aside from the studies on Japan, Hooper and Mann (1989) is an important predecessor that examines the stability of the US import pass-through. In examining price movements of manufacture goods, they find little evidence against stability of the pass-through coefficients in the 1980s. Since Taylor (2000) put forth his view, the literature has

seen a rejuvenated interest in stability of ERPT. Recent studies address-
ing the issue include Bailliu and Fujii (2004), Campa and Goldberg
(2002), Choudhri and Hakura (2001), Gagnon and Ihrig (2001), and
McCarthy (1999). The empirical evidence reported in these studies is
mixed, and thus the declining pass-through remains a proposition
rather than an indisputable fact.

8.3 Data Description

We examine responses of imported product prices to exchange rate
movements in Japan, especially in the recent deflationary era, using
two different panels of disaggregated wholesale price index data.[14]
The first panel contains the price indexes on imported and domestic
products, which are disaggregated by stage of use and demand. The
product categories consist of raw materials (raw materials for processing, construction materials, fuel), intermediate inputs (semifinished
goods, construction materials, fuel and energy, other intermediate
materials), and final goods (capital goods, consumer durables, consumer nondurables).[15] The panel spans the post–Bretton Woods period
(1973:3–2001:12), and thus it enables us to contrast ERPT estimates
under alternative inflation environments such as the high inflation era
of the 1970s to the early 1980s and the more recent deflationary circumstances.[16] Another merit of the panel is that it allows us to compare
the degrees of ERPT at different stages of goods production by separat-
ing the price indexes of raw materials, intermediates, and finished
goods from each other. This form of data disaggregation enables us to
study the hypothesized decline of the firms' pricing power as a universal phenomenon across all stages of goods production.

The second panel contains shorter time series of import and domestic product price indexes but with a finer level of disaggregation by
industry. The price indexes are available for sixteen manufacturing sectors, two agricultural, forestry, and fishery sectors, one mining sector,
and one scrap and waste sector.[17] As the microeconomic factors related
to the industry market structure are known to be important determinants of ERPT, use of the by-sector data should help increase the accuracy of estimations.[18] However, the data start only in 1995, and thus no
direct reference can be made to preceding periods of more inflationary
environments.

All data are in a monthly frequency and are extracted from the Bank
of Japan Financial and Economic Data (the 2002 version). The price

data include the wholesale price indexes for imported products, domestic products, and overall products, respectively. In addition we
use the data on the nominal and real effective exchange rates, and the
industrial production index. We emphasize the necessity of price index
data of imported and domestic products in separation. According to
(2) and (3), exporting firms' decision should depend on the price of
domestic competing products as well as the exchange rate. Without
controlling for the movements of domestic competitors' price, the
ERPT estimates are likely to be biased. By exploiting the fact that
the BOJ report the price indexes of domestic and imported products in
separation, we are able to control for the effect to enhance the accuracy
of ERPT estimation.

8.4   Empirical Model Specification

Based on the pricing model of exporting firms described by (2) in section 8.2, we construct an empirical specification of the logged import
price. Specifically, we model the import price as a function of the exchange rate and a set of additional variables that affect the demand
elasticity and the marginal cost of the imported product. By also incorporating price inertia and allowing for lags in the exchange rate effects,
we obtain

$$p_t = c + \phi(L)p_{t-1} + \lambda(L)s_t + \delta p_t^d + \tau w_t^* + \varphi y_t + \varepsilon_t, \tag{4}$$

where c is a constant, p_t is the import price index of a given product,
s_t is the nominal effective exchange rate in units of yen per unit of
the foreign currency, p_t^d is the price index of the competing domestic
product, w_t^* and y_t are control variables for the exporter's cost shifter
and the importer's demand conditions, respectively, and ε_t is a distur-
bance term. All variables are in logarithms, and $\phi(L)$ and $\lambda(L)$ are lag
polynomials. The lagged import prices are included as regressors to
account for price inertia and to capture, at least in part, expectations
for future price movements. The lagged exchange rate terms are also
allowed since responses of import prices to exchange rate changes
may not be fully manifested instantaneously.

   As indicated by (2) and (3), in estimating ERPT it is necessary to iso-
late the exchange rate effect from a few other effects: the exporter's cost
shifter, importer's demand conditions, and the price of the domestic
competitor. Controlling for additional effects is considered critical, especially for Japan in recent years, where the domestic prices have been

declining and the demand condition has been rather weak. Since both of the data panels report the price indexes of imports and domestic products separately, p_t^d is directly observed. Movements of the exporters' cost are harder to measure, and we resort to constructing a proxy variable. Specifically, we adopt the wholesale price movements of Japan's major trade partners derived implicitly from the nominal and real effective exchange rate series:

$$w_t^* = q_t - s_t + \tilde{p}_t, \tag{5}$$

where q_t is the real effective exchange rate, and $\tilde{p}_t$ is Japan's overall wholesale price index. Finally, to capture the domestic demand conditions, we employ the Japanese industrial production index as y_t.

To avoid well-known problems in statistical inferences associated with nonstationary variables, we specify the equation in terms of first differences of the logged variables:[19]

$$\Delta p_t = c + \sum_{i=1}^{j} \phi_i \Delta p_{t-i} + \sum_{i=0}^{k} \lambda_i \Delta s_{t-i} + \delta \Delta p_t^d + \tau \Delta w_t + \varphi \Delta y_t + \varepsilon_t \tag{6}$$

for which the lag orders j and k are determined by Akaike information criteria.[20] In estimating (6), we need to treat Δp_t^d as an endogenous regressor, since the domestic firms compete against the exporting firm taking Δp_t into account. Therefore we adopt the instrumental variable technique using lagged domestic product prices as instruments.[21]

The coefficient $\hat{\lambda}_0$ gauges the instantaneous effect of exchange rate changes on import inflation.[22] Prices of goods can be rigid, however, and the effects of exchange rate fluctuations are not necessarily translated into the local prices in an immediate fashion. This is a valid concern particularly for the current study since our data are observed in a monthly frequency. Given the price dynamics of (6), the total effects of exchange rate movements on the import inflation can be gauged by $\sum_{i=0}^{k} \hat{\lambda}_i / (1 - \sum_{i=1}^{j} \hat{\phi}_i)$. For the remainder of this study, we refer to $\hat{\lambda}_0$ and $\sum_{i=0}^{k} \hat{\lambda}_i / (1 - \sum_{i=1}^{j} \hat{\phi}_i)$ as short-run ERPT and long-run ERPT, respectively.

Unfortunately, the perceived persistence Taylor (2000) refers to is not directly observable, and thus, it is not easily incorporated into the model specification in an explicit fashion. In what follows we take an indirect approach of estimating the short-run and long-run ERPT for different sample periods, and then contrasting the obtained pass-through coefficients across periods under alternative inflation environments. If Taylor's supposition is right, the pass-through estimates should exhibit a decline in magnitude as we move from a highly persistent inflationary era to a less persistent deflationary period.

8.5   Empirical Results: By-Stage-of-Use-and-Demand Estimates

Tables 8.2 and 8.3 report the estimated short-run and long-run pass-through coefficients using the first panel of price index data that categorizes products by stage of use and demand. For each product category in both tables, the entries in the first column denote the full sample estimates of ERPT. The next five columns contain the subsample estimates for 1973:3 to 1979:12, 1980:1 to 1984:12, 1985:1 to 1989:12, 1990:1 to 1994:12, and 1995:1 to 2001:12.

To infer the current degree of ERPT in Japan, it is pertinent to refer to the 1995:1 to 2001:12 estimates. However, the 1997 Asian crisis exerted a significant effect on the import prices from neighboring economies, which could have altered the Japanese inflation environment considerably. To take into account this possibility, we provide additional estimates in the last column using only the 1997:7 to 2001:12 data.

Starting with the short-run ERPT in table 8.2, the full sample estimates show that exchange rate changes exert significant and immediate effects on the imported product price movements at all stages. The pass-through coefficients are, however, significantly less than unity suggesting that only part of the exchange rate changes are passed instantaneously to the import prices. In comparing the estimates in panels A, B, and C of the table, we find no clear pattern of difference in the short-run ERPT among raw materials, intermediate materials, and final goods.

In contrasting the estimates across subperiods, we observe that the short-run pass-through is reasonably stable for some product categories while rather unstable for others. For instance, the estimates for consumer nondurable goods are largely stable across periods. On the other hand, the coefficients for construction materials (under both raw materials and intermediate materials) and fuel and energy appear to be decreasing over time. There is yet another group including fuel and capital goods of which short-run ERPT has been increasing over time. It is noted, however, that these mixed results should not be interpreted as evidence for or against declining pass-through since the short-run coefficients represent only part of the overall effects that are more pertinent to Taylor's insight.

Table 8.2
Short-run pass-through estimates

	Full sample[a]	1973:3– 1979:12	1980:1– 1984:12	1985:1– 1989:12	1990:1– 1994:12	1995:1– 2001:12	1997:7– 2001:12
A. Raw materials							
Raw material for processing	0.630** (0.048)	0.586** (0.084)	0.535** (0.083)	0.582** (0.163)	0.473** (0.118)	0.602* (0.257)	0.425 (0.260)
Construction materials	0.270** (0.069)	na	0.990**,b (0.154)	0.363** (0.114)	−0.229 (0.288)	0.236** (0.073)	0.261** (0.091)
Fuel	0.676** (0.066)	na	0.626** (0.086)	0.561** (0.135)	0.580** (0.128)	0.817**,b (0.146)	0.689**,b (0.229)
B. Intermediate materials							
Semifinished goods	0.529** (0.035)	0.476** (0.116)	0.422** (0.113)	0.437** (0.065)	0.753** (0.079)	0.573** (0.042)	0.552** (0.056)
Construction materials	0.633** (0.059)	0.219 (0.190)	0.832*,b (0.189)	0.916**,b (0.176)	0.537** (0.121)	0.549** (0.078)	0.554** (0.081)
Fuel and energy	0.348** (0.089)	0.277 (0.119)	0.306* (0.133)	0.502* (0.203)	0.191 (0.272)	0.292 (0.225)	−0.069 (0.368)
Other intermediate materials	0.492** (0.037)	na	0.081 (0.089)	0.544** (0.080)	0.898**,b (0.071)	0.475** (0.095)	0.355** (0.118)
C. Final goods							
Capital goods	0.409** (0.030)	0.101 (0.082)	0.355** (0.094)	0.524** (0.098)	0.433** (0.056)	0.551** (0.045)	0.618** (0.050)
Consumer durable goods	0.390** (0.034)	0.094 (0.064)	0.183 (0.134)	0.279** (0.082)	0.707** (0.084)	0.488** (0.033)	0.532** (0.051)
Consumer nondurable goods	0.432** (0.027)	0.409** (0.092)	0.418** (0.057)	0.545** (0.068)	0.303** (0.054)	0.498** (0.040)	0.464** (0.063)

Notes: ** and * indicate statistical significance at the 1 and 5 percent levels, respectively. Due to data limitations, 1980:1–2001:12 applies to the three categories.
a. The full sample period is 1973:3 to 2001:12 except for construction materials and fuel in panel A and other intermediate goods in panel B.
b. Statistically significant coefficient, which denotes acceptance of the null hypothesis of a full pass-through (i.e., the estimated pass-through coefficient being equal to one) at the 5 percent level.

Table 8.3
Long-run pass-through estimates

	Full sample[a]	1973:3– 1979:12	1980:1– 1984:12	1985:1– 1989:12	1990:1– 1994:12	1995:1– 2001:12	1997:7– 2001:12
A. Raw materials							
Raw material for processing	0.938**,b (0.111)	1.128**,b (0.154)	0.932**,b (0.143)	1.053**,b (0.354)	0.402 (0.288)	0.001 (0.552)	0.159 (0.415)
Construction materials	0.394** (0.095)	na	1.121**,b (0.175)	0.582** (0.160)	−0.213 (0.390)	0.419** (0.076)	0.408** (0.097)
Fuel	0.904**,b (0.225)	na	1.145**,b (0.203)	0.937*,b (0.371)	−0.050 (0.511)	0.679* (0.326)	0.345 (0.397)
B. Intermediate materials							
Semifinished goods	0.610** (0.053)	0.842**,b (0.186)	0.517** (0.127)	0.401** (0.104)	0.925**,b (0.166)	0.593** (0.048)	0.501** (0.062)
Construction materials	0.388** (0.133)	0.168 (0.752)	0.862**,b (0.270)	−0.097 (0.413)	0.200 (0.503)	0.385* (0.183)	0.383* (0.182)
Fuel and energy	1.296**,b (0.374)	1.521**,b (0.482)	0.875**,b (0.206)	1.624 (1.229)	−0.248 (0.630)	0.960 (0.493)	0.384 (0.921)
Other intermediate materials	0.519** (0.052)	na	0.021 (0.102)	0.565** (0.092)	1.032**,b (0.126)	0.448** (0.109)	0.241 (0.157)
C. Final goods							
Capital goods	0.655** (0.056)	0.693**,b (0.191)	0.761**,b (0.145)	0.772**,b (0.187)	0.621** (0.095)	0.598** (0.059)	0.654** (0.087)
Consumer durable goods	0.464** (0.055)	0.210* (0.095)	0.473** (0.140)	0.384** (0.142)	0.660** (0.154)	0.553** (0.045)	0.552** (0.090)
Consumer nondurable goods	0.650** (0.053)	0.790**,b (0.180)	0.696**,b (0.107)	0.730*,b (0.143)	0.352** (0.074)	0.641** (0.064)	0.607** (0.096)

Notes: ** and * indicate statistical significance at the 1 and 5 percent levels, respectively. Due to data limitations, 1980:1–2001:12 applies to the three categories.
a. The full sample period is 1973:3 to 2001:12 except for construction materials and fuel in panel A and other intermediate goods in panel B.
b. Statistically significant coefficient, which denotes acceptance of the null hypothesis of a full pass-through (i.e., the estimated pass-through coefficient being equal to one) at the 5 percent level.

The coefficient estimates in the last two columns in table 8.2 provide us with an idea on the magnitude of the immediate effect of the yen's depreciation in terms of import inflation. The magnitude of instantaneous inflation ranges from zero (for fuel and energy) to 70 to 80 percent of the depreciation rate (fuel under the raw materials), with many product categories between 45 and 60 percent of the depreciation rate.

To account for the full effect of exchange rate changes on import prices, we now turn to the long-run ERPT estimates in table 8.3. Overall, the full-sample estimates reveal that the effects of exchange rate movements on import prices are magnified as the lagged price adjustments are being completed.[23] For raw materials for processing, fuel, and fuel and energy, the pass-through coefficients are statistically indistinguishable from unity, suggesting that effects of exchange rate changes are completely passed through to the import prices over time. That is, the import price of these products will rise sooner or later at the same rate as the yen's depreciation.

Comparing the coefficient estimates across subperiods, however, we find the long-run ERPT declining in numerous product categories. Full pass-through is a phenomenon mostly of the 1970s and the 1980s. By the second half of the 1990s there is no full pass-through observed for any product category. In seven product categories out of ten, the long-run pass-through coefficients in the 1990s are substantially smaller than those for the 1973:3 to 1979:12 and/or 1980:1 to 1984:12 samples. In particular, for all three raw material categories the long-run pass-through, which was virtually 100 percent in the 1970s and/or the early 1980s, has been reduced substantially to a range of zero to 68 percent. Similarly, the long-run pass-through has declined substantially for construction materials, and fuel and energy of intermediate materials as well as for capital goods and consumer non-durables of final goods.

The most recent estimates in the last two columns suggest that exporting firms of final goods maintain a relatively high degree of long-run pass-through even in the recent deflationary periods as compared to those of raw materials and intermediates. Since the onset of the Asian crisis the final goods exporters to Japan have managed to pass 55 to 65 percent of the exchange rate changes to the importers and consumers. We conjecture that a high degree of product differentiation generally associated with final goods may be part of the reason for the maintained pricing power by exporters.

Overall, the empirical results obtained thus far are largely consistent with Taylor's conjecture. As the Japanese economy left the high inflation periods of the 1970s to the early 1980s and entered the deflation-ary 1990s, the inflation persistence has been reduced and the degree of long-run ERPT has declined in many product categories. In other words, for many products the yen's depreciation in recent years is not as inflationary as it was in the 1970s and the early 1980s. To elaborate on this point further, we calculate the effects of a 1 percent depreciation of the yen on the overall wholesale inflation using the estimated ERPT coefficients and the weights assigned to each product category in the overall wholesale price index.[24]

The results are reported in panel A of table 8.5.[25] The reported fig-ures represent overall wholesale price inflation in percentage terms caused solely by import inflation as a result of a 1 percent depreciation of the yen.[26] From the figures it is unambiguous that the long-run infla-tionary effects of the yen's depreciation have been weakened over time. The scale of its decline is in fact striking. In the first half of the 1980s, a 1 percent depreciation led to 0.092 percent inflation of the overall Japa-nese wholesale price. Depreciation of the same scale, however, gener-ated only 0.065 percent inflation in the second half of the same decade. The effect declines further to 0.047 percent in the first half of the 1990s. In the most recent periods the estimates turn out to be only slightly more than 0.050 percent. Overall, we find that the long-run inflationary effect of the yen's depreciation has been reduced in its magnitude by 40 to 45 percent as compared to what it was in the early 1980s.

The calculated short-run effect is probably somewhat more comfort-ing to the proponents of *yenyasu-yudo* since decline is not obvious. The calculation based on the 1995:1 to 2001:12 data suggest that a 1 percent depreciation would generate an immediate inflation of 0.069 percent. The corresponding figure for 1980:1 to 1984:12 and 1985:1 to 989:12 are 0.063 and 0.074 percent, respectively. When we constrain the sample to the post–Asian crisis period, however, the inflationary effects, both short-run and long-run, appear substantially weaker. In this latest period the short-run effect is estimated to be 0.056 percent, indicating a reduction in its magnitude by 11 and 24 percent from the first and second halves of the 1980s, respectively.

8.6   Alternative Estimates by Industry

The long-run results in the previous section suggest that a 1 percent depreciation should translate eventually to an overall inflation of only about 0.05 percent. While the results are indicative of a decline in the inflationary effects of yen's depreciation, the calculation is based on the price indexes that are disaggregated relatively coarsely by stage of use and demand. In this section we use the second panel of price index data to obtain ERPT estimates for the most recent periods by finer industry categories. The purpose of this exercise is to supplement the results of the previous section by providing alternative pass-through estimates for the most recent period.

Table 8.4 summarizes the estimation results. Since the by-industry price index data are available only from 1995:1, the full sample is defined by 1995:1 to 2001:12. In addition to the full-sample estimates, we provide estimates using only the 1997:7 to 2001:12 data. The first two columns contain full-sample estimates. The short-run coefficients in the first column show that the import prices of all sectors respond to exchange rate changes significantly and immediately. For nonferrous metals, other manufacturing industry products, inedible agricultural and forestry products, and forestry products (under mining products), the short-run pass-through is complete. This result seems reasonable since some of these sectors are heavily import-reliant, and thus the exporters tend to face a fairly inelastic demand in Japan. In contrast, the iron and steel sector has the lowest short-run pass-through rate of 0.172. The sector is associated mainly with a low level of product differentiation and dominant presence of Japanese domestic firms, which can constrain exporting firms' pricing power.

The long-run ERPT estimates are reported in the second column. Generally, more of the exchange rate changes are passed-through to import prices as the price adjustment processes are completed. For instance, the rate of pass-through reaches unity for the processed foodstuffs, precision instruments, and edible agricultural, livestock, and fishery products. At the other extreme, the long-run pass-through is indistinguishable from zero for pulp, paper, and related products, iron and steel, and nonferrous metals. It is noted that depending on how exporters would adjust their product prices, the long-run ERPT could be larger or smaller than the short-run counterpart. If price rigidity exists primarily in the producers' currency terms, exporters may initially pass a substantial portion of the yen's depreciation effect to the importers. Then they may lower the yen prices of their products over time so as not to lose their market shares to the Japanese competitors. Under such circumstances the degree of ERPT declines to make the long-run coefficient smaller than the short run. If exporting firms initially find it in their interest not to immediately adjust yen prices fully

Table 8.4
Pass-through estimates by industry

	1995:1–2001:12		1997:7–2001:12	
	Short run	Long run	Short run	Long run
A. Manufacturing				
Processed foodstuffs	0.607**	0.846**,a	0.671**	0.927**,a
	(0.056)	(0.150)	(0.067)	(0.177)
Textile products	0.487**	0.551**	0.463**	0.533**
	(0.052)	(0.056)	(0.076)	(0.078)
Lumber and wood products	0.738**	0.595**	0.791**	0.602**
	(0.072)	(0.097)	(0.078)	(0.103)
Pulp, paper, related products	0.442**	−0.432	0.541**	0.066
	(0.131)	(0.308)	(0.121)	(0.237)
Chemicals	0.365**	0.465**	0.402**	0.447**
	(0.057)	(0.069)	(0.060)	(0.099)
Plastic products	0.796**	0.742**	0.860**,a	0.685**,a
	(0.098)	(0.100)	(0.124)	(0.153)
Petroleum and coal products	0.544**	0.291	0.242	0.004
	(0.202)	(0.269)	(0.233)	(0.334)
Ceramic, stone, clay products	0.597**	0.713**	0.518**	0.704**
	(0.048)	(0.072)	(0.069)	(0.082)
Iron and steel	0.172**	0.117	0.296**	0.293*
	(0.064)	(0.105)	(0.077)	(0.137)
Nonferrous metals	0.717**,a	0.268	0.942**,a	0.287
	(0.145)	(0.203)	(0.229)	(0.311)
Metal products	0.478**	0.493**	0.372**	0.454**
	(0.063)	(0.101)	(0.113)	(0.118)
General machinery	0.752**	0.789**	0.783**	0.823**,a
	(0.056)	(0.078)	(0.049)	(0.082)
Electrical machinery	0.598**	0.629**	0.687**	0.741**
	(0.041)	(0.050)	(0.056)	(0.091)
Transportation equipment	0.473**	0.525**	0.463**	0.487**
	(0.040)	(0.052)	(0.047)	(0.057)
Precision instruments	0.683**	0.853**,a	0.690**	0.811**,a
	(0.051)	(0.088)	(0.072)	(0.116)
Other manufacturing industry products	0.803**,a	1.178*,a	0.714**	0.817**,a
	(0.125)	(0.542)	(0.065)	(0.109)
B. Agricultural, forestry, fishery products				
Edible agricultural, livestock, fishery products	0.614**	0.894**,a	0.657**	0.925**,a
	(0.081)	(0.131)	(0.100)	(0.158)
Inedible agricultural and forestry products	0.920**,a	0.876**,a	0.936**,a	0.805**,a
	(0.074)	(0.138)	(0.098)	(0.139)

Table 8.4

(continued)

	1995:1–2001:12		1997:7–2001:12	
	Short run	Long run	Short run	Long run
C. Mining products				
Forestry products	0.925**,a	0.998**,a	0.868**,a	0.906*,a
	(0.144)	(0.356)	(0.266)	(0.489)
D. Scrap and waste				
Scrap and waste	0.568**	0.270	0.610**	0.567**
	(0.100)	(0.151)	(0.101)	(0.155)

Notes: ** and * indicate statistical significance at the 1 and 5 percent levels, respectively.
a. Statistically significant coefficient, which denotes acceptance of the null hypothesis of a full pass-through (i.e., the estimated pass-through coefficient being equal to one) at the 5 percent level.

Table 8.5

Estimated effects of 1 percent depreciation on the overall wholesale price inflation

	Short run	Long run
A. By-stage-of-use calculation		
Full sample	0.0668	0.0785
1980:1–1984:12	0.0628	0.0918
1985:1–1989:12	0.0738	0.0646
1990:1–1994:12	0.0672	0.0474
1995:1–2001:12	0.0691	0.0559
1997:7–2001:12	0.0560	0.0503
B. By-industry calculation		
1995:1–2001:12	0.0653	0.0664
1997:7–2001:12	0.0660	0.0493

Notes: The entries denote estimated overall wholesale price inflation in percentage terms resulting from 1 percent depreciation of the yen. The exchange rate pass-through coefficient estimates are used for the calculation while assuming no change in domestic product prices.

in response to exchange rate changes, they may decide instead to alter the yen prices to shift more of the depreciation effect to consumers in phases. In this case prices tend to be rigid in consumers' currency terms.

Constraining the data to the post–Asian crisis sample rarely affects the significance of the pass-through estimates. On the other hand, the sizes of the coefficients are affected to various degrees as seen in the last two columns of table 8.4. To assess the extent of an overall inflationary effect, we proceed to calculate the weighted sum of the pass-through coefficients using the by-industry weights listed in panel B of table 8.6. The results are displayed in panel B of table 8.5. For 1995:1 to 2001:12 the inflationary effects are estimated to be around 0.065 percent both in the short-run and the long-run. When constrained to the 1997:7 to 2001:12 sample, however, the long-run effects decline substantially to 0.049 percent while the short-run effects remains at the same magnitude.

Unfortunately, due to the data constraints we are not able to obtain corresponding figures for earlier sample periods. Thus no direct implications are drawn on the magnitude of decline in the pass-through coefficients. Nevertheless, the by-industry results also suggest that depreciation is only partially transmitted into an inflation pressure. In particular, for the post–Asian crisis we note that both the by-industry estimates in this section and the by-stage-of-use-and-demand estimates in the previous section suggest that a 1 percent depreciation eventually translates to only a 0.05 percent overall inflation. In other words, to generate a 1 percent inflation, the yen needs to depreciate by 20 percent.

8.7 Extended Discussion

The empirical results reported in the previous two sections motivate some additional questions and discussion. First, the fact that the pattern of changes in the ERPT varies significantly across product categories (as seen in tables 8.2 and 8.3) implies roles of product/sector-specific factors in determining the extent to which the underlying force to reduce the ERPT can work through. As mentioned in section 8.2, it is widely acknowledged that the rate of ERPT depends on industry-specific factors. In the current case, however, our interest is in identifying the factors that determine the extent of *decline* in ERPT. Particularly, we are interested in roles of the domestic deflationary environment in generating a decline in ERPT. In this regard we

Table 8.6
Product categories and assigned weights in the overall wholesale price index

	Domestic products	Imports
A. By-stage-of-use and demand		
Raw materials	20.40	21.75
Raw material for processing	12.30	18.28
Construction materials	4.22	0.11
Fuel	0.33	3.36
Other raw materials	3.55	0
Intermediate materials	405.74	30.28
Semifinished goods	242.32	25.42
Construction materials	68.81	25.42
Fuel and energy	42.77	1.06
Other intermediate materials	51.84	0.51
Finished goods	366.72	35.77
Capital goods	129.35	10.42
Consumer durable goods	69.54	7.62
Consumer nondurable goods	167.83	17.72
Total	792.86	87.79
B. By industry		
Manufacturing	725.42	63.68
Processed foodstuffs	87.97	4.22
Textile products	22.05	7.30
Lumber and wood products	12.96	3.06
Pulp, paper, related products	25.30	1.48
Chemicals	61.77	6.61
Plastic products	29.21	0.26
Petroleum and coal products	22.51	2.78
Ceramic, stone, clay products	27.92	0.91
Iron and steel	34.33	1.64
Nonferrous metals	16.71	4.83
Metal products	36.32	0.86
General machinery	82.45	3.81
Electrical machinery	122.30	14.80
Transportation equipment	65.07	4.32
Precision instruments	9.05	1.88
Other manufacturing industry products	69.50	4.92
Agricultural, forestry, fishery products	23.61	8.16
Edible agricultural, livestock, fishery products	21.70	4.67
Inedible agricultural and forestry products	1.91	3.49
Mining product	6.97	15.53

Table 8.6
(continued)

	Domestic products	Imports
Forestry products	6.97	15.53
Electric power, gas, water	34.62	0
Scrap and waste	2.24	0.42
Scrap and waste	2.24	0.42
Total	792.86	87.79

Source: Bank of Japan, *Financial and Economic Data 2002.*

conjecture that the differences in the price movement of the competing domestic products have played a significant role in generating the various degrees of changes in ERPT. For instance, a significant domestic product deflation can be an indication of increased competition under weak demand conditions. Under the circumstances the foreign exporters in the same product category may decide to absorb more of the effects of yen's depreciation than otherwise, reducing the rate of ERPT.

To evaluate the conjecture, we conduct a cross-product category analysis of the ERPT estimates. Specifically, we explore possible relationships between the price behavior of the competing domestic products and the rate of decline in the pass-through. For each product category, we obtain the sample mean and variance of the domestic product inflation. We also calculate the rate of decline in the ERPT based on the estimates for the 1980s and the late 1990s.[27] We then examine if the differences in the rate of decline in ERPT can be explained by the domestic inflation measures.

The exercise, however, fails to identify any significant effect of either of the domestic inflation variables on the rate of ERPT reduction.[28] Given the small size of the sample (i.e. the number of product categories), perhaps the result is not surprising. We nevertheless consider extending such cross-product category/sector analysis to be potentially informative, and wish to conduct a more extensive examination in the future as the paucity of data is resolved.

Second, one may wonder how unique Japan's experience of the declining pass-through appears in the global economy. In other words, is the underlying force specific to Japan, or is it something shared by other industrialized nations? Answering this question thoroughly will require a detailed multicountry analysis using similarly disaggregated data, which is beyond the scope of the current study. We instead draw on Bailliu and Fujii (2004) that provides panel estimates of the average pass-through of 11 OECD countries excluding Japan. Their estimates, based on aggregate import price data in an annual frequency, suggest that a decline in the import pass-through is actually a common phenomenon of the 1990s among the OECD countries. A rough estimate based on their results points to a decline of the average aggregate long-run ERPT by approximately 20 percent. This is comparable to the magnitude of the decline experienced by Japan for capital goods and consumer nondurables but is significantly less substantial than that for raw materials and intermediate materials. The finding suggests that while a decline in ERPT is not necessarily a phenomenon restricted to Japan, it has been manifested quite markedly by the deflationary economy.

8.8   Conclusion

The prolonged economic malaise has put the Japanese economy in a rather unusual and problematic situation where general prices decline on a continual basis. There is no doubt that the ongoing deflation has been exerting a detrimental effect on the ailing economy. It is therefore essential that an effective deflation-combating policy be prescribed immediately. In the current policy debate the yen's depreciation seems to be gaining popularity as a candidate for an effective deflation-taming tool. Aside from whether or not the BOJ can drive the exchange rate in a particular direction, however, the idea of fighting deflation by depreciation presupposes that exporters to Japan shift most of the effects of depreciation to the Japanese importers and consumers. While the assumption of complete pass-through is routinely adopted by traditional open economy models, its empirical validity remains controversial. This is particularly so for Japan today where foreign exporters observe a continual decline in the product prices of the domestic competitors. As Taylor (2000) argues, the degree of ERPT may depend not only on the microeconomic factors, but also macroeconomic factors such as the domestic inflation environment.

In this chapter we estimated the degrees of pass-through to the Japanese imports over alternative sample periods using two sets of disaggregated price indexes. From these pass-through estimates we calculated how much of a general inflation the yen's depreciation generates via import inflation. The subsample estimates suggest that in many product categories ERPT has declined in recent periods consistently with Taylor's (2000) conjecture. Our calculation further confirms a reduction in the magnitude of the overall wholesale inflation attained by the yen's depreciation.

The findings provide some cautionary notes regarding the expected effectiveness of the yen's depreciation in fighting the Japanese deflation. Suppose that the BOJ can induce the yen's effective depreciation by 10 percent. In the early 1980s this would have created overall wholesale inflation by the rate of 0.92 percent in the long run. However, our estimates for the most recent period suggest that the same 10 percent depreciation is expected to lift the wholesale price only by 0.50 to 0.56 percent. These changes are well illustrated by figure 8.3, which describes how the inflation persistence and the effects of depreciation have been shifting. In short, the yen's depreciation is not as effective as it was in earlier periods in creating an inflationary pressure. Clearly,

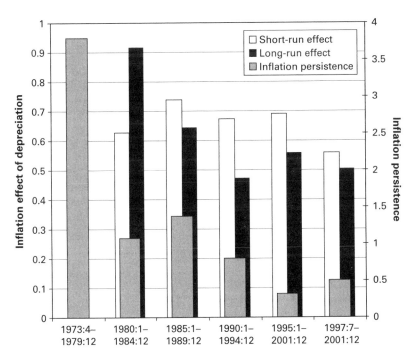

Figure 8.3
Inflation persistence and effects of depreciation. The short-term and long-term effects are estimated by 10 percent depreciation of full inflation using pass-through coefficients. Price data are disaggregated by the stage of use and demand. Inflation persistence is measured axially in months as the half-life of full inflation.

this conclusion alone does not constitute either thorough refutation or endorsement of a particular policy prescription. Rather, it is meant to provide some useful information to enhance our understanding of this critical issue.

In documenting the recent Japanese experience, this study also serves as a unique evaluation of the intriguing proposition Taylor (2000) put forth on the relationship between degrees of pass-through and inflation environment. In that sense the findings of the current study are meant also to help illuminate a larger picture of price behavior in open economies in general.

Meanwhile we also recognize the limitations of the current analysis. The subsample comparison of ERPT is based on the price indexes that are only crudely disaggregated. Although we supplement it by using the industry data, it is desirable to examine the import price movements over the long horizon with more finely disaggregated data. Such data should also enable us to extend our preliminary cross-product category analysis to identify the determinants of the rate of decline in ERPT.

Finally, it will be informative to study the responses of the consumer prices to exchange rate changes, in addition to those of the wholesale prices. These avenues may be pursued as a future extension when the present data limitations are removed.

Notes

I am grateful to two anonymous referees, Jeannine Bailliu, Yin-Wong Cheung, Menzie Chinn, Takatoshi Ito, Fukunari Kimura, Nikolas Müller-Plantenberg, and Frank Westermann for invaluable comments and discussions. I also wish to acknowledge helpful comments from the participants of the 2003 Venice Summer Institute and the 2003 Japanese Economic Association meeting. The usual disclaimer applies.

1. For instance, according to the *Nikkei Shimbun* (February 22, 2003), at the meeting hosted by the Policy Research Institute of the Ministry of Finance, Hiroshi Yoshikawa, a member of the Council on Economic and Fiscal Policy of the Cabinet Office and the former Vice Minister of Finance Haruhiko Kuroda agreed on that a depreciation to 130 to 140 yen per dollar level will have an immediate and significant effect on the deflation by raising the import price. The yen-dollar rate then was 118.90, so the suggested depreciation is by approximately 9 to 18 percent. The media also reports that a similar view to support *yenyasu-yudo* has been expressed at the Monetary Policy Meeting of the BOJ by some of its constituents.

2. Svensson (2003), for example, suggests a substantial depreciation and a temporary crawling peg as a devise to escape from a liquidity trap and deflation. Although import inflation is not the primary focus in his recommendation, he refers to it as a "direct channel" and notes its desirable effects.

3. More fundamentally, it is questionable if the BOJ can actively drive the exchange rate to a desired level. While effectiveness of market intervention remains controversial in general, it is even more so in the current scenario because (1) Japan has no room to reduce its interest rates, (2) massive-scale sale of the domestic assets can have a serious negative impact on the economy, and (3) the United States and the European Union do not appear to be particularly enthusiastic about cooperative interventions. However, we assume that the BOJ is capable of at least inducing depreciation, if not depreciation, by a desired amount, and ask how effective it would be in terms of reversing the downward trend of domestic prices.

4. Another implicit assumption is that movements of import price have sizable effects on Japan's overall inflation.

5. The yen's depreciation is expected to have also an export-boosting effect that partially makes up for the frail domestic demand. This is one reason that the proposal for weaker yen is gaining popularity. In this chapter, however, we limit our scope to its effects on the domestic inflation.

6. The other possibility is the case where the marginal cost and the markup moves by the same amount but in the opposite directions.

7. In particular, the nature of market competition and the cost structure have been examined as a determinant of ERPT. See, for instance, Dornbusch (1987), Feenstra (1989), Goldberg and Knetter (1997), and Yang (1997).

8. Similarly an increase in (perceived) persistence in exchange rate changes leads to a greater price response by a firm. See Taylor (2000) for further details.

9. The indexes are normalized to be one in 1973:3.

10. In this paper, inflation is measured in terms of a nonannualized monthly rate.

11. The wholesale inflation process is modeled as a first order autoregressive process, and the coefficient estimate is used to calculate its half-life.

12. The exchange rate is measured in units of yen per unit of the foreign currency.

13. See, for instance, Gagnon and Knetter (1995), Giovannini (1988), Marston (1990), and Ohno (1989) for analyses on the Japanese exporting firms' pricing behavior.

14. Price responses at the retail level may be a better indicator of overall effects of depreciation, since they also reflect movements of additional price markups by domestic distributors and retailers. However, with consumer price indexes, we are unable to separate changes in import prices from those in domestic prices. Also the wholesale price data allows us to quantify ERPT to imported input prices, which is consistent with Taylor's theoretical framework. For these reasons we choose to work with the wholesale price index data.

15. See table 8.6 for details.

16. While the series goes further back to the 1960s at the source, we utilize only the Post-Bretton Woods period so as to control for potential effects of alternative exchange rate regimes. Also note that our primary focus is on Japan's experience in the recent deflationary period.

17. All sectors in the wholesale price index are covered. See table 8.6 for a detailed description of the sectors.

18. Relevant factors include demand elasticity and production cost structure. See Feenstra (1989), Giovannini (1988), Marston (1990), and Yang (1997) among others.

19. The augmented Dickey-Fuller test results suggest that the series, except for some of the domestic product prices, contain a unit root. Since the domestic price series yield mixed results, we also estimated (6) while replacing Δp_{t-i}^d with p_{t-i}^d. The results are similar, and do not alter the story significantly. Assuming nonstationarity of the variables, we also test for cointegration between p_t and s_t. The evidence is generally insignificant, and hence an error correction term is not included in (6).

20. We check the serial correlations in the resulting residuals to ensure the adequacy of the specifications selected by the information criteria.

21. First through sixth lags of the domestic product price series and a linear trend are used as instruments.

22. The inclusion of the contemporaneous exchange rate term on the right hand side may raise some concerns about endogeneity. However, the use of disaggregated price data enables us to avoid the potential problem given that no single sector is large enough to drive the exchange rate movements by itself.

23. This is observed by comparing the long-run coefficients with the corresponding short-run coefficients in table 8.2.

24. Table 8.6 contains the weights assigned to each category at the data source.

25. The subsample calculations for 1973:3 to 1979:12 are not available since some price indexes start only from 1980:1.

26. In the calculation we assume that the prices of domestic products (for domestic consumption) stay constant following the depreciation.

27. To calculate the rate of decline in ERPT, we use primarily the 1980 to 1984 and 1995 to 2001 estimates. While we also incorporate the 1985 to 1989 and 1997 to 2001 estimates, using the alternative subsamples does not alter the conclusion.

28. This applies to both the short-run and long-run ERPT. To conserve space, the results are not reported but are available upon requests.

References

Bailliu, J., and E. Fujii. 2004. Exchange rate pass-through and the inflation environment in industrialized countries: An empirical investigation. Bank of Canada Working Paper 2004-21.

Campa, J. M., and L. S. Goldberg. 2002. Exchange rate pass-through into import prices: A macro or micro phenomenon? NBER Working Paper 8934.

Choudhri, E. U., and D. S. Hakura. 2001. Exchange rate pass-through to domestic prices: Does the inflationary environment matter? IMF Working Paper 01/194.

Dornbusch, R. 1987. Exchange rate and prices. *American Economic Review* 77: 93–106.

Feenstra, R. C. 1989. Symmetric pass-through of tariffs and exchange rates under imperfect competition: An empirical test. *Journal of International Economics* 27: 25–45.

Gagnon, J. E., and J. Ihrig. 2001. Monetary policy and exchange rate pass-through. Board of Governors of the Federal Reserve System, International Finance Discussion Paper 704.

Gagnon, J. E., and M. M. Knetter. 1995. Markup adjustment and exchange rate fluctuations: Evidence from panel data on automobiles and total manufacturing. *Journal of International Money and Finance* 14: 289–310.

Giovannini, A. 1988. Exchange rates and traded goods prices. *Journal of International Economics* 24: 45–68.

Goldberg, P. K., and M. M. Knetter. 1997. Goods prices and exchange rates: What have we learned? *Journal of Economic Literature* 35: 1243–72.

Hooper, P., and C. Mann. 1989. Exchange rate pass-through in the 1980s: The case of U.S. imports of manufacturing. *Brookings Papers on Economic Activity* 1: 297–337.

Marston, R. C. 1990. Pricing to market in Japanese manufacturing. *Journal of International Economics* 29: 217–36.

McCarthy, J. 1999. Pass-through of exchange rates and import prices to domestic inflation in some industrialized countries. Federal Reserve Bank of New York, New York.

Ohno, K. 1989. Export pricing behavior of manufacturing: A U.S.–Japan comparison. *IMF Staff Papers* 36: 550–79.

Otani, A., S. Shiratsuka, and T. Shirota. 2003. The decline in the Exchange Rate Pass-Through: Evidence from Japanese Import Prices. *Monetary and Economics Studies* 21: 53–81.

Sazanami, Y., F. Kimura, and H. Kawai. 1997. Sectoral price movements under the yen appreciation. *Journal of the Japanese and International Economics* 11: 611–41.

Svensson, L. E. O. 2003. Escaping from a liquidity trap and deflation: The foolproof way and others. *Journal of Economic Perspectives* 17: 145–66.

Taylor, J. B. 2000. Low inflation, pass-through and the pricing power of firms. *European Economic Review* 44: 1389–1408.

Yang, J. 1997. Exchange rate pass-through in U.S. manufacturing industries. *Review of Economics and Statistics* 79: 95–104.

9   Japan's Imbalance of Payments

Nikolas Müller-Plantenberg

9.1   Introduction

9.1.1   Global Financial Imbalances

The financial imbalance between America and Asia has reached a critical level in recent years. Since the mid-1990s, the United States has been running an enormous deficit on its balance on current account (in recent years to the tune of $500 billion, or 6% of world trade), piling up foreign debt on an unprecedented scale. Among America's most generous lenders are the East Asian economies, particularly Japan and China. However, the sustained slide of the dollar that started in early 2002 is a sign that the country finds it now much harder than before to attract foreign capital.

That the dollar did not fall more quickly is in large part due to the heavy intervention by the central banks of Japan, China, Hong Kong, Taiwan, and South Korea, who have become passionate purchasers of American government debt of late. Collectively, these five central banks hold around $1.5 trillion in official reserves, almost half the global total, most of them in dollar assets; in 1990 for comparison, the same share had been only 24 percent. Between 2000 and 2004 China's reserves have tripled and Japan's doubled.

By now, many observers see a problem in those developments. They point out that by buying dollars and keeping the dollar strong, the Asian economies are delaying the inevitable adjustment in the US trade balance. In other words, allowing America to continue to accumulate foreign debt at an ever faster rate means that the eventual adjustment will be correspondingly bigger.

However, it would be wrong to portrait current developments as an isolated episode. What this chapter seeks to show instead is that the interaction between current account imbalances, capital flows and exchange rates is but a recurrent economic phenomenon. One country where this is particularly evident, and which this chapter focuses on, is Japan, the by far biggest economy in East Asia. Studying the experience of this country is interesting since it has been running the world's largest current account surplus since 1981, with strong fluctuations over the years. As we will see, there has been a close link between Japan's balance of payments and the movements of the yen.

9.1.2 International Cash Flow and Exchange Rates

An important hypothesis of this chapter is that international payment flows are a central determinant of exchange rates. In business terms, cash flow is the flow of liquid assets in and out of a company over a period of time, after deduction of expenses and debt service payments. Similarly one can think of a country's international cash flow as the sum of cross-border monetary payments arising from its commercial and financial transactions. Since a country's international cash flow shapes the demand and supply conditions of its currency in the foreign exchange market, we should expect it to play a central role in the determination of exchange rates.

In practice, the problem is that a country's cash flow cannot be easily measured. It is neither determined solely by the current account nor solely by the capital account. Most of the monetary transactions are recorded in a subcategory of the financial account of the balance of payments, the so-called other investment balance. However, "other investment" also includes other, less liquid, means of international financing, such as bank loans. Disaggregated data are hard to come by, even for a country like Japan. This means that it is normally impossible to construct international cash flow series directly from balance of payments data.

This chapter develops a methodology to infer the likely movement of a country's cross-border payment flows from the joint fluctuations of its current account and debt balance. Applying the method to Japan, it finds that the Japanese cash flow variable traces the movements of the yen exchange rate remarkably well over recent decades.

9.1.3 Plan of the Chapter

The chapter is organized as follows. Section 9.2 develops a simple model to capture the dynamic interaction between the balance of payments, international cash flow and the exchange rate, highlighting, in particular, the role of foreign debt and lending in the adjustment of the exchange rate. Section 9.3 provides time series evidence from Japan, Germany, and Korea corroborating the model's conclusions. Section 9.4 presents the methodology for simulating cross-border payment flows and applies it to the case of Japan. Section 9.5 considers the implications of the chapter's analysis for Japan's persisting economic crisis. Section 9.6 provides overall conclusions.

9.2   A Model of International Cash Flow

Most financial analysts and economic journalists carry in the back of their heads a basic model of international adjustment featuring a two-way feedback between the balance of payments of a country and its exchange rate. On the one hand, it is generally taken for granted that the real exchange rate influences the trade balance, and thus the current account. By making a country more competitive, a weak currency encourages exports and discourages imports and thus improves the trade balance. On the other hand, it is believed that current account surpluses, and likewise capital inflows, generate inflows of foreign currency, which push up a country's currency.

Leaving capital flows aside for a moment, the common premise is that there is a negative effect of the real exchange rate on the current account and a positive effect of the current account on the nominal exchange rate. These economic mechanisms are not new. For instance, both were already present in the traditional flow market model of the exchange rate, which was first formalized by Robinson (1937) and Machlup (1939, 1940). In this model the exchange rate is determined by the supply and demand conditions in the foreign exchange market, which in turn depend on the trade balance. Up to the 1970s the flow market model was very popular, and economists applying it spent considerable time estimating the exchange rate sensitivities of exports and imports in order to determine the equilibrium in the foreign exchange market. Although authors also considered various shifts of the supply and demand curves of the currency market, the model remained essentially static in nature (e.g., for textbook treatments, see Kenen 2000; Abel and Bernanke 2003).

The static nature of the flow market model is unsatisfactory for two reasons. First, empirical and theoretical evidence suggests that trade flows adjust only gradually to exchange rate changes (e.g., see Dixit 1989). Second, what we really want to know are answers to dynamic questions. For example, we are often interested to know for how long a current account deficit of a particular country will persist, or how fast its currency will depreciate. The duration and magnitude of a current account deficit matters, since it determines the amount of external finance a country requires. And the rate of depreciation matters, since a rapidly depreciating exchange rate calls for much larger economic adjustments than a gradually falling one.

In this section we will look at ways to model the bidirectional relationship between the current account and the exchange rate in a dynamic fashion. We will examine a simple benchmark model of an open economy in which the capital account of the balance of payments consists only of direct monetary payments, as well as a variant of the model where current account imbalances are financed by foreign debt.

9.2.1 A Benchmark Model

The benchmark model consists of the following equations:

$$s_t = -\xi c_t, \tag{1}$$

$$q_t = s_t, \tag{2}$$

$$z_t + c_t = 0, \tag{3}$$

$$z_t = z_{t-1} - \phi q_{t-1}, \tag{4}$$

where q_t is the real exchange rate, s_t is the nominal exchange rate, z_t is the current account, c_t is the monetary account, or minus the country's cash flow, and ξ and ϕ are positive constants. Note that the exchange rate is defined as the price of the domestic currency in terms of a foreign currency; that is, a rise in the nominal exchange rate implies a nominal appreciation of the currency, and similarly for the real exchange rate.

The four equations are interpreted as follows: Equation (1) assumes that the nominal exchange rate is driven by international payment flows in the foreign exchange market. The domestic currency appreciates when a country receives payments for its exports from abroad, and vice versa. (Note that the alternative assumption that exchange rates are driven by cumulative payment flows would also be plausible; however, it is not adopted here.) Equation (2) states that the real and nominal exchange rates are equal, implying similar inflation rates at home and abroad. Equation (3) is the balance of payments. The current account balance, which comprises only the trade balance, is equal to the country's international cash flow since exports and imports are paid for in cash. Equation (4) describes the dynamic adjustment process of the current account. Net exports rise gradually when the local currency is cheap, and vice versa.

The model can be transformed into a first-order difference equation in the current account variable, z_t:

$$z_t = (1 - \phi\xi)z_{t-1}. \tag{5}$$

The solution to this equation is

$$z_t = A(1 - \phi\xi)^t, \tag{6}$$

where A is an arbitrary constant. The dynamic behaviour of the nominal and real exchange rate, s_t and q_t, and the international cash flow variable, c_t, is then readily derived from equations (1), (2), and (3). The movements of the current account and the international cash flow variable mirror each other, and up to a scaling factor, all variables follow the same dynamic process.

Three things are worth noting regarding the dynamic behaviour of the variables in this model. First, when the product of the model's coefficients is greater than one—that is, when $\phi\xi > 1$—the current account and all the other variables in the model start to oscillate from one period to the next. This is intuitive, since $\phi\xi$ is measuring the feedback between the current account and the exchange rate. When $\phi\xi > 1$, either international cash flow strongly influences the nominal exchange rate or the real exchange rate has a big impact on the current account, or both. So there may be cycles as an external surplus generates payment inflows that lead to a strong appreciation; this in turn gives rise to a deficit in the current account, and so on.

The parameters ϕ and ξ will generally take different values across countries and may even change over time. The parameter ϕ measures the exchange rate sensitivity of trade flows and depends for instance on the openness of a country, the shares of exports and imports relative to GDP and the degree of exchange rate pass-through. The parameter ξ describes the setting of the exchange rate in the foreign exchange market and may be related, among other things, to the level of intervention by the monetary authorities. It depends mostly on the institutional setting of the foreign exchange market and thus probably varies less than ϕ. However, given the worldwide liberalization of trade flows over the past decades, we should expect ϕ to have risen in many countries. Large swings in the external accounts and in exchange rates are therefore more likely than they were a few decades ago.

The second point to note regarding the model's dynamics is its potentially explosive behavior. As soon as $\phi\xi$ exceeds two, mutual feedbacks reinforce each other so that the balance of payments and the exchange rate fluctuate more and more strongly over time. According to the model, countries are risking economic and financial instability when they open up their markets to the outside world.

A third and final conclusion from the model is that the current account, z_t, and the real exchange rate, q_t, are positively correlated. This theoretical finding is in direct contradiction to the widespread belief that the relationship is negative, that is, that strong exports are associated with a weak, competitive exchange rate.

Thanks to its dynamic nature, this introductory model yields predictions that could not be obtained with the conventional flow market approach. Because of its fundamentally static perspective, the flow market model can neither account for dynamic adjustment paths—whether they are smooth, oscillatory, or explosive—nor does it in general predict a positive association between the current account and the exchange rate.

9.2.2 A Model with International Debt

Direct monetary payments form only a fraction of countries' financial transactions. Countries normally finance a large part of their external deficits by borrowing from abroad. The fact that gross foreign asset positions in a worldwide cross section of countries consist mostly of foreign loans rather than foreign equity (Kraay et al. 2000) implies that countries prefer trade credits, bank loans, or bond issuance to other forms of external finance. In the following model, which is a variant of the previous benchmark model, we therefore consider what happens when a country uses debt to cover its financing requirements.

Another assumption that we will adopt in the new model is that debt flows are accommodating imbalances on the current account side of the balance of payments. This is in line with the old view that the capital account adjusts to movements in the current account, rather than vice versa (Keynes 1929). The assumption is still often realistic despite the recent rise in capital mobility worldwide. However, as our empirical examples in the next section will show, there are occasions when capital flows are obviously moving in an independent fashion. Further below, we will discuss the implications of such autonomous capital flows.

Accommodating debt flows can be introduced into the previous model as follows:

$$s_t = -\xi c_t, \tag{7}$$

$$q_t = s_t, \tag{8}$$

$$z_t + d_t + c_t = 0, \tag{9}$$

$$d_t := d_t^1 - d_{t-1}^1, \tag{10}$$

$$c_t = d_{t-1}^1, \tag{11}$$

$$z_t = z_{t-1} - \phi q_{t-1}, \tag{12}$$

where d_t is the debt balance in the balance of payments and d_t^1 is the flow of foreign debt with a one-period maturity that is created in period t. Equations (7), (8), and (12) are the same as equations (1), (2), and (4), respectively. Equation (9) is the balance of payments, which now includes the debt balance. Equation (10) defines the debt balance as the difference between newly incurred foreign debt and foreign debt incurred in period $t-1$ and falling due in period t. Equation (11) states that in each period, all of the debt incurred in the previous period is repaid.

It should be noted that the assumption that foreign debt has a fixed, one-period maturity is made for simplicity only and that it does not affect the model's conclusions. Moreover it is always possible to redefine the maturity length by changing the unit of time, say from one year to two years or to six months.

In analyzing the model, we observe that equations (9), (10), and (11) imply that countries pay for their imports and receive payments for their exports always after one period:

$$c_t = -z_{t-1}. \tag{13}$$

The deferred payments imply that the model can now be reduced to a second-order difference equation in the current account variable, z_t:

$$z_t = z_{t-1} - \phi \xi z_{t-2}. \tag{14}$$

As long as $\phi \xi > \frac{1}{4}$, the solution to this equation is the following trigonometric function:

$$z_t = B_1 r^t \cos(\theta t + B_2),$$
(15)

where

$$r := \sqrt{\phi \xi},$$

$$\theta := \arccos\left(\frac{1}{2\sqrt{\phi \xi}}\right),$$

$\theta \in [0, \pi]$.

There are important parallels, as well as differences, between this model, which incorporates international debt flows, and the previous model, which assumed away those flows. First, the variables of the model are again moving in a cyclical fashion. In contrast to the previous model, however, oscillating behavior occurs already when the product of ϕ and ξ exceeds one-fourth. The higher tendency of the variables to move in a cyclical manner results from the desynchronization of the current account and the exchange rate: A strong current account, for instance, produces payment inflows in the next, rather than the current, period. Consequently it takes longer for the exchange rate to appreciate and to reverse the export boom. Eventually though, the trade balance, and thus the current account, move into deficit. The same process starts again, this time with opposite sign.

The cyclical movements occur even if the exchange rate sensitivity of trade flows is low or if the influence of changing demand and supply conditions in the currency market on the exchange rate is weak. Low values of the parameters ϕ and ξ simply mean that the mutual, non-synchronous feedbacks between the current account and the exchange rate are weaker, making the adjustments of those variables more protracted and their cycles longer. In fact, since θ is proportional to the frequency of those cycles, and since the product of the parameters, $\phi \xi$, is positively related to θ, it follows that the frequency of the cycles, say ω, rises with the value of that product. Whereas ω was one-half in the previous model—the variables were oscillating from one period to the next, completing one cycle in two periods—it is easily established that in the model with international debt, ω will always be less than one-half.

The second parallel between this and the previous model concerns the stability of the solution. The present model becomes unstable when the product of ϕ and ξ exceeds one. In the previous model by contrast, the corresponding condition was that the product had to be greater than two. In other words, balance of payments and exchange rate fluctuations are potentially less stable when countries borrow from, and lend to, each other. Intuitively, international borrowing and lending delays the—inevitable—adjustment of the exchange rate. Therefore balance of payments imbalances can grow larger, implying eventually even bigger exchange rate changes.

A third and final aspect in which the two models are comparable concerns the correlation between the current account and the exchange rate. In the previous model, we established a positive, contemporaneous correlation between both variables. In the model with international debt, the positive relation still holds, except that the exchange rate now lags the movements of the current account. In the following section we will see that the delayed response of the exchange rate to current account movements is an empirically important phenomenon. For terminological simplicity we will refer to it as the adjustment delay.

9.2.3 Accommodating versus Autonomous Capital Flows

When a country's capital flows are autonomous—that is, not just adapting to the country's financing needs—the analysis obviously changes. We will not enter upon a formal analysis here (for a dynamical system analysis, see Müller-Plantenberg 2004) but rather build on the intuition from our previous two models.

Autonomous capital flows are driven by a variety of factors. Whatever the underlying cause, capital inflows induce extra cash flow for the recipient country, which pushes up the domestic currency. Capital outflows have just the opposite effects.

Depending on their intensity, capital flows will generally distort the cyclical movements of the current account and exchange rate. Consider capital inflows, for example. By keeping the currency strong, capital inflows can make a current account deficit more persistent. Moreover, apart from the exchange rate channel, capital inflows often coincide with booms in domestic consumption and investment (Calvo, Leidermann, and Reinhart 1996) and thus have adverse effects on the current account (which is defined as the gap between a country's savings and investment).

When a country receives significant capital inflows, we should therefore not be surprised to see an appreciation of the currency even though the current account is weak or deteriorating. On the other hand, due to the buildup of foreign claims we should expect an even bigger adjustment of the exchange rate sooner or later—once capital flows cease or when they become insufficient to finance the external deficit.

9.3   Empirical Evidence

The purpose of this section is to compare the time series evidence on Japan's external performance with the theoretical predictions of the previous section. To anticipate the outcome, the model with international debt of the previous section fits the data remarkably well— better than one might have expected in fact, given that one would never expect economic relationships to match the real world exactly. This section also takes a look at a number of other countries and episodes to show that the model's conclusions hold elsewhere, too.

9.3.1   Japan

Over the last half-century the yen has been appreciating persistently, in nominal and in real terms. This development has attracted considerable attention, and various theories for it are on offer. What has also been remarkable—and what consequently merits an explanation as well—is that there have been massive fluctuations of the Japanese currency over the years. For instance, between 1985Q3 and 1988Q4, the yen's value shot up by 61 percent in trade-weighted terms (39 percent in the year from 1985Q3 through 1986Q3 alone). In the 1990s, to take another example, the yen rose by 52 percent from 1992Q3 through 1995Q2, then dropped by 35 percent in the following three years through 1998Q3, only to be pushed up once more by 40 percent in the two years thereafter. Fluctuations of these magnitudes can be observed all the way back to the early 1970s when the yen started to float.

Current Account and Exchange Rate Movements
The model in section 9.2 suggests that the large swings in the yen were primarily the result of similarly impressive movements of the Japanese current account. Consider figure 9.1, which plots the current account balances (in US dollar terms) of a number of countries that have, at some stage, achieved high surpluses during the past twenty-five years. It is evident that Japan's surplus—which mirrored the equally impressive current account deficit of the United States—has dwarfed the surpluses of all its competitors; even Germany's export boom of the 1980s

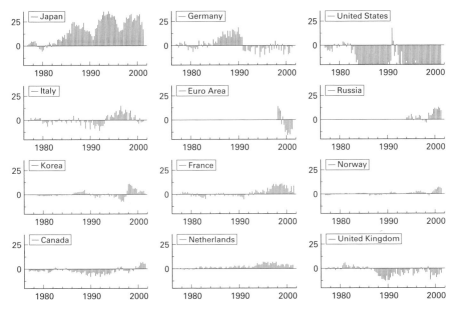

Figure 9.1
Large current account surpluses from 1977Q1 to 2001Q3. Current account balances of countries with large current account surpluses are in billions of US dollars. Countries are selected and ordered according to the highest current account balance they achieved in any single quarter. Source: IMF, *International Financial Statistics*.

appears modest compared with what Japan achieved during the last two decades.

Figure 9.2 illustrates the link between the current account and the nominal effective exchange rate in Japan. It plots the time series of both variables over a period of more than thirty years. As in the text, the nominal exchange rate is defined as the foreign currency price of the domestic currency, that is, a rise in the nominal exchange rate implies an appreciation of the domestic currency.

A remarkable feature of the data is the recurrent oscillation of both variables. The current account, in particular, experienced five large upswings and downswings, with clear turning points. The exchange rate went through similar upward and downward movements. In general, the exchange rate seems to have followed the movements of the current account, normally with a lag of up to two years. Another way to see this is by noting that the exchange rate increased most strongly in the years when the current account reached a peak. These peaks occurred in 1971–1972, 1977–1978, 1985–1986, 1992–1993, and in 1999.

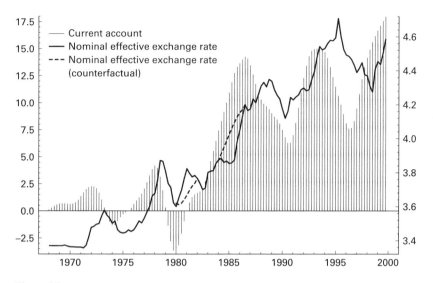

Figure 9.2
Japanese current account and counterfactual exchange rate. Japanese current account (left scale) in trillions of yen, transformed from biannual to quarterly frequency data using a natural cubic spline smooth, and nominal effective exchange rate (right scale, in logarithms) from 1968Q1 to 1999Q4. The exchange rate is plotted along with counterfactual estimates for 1980Q1 to 1981Q4 and 1984Q2 to 1986Q2 when measures to liberalize Japan's capital account started to take effect. The counterfactual series was calculated by removing the exchange rate observations during years of increased capital in- and outflows and filling the missing values with the estimates from a natural cubic spline smooth based on all remaining observations. Sources: OECD, *Economic Outlook*, IMF, *International Financial Statistics*, and own calculations.

The time series plot in figure 9.2 thus confirms central predictions of the model in section 9.2.2. First, we can observe that the current account and exchange rate are jointly going through long cycles. Second, the exchange rate is positively correlated with the current account during those swings. Third, the exchange rate has lagged the current account due to the adjustment delay.

Liberalization of the Capital Account
Important changes were brought to Japan's economic environment in the early and mid-1980s when the country opened its financial markets to the outside world. The tight regulation of the financial system, which Japan had maintained from the end of World War II to the mid-1970s, was significantly reduced in two phases. The first phase of liberalization started in the late 1970s. As late as in early 1979, Japan still retained formidable restrictions on foreign purchases of domestic

assets, not least in view of the yen's extraordinary appreciation in 1977 and 1978. However, when the yen depreciated rapidly in 1979, the Japanese moved quickly to reduce controls on capital inflows, making it possible for foreigners to hold Japanese securities (Frankel 1984). The liberalization of capital inflows appears to have been particularly effective: portfolio inflows rose substantially between 1980Q1 and 1981Q4, putting upward pressure on the yen.

The second phase of liberalization started when the Japanese—following requests of the US Treasury—began to remove restrictions on international capital flows further in May 1984. This time the removal of capital controls triggered strong capital outflows, mainly between 1984Q2 and 1986Q2, contributing to the remarkable strength of the US dollar at the time.

The capital flows that were set off by the Japanese liberalization measures are typical examples of autonomous capital flows. No one knows how the yen would have behaved without those additional flows. However, figure 9.2 illustrates what happens when we remove the exchange rate data during the episodes of increased capital inflows and outflows and simply link up the remaining observations. Manipulating the original exchange rate series in this way, what we obtain is a counterfactual exchange rate series that follows the movements of the current account even more smoothly. Instead of being subject to various shifts as in the original time series, the yen is now appreciating steadily between 1980 and 1988 and gradually following the movement of the current account during the early and mid-1980s.

The model with accommodating capital flows from section 9.2.2 thus seems to be confirmed once more. Another prediction of the model—namely that the introduction of debt flows can lead to greater cyclical movements of the variables over time—appears to be borne out by the data, too: the swings in the Japanese current account have by and large become greater over time.

9.3.2   Other Countries

We conclude this section by considering evidence from a few other countries. One conclusion from the model in section 9.2.2 was that the cycle frequency should increase with the product of the two parameters, ϕ and ξ. Note that ϕ is measuring the impact of the exchange rate on net exports. We said that this parameter should rise with a country's share of trade in GDP, since a proportional change in exports and

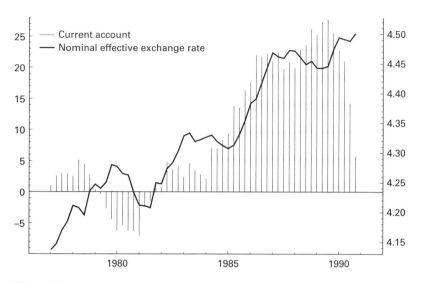

Figure 9.3
German current account and nominal exchange rate in the 1980s. German current account (left scale, in German marks) and nominal effective exchange rate (right scale, in logarithms) from 1977Q1 to 1990Q4. Source: IMF, *International Financial Statistics*.

imports leads to a greater movement in the trade balance when this share is large than when it is small.

Between 1980 and 2003 Japan's shares of exports and imports relative to GDP have been 10 and 8 percent respectively on average. Now consider Germany, the world's next-strongest export performer, where the same shares were 26 and 23 percent. From figure 9.3 we see that Germany experienced similar swings in the current account and the exchange rate during the 1980s. In line with our theoretical prediction, however, the swings were of a higher frequency—and thus of a shorter duration—than in Japan.

Another aspect of the theoretical model for which we find even more evidence in the data of other countries is the role of autonomous capital flows. An interesting example is South Korea, Japan's neighbor. Figure 9.4 plots the Korean current account and exchange rate series, with the data spanning almost two and a half decades. Throughout the whole period current account deficits are accompanied by (or due to the adjustment delay followed by) depreciations of the won, and vice versa. This is true for the two episodes during which the Korean currency declined substantially—first in 1985–1986 and later in 1987 during the Asian crisis—and likewise for the two episodes during

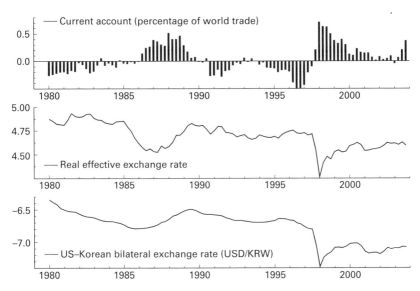

Figure 9.4
Korea's current account and exchange rate. South Korean current account, South Korean real effective exchange rate, and US–Korean bilateral exchange rate from 1980Q1 to 2003Q3. The current account variable is measured as a percentage of world trade. Sources: OECD, *Economic Outlook* and *Main Economic Indicators*.

which the currency rose strongly—namely in the late 1980s and from 1998 to 2000. What merits attention, though, is the fact that the won kept strong during most of the 1990s despite a rapidly worsening current account deficit. Clearly, the explanation lies in the strong private capital inflows that Korea and other East Asian economies received in the years before the Asian crisis (Grenville 1998). In keeping the won strong, these capital inflows contributed to the deterioration of the current account. The inevitable result was the Korean currency crisis in 1987, which was made worse through the panic among foreign investors.

Looking at currency crises more generally, it is rather common that countries run large current account deficits prior to their crises, which are only sustained due to large capital inflows. When capital inflows dry up, however, the national currencies tend to get into trouble. Eichengreen (2003, ch. 8) and Bussiere and Mulder (1999), for instance, have shown that a small set of variables—including the current account as a percentage of GDP, export growth, international reserves, and short-term foreign debt relative to reserves—do a very good job in predicting the EMS crisis in 1992–1993, the Mexican crisis in 1994–1995 as well as the Asian crisis in 1997.

As a final example of how autonomous capital flows matter for a country's external performance, consider the United States. In the early 1980s a massive deficit emerged in the US current account balance. Thanks to strong capital inflows, the dollar appreciated considerably until 1985. In that year, however, the adjustment could no longer be delayed, with the result of a sustained depreciation of the dollar, which lasted several years. An even larger deficit in the US current account developed in the latter half of the 1990s. Again, the deficit did not seem to harm the dollar, which once more kept on appreciating. Yet things eventually changed in early 2002 when the dollar started to depreciate rapidly.

9.4 Simulating International Cash Flow

9.4.1 A Model of International Cash Flow

The goal of this section is to simulate the flows of monetary payments between Japan and the rest of the world. For this purpose the following empirical model has been set up. As in the theoretical models of section 9.2, z_t denotes the current account, d_t the debt balance, and c_t the flow of cross-border payments, or cash flow. Suppose that current account transactions in a given period are either immediately paid for or financed through debt of different maturities:

$$c_t^0 = -\mu_0 z_t,$$
$$d_t^1 = -\mu_1 z_t,$$
$$d_t^2 = -\mu_2 z_t, \qquad\qquad\qquad (17)$$
$$d_t^3 = -\mu_3 z_t,$$

$$\ldots,$$

where debt issued in period t is indexed by its maturity and denoted as d_t^i, with $i = 1, 2, \ldots, \infty$. Debt maturity is defined here as the actual, or ex post, maturity. For example, if foreign debt held by Japanese investors has a one-year maturity and is rolled over twice, the actual maturity is taken to be three years.

Consequently cash payments in any given period have to be made for part of the current commercial transactions as well as for any debt falling due:

$$c_t^0 = -\mu_0 z_t,$$
$$c_t^{-1} = d_{t-1}^1,$$
$$c_t^{-2} = d_{t-2}^2, \qquad\qquad (18)$$
$$c_t^{-3} = d_{t-3}^3,$$

. . . .

Here c_t^{-i} represents that part of the cash flow in period t that results from debt issued i periods ago. It follows from equations (17) and (18) that the overall cash flow in period t depends on all the present and past current account balances:

$$c_t = \sum_{i=0}^{\infty} c_t^{-i} = -\mu_0 z_t + \sum_{i=1}^{\infty} d_{t-i}^i = -\sum_{i=0}^{\infty} \mu_i z_{t-i}. \qquad (19)$$

The debt balance, d_t, is the sum of the debt incurred in period t, less all debt repaid in that period:

$$d_t = \sum_{i=1}^{\infty} d_t^i - \sum_{i=1}^{\infty} c_t^{-i}$$

$$= -\sum_{i=1}^{\infty} \mu_i z_t + \sum_{i=1}^{\infty} \mu_i z_{t-i}. \qquad (20)$$

The debt balance is thus also a function of present and past current account balances:

$$d_t = \sum_{i=0}^{\infty} \alpha_i z_{t-i} = \alpha(L) z_{t-i}, \qquad\qquad (21)$$

where

$$\alpha_0 = -\sum_{i=1}^{\infty} \mu_i \quad \text{and} \quad \alpha_j = \mu_j \quad \text{for } j = 1, 2, \ldots. \qquad (22)$$

In equation (21), L is the lag operator and $\alpha(L) = \alpha_0 + \alpha_1 L^1 + \alpha_2 L^2 + \cdots$.

The problem is that the cash flow variable, c_t, is not directly observed. As mentioned in the introduction, payment flows across international borders do not enter the balance of payments as a separate

item. Instead, they enter various subcomponents. For example, some
cash flows, such as changes in bank balances, appear in the "other investment" item in the financial account. However, "other investment"
also includes trade credits and loans, thus making it impossible to infer
cash flow movements from the movements of the "other investment"
balance unless disaggregated data is available.

With knowledge of μ_i, $i = 1, 2, \ldots$, however, c_t can be indirectly
obtained from equation (19). For $i = 1, 2, \ldots$, the parameters μ_i coincide with the parameters α_i of the infinite lag polynomial in equation
(21).

In principle, the current account, z_t, and the debt balance, d_t, could
fluctuate independently over time, as long as the gap between the two
is made up by movements in other components of the capital account.
However, our goal is to simulate the international cash flow of Japan
and, as figure 9.5 shows, in this country both the current account
and the debt securities balance have moved quite closely together
over time. This suggests that other balance of payment components

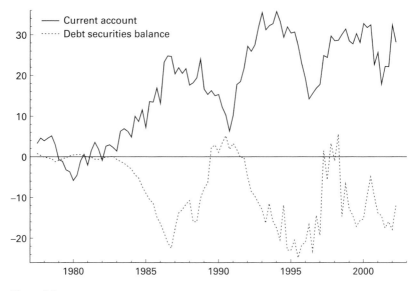

Figure 9.5
Current account and lending to Japan from 1970 to 1998. Japanese current account (left
scale) and debt balance (right scale, with reversed sign) in billions of US dollars. The
debt balance is defined as the sum of the debt securities balance, other investment, and
net errors and omissions. Sources: IMF, *International Financial Statistics*, and Lane and
Milesi-Ferretti (1999).

canceled each other out, at least roughly; thus, to keep things simple, they are not further considered here.

The reader might wonder why only the debt securities balance is considered at this point. It is certainly the case that the overall debt balance, d_t, contains other components, such as trade credits and loans, in addition to debt securities. The simple reason for not considering those items is that the data for Japan are incomplete. While ignoring certain flows of foreign debt is of course not very satisfactory, it should be pointed out that the debt securities balance—which recorded, for instance, the huge purchases of American bonds by the Japanese since the mid-1980s—has arguably been the most important debt-related item in Japan's balance of payments in the recent decades.

Augmented Dickey-Fuller tests (not reported) show that the null hypothesis of a unit root cannot be rejected for z_t nor for d_t (where d_t is from now on taken to comprise flows of debt securities only). While individually $I(1)$, the Japanese current account and debt securities balance appear to be cointegrated, that is, a linear combination of both variables exists that is $I(0)$. To test for cointegration, Johansen's (1988) procedure is applied, and it is found that the null hypothesis of no cointegration can be rejected at the 1 percent significance level (see table 9.1).

From these results the relationship between the two balance of payments components can be modeled as an autoregressive distributed lag (ARDL) model:

$$d_t = \kappa + \sum_{i=1}^{p} \gamma_i d_{t-i} + \sum_{i=0}^{q} \beta_i z_{t-i} + \varepsilon_t, \qquad \varepsilon_t \sim N(0, \sigma^2). \tag{23}$$

The infinite lag polynomial in equation (21) can then be obtained by dividing the distributed lag polynomial by the autoregressive lag polynomial of the ARDL model:

Table 9.1
Testing for cointegration

H_0	H_A	Trace test	p-Value
$r = 0$	$r > 0$	22.750	[0.003]**
$r \leq 1$	$r > 1$	2.2928	[0.130]

Notes: Testing for the number of distinct cointegrating vectors, using 2 lags. Double asterisks (**) mark significance at the 1 percent level.

$$\alpha(L) = \frac{\beta(L)}{\gamma(L)}, \tag{24}$$

where $\gamma(L) = 1 - \gamma_1 L - \gamma_2 L^2 - \cdots - \gamma_p L^p$ and $\beta(L) = \beta_0 + \beta_1 L + \cdots + \beta_q L^q$.

Quarterly data from 1977 to 2002 were used in the estimation. The data were taken from the IMF's Balance of Payments Statistics. The lag lengths, p and q, in the ARDL model were both set to 3.

9.4.2   Simulation Results

The values of c_t were now simulated, based on equations (19), (22), and (24). Note that we do not have an estimate of μ_0. The solution adopted here is to simply set it equal to α_0, suggesting that current accounts are financed to one-half by direct cash payments, to the other half by debt. This is but a convenient assumption; it was found that raising μ_0 above or below this value does not affect the results too much.

Quarterly data on the Japanese current account from 1968Q1 to 1999Q4 were used in the simulation. These data had previously been constructed from a biannual current account series contained in the OECD's Economic Outlook database. Only the first 8 lags of the polynomial $\alpha(L)$ were used for the simulation, to avoid losing too many observations for the simulation.

The outcome of the simulation is shown in figure 9.6. The movements of Japan's international cash flow coincide remarkably closely with those of the Japanese exchange rate. The mean lag of $\alpha(L)$, which indicates the average maturity of foreign debt, is 1.653 quarters. The figure also plots net sales of Japanese reserve assets, which appear relatively small compared with the aggregate cash flow facing the Japanese economy.

9.5   Japan's Economic Stagnation

If the proposition underlying the previous three sections is correct—namely that the yen's nominal exchange rate was, by and large, driven by trade and capital flows over the years—what does this imply for the analysis of Japan's current economic problems? And what should we think of proposals to devalue the yen to revive the Japanese economy?

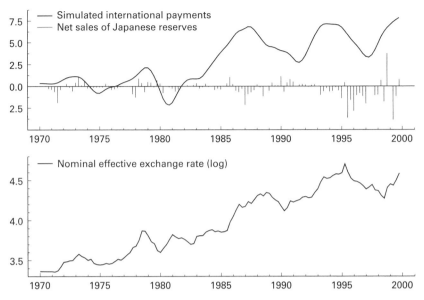

Figure 9.6
Japan's imbalance of payments. Simulated net international payments to Japan, as an indicator of yen order flow, shown together with net sales of reserves (top panel, in trillions of yen, reserve sales drawn as index bars), and nominal effective exchange rate (bottom panel, in logarithms). Sources: OECD, *Economic Outlook*, IMF, *International Financial Statistics*, and own calculations.

9.5.1 The Downside of Success

A Hard Landing

Japan has for a long time been admired across the globe for its economic performance and, in particular, for its international competitiveness and export strength. The traditionally high saving rate helped Japan to become the largest creditor nation in the world. The unhappy end of this success story is now evident to everyone. The analysis of this chapter can shed some light on where the downside of success lies.

As I suggested earlier, notwithstanding other factors, Japan's large and sustained current account surpluses are at the root of its current economic problems. By pushing up the yen very strongly over decades, Japan's export boom has contributed to the deflationary pressures from which the economy has been suffering from for quite some time.

Of course, removing the external surplus would fix the problem according to the logic applied here. Yet the current account is not a policy variable, and at any rate a strong demand for Japanese exports seems to provide a welcome stimulus for the economy. Policy makers naturally look for other kinds of remedies, namely for measures they can potentially control.

What Scope for Monetary Policy?
Consider monetary policy. With interest rates hitting zero, the Bank of Japan's only way to induce money growth is to keep printing money. But the BOJ has already bought government bonds, and thus created money, on a large scale. The monetary base has increased at an annual rate of almost 25 percent over the two years to 2003 (*The Economist*, June 19, 2003). Yet this has not led to higher growth in broad money. Instead, bank lending has continued to fall. Banks are reluctant to lend, as they are already piled up with bad loans, a problem that is only slowly being overcome. Moreover indebted firms are unwilling to borrow as long as the deflation environment persists.

An equally important question is whether monetary policy had been too strict prior to the crisis, and thus to what extent it could have been contributing to the overly strong yen. This chapter cannot give a detailed answer to this question. However, an examination of the data suggests that money growth in Japan was actually quite strong in comparison with other countries. According to the OECD's Economic Outlook, the money stock in Japan grew at an annual average of 9.1 percent from 1970 to 2000, compared with 7.3 percent and 7.8 percent in the United States and Germany respectively. For comparison, the volume of GDP in Japan rose on average by 3.2 percent per year, whereas in the United States and Germany, it increased by 2.9 and 2.7 percent, respectively.

There is an interesting parallel to currency crises. In the aftermath of such crises, it is tempting to put the blame on fiscal and monetary policies for being too loose. Yet during the currency crises of the 1990s, macroeconomic policies prior to those crises had been considered sound in many of the countries affected. Instead, currencies collapsed following sharp withdrawals of foreign funds after long periods of foreign lending. There is thus a lesson for Japan. When external imbalances start to shift the relative demand for national monies, it can be just as hard to defend a currency as to keep it from rising.

9.5.2   *Devalue the Yen?*

Many economists advocate a big depreciation of the yen through intervention in the foreign exchange markets in the current situation (e.g., Svensson 2001). Japanese prices have been falling since 1995, and devaluation is viewed by many as one of the few policy tools left to fight deflation. First, a cheaper yen would boost exports, and this would stimulate the economy. Second, through higher import prices, it would presumably push up inflation, stimulating consumption and investment and decreasing the real value of debt in the economy. However, given that Japan's imports account for only 10 percent of GDP, an ordinary devaluation would not suffice—it would have to be substantial.

The rest of this section will address two questions: First, is a devaluation of the yen feasible? And second, how much would it help, or might it even be harmful?

Magnitude of Intervention

Using foreign exchange intervention to lower the yen seems straightforward. All there is to do for the Japanese authorities is to print large amounts of yen to buy dollar bonds. So isn't this the point where the parallels with currency crises end? When a central bank tries to support a currency, it quickly runs out of reserves. In Japan, however, it would appear that intervention does not face similar limitations.

Yet the facts are that Japan has been acquiring reserves on an unprecedented scale in recent years. What is more, Japan's share of all reserves held worldwide has risen substantially since 1993, as can be seen from figure 9.7. Interestingly, reserve holdings by other industrial countries have declined sharply over the same period. Out of industrial countries' reserves, Japan now holds a share of 45.6 percent (2001M11), up from only 12.0 percent nine years back (1992M9).

In the past, strong appreciations of the yen were almost always associated with increases in reserves. Yet even large interventions did not appear to help much to prevent the yen from rising. From the empirical analysis in this chapter, it is clear why. Consider once more figure 9.6, which plots the simulated cash flow together with the changes in Japanese reserves. The impression is that intervention has seldom been more than a small fraction of the economywide payments across the border. It is therefore not surprising that their impact should have been limited.

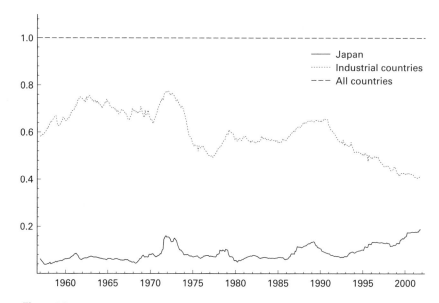

Figure 9.7
Japan's share of world reserves. Japan's share of total reserves of all countries, plotted alongside the industrial countries' share of worldwide reserves (monthly data, excluding gold reserves). Source: IMF, *International Financial Statistics*.

What do the actual market participants think? Cheung and Wong (2000) have recently carried out a survey of practitioners in the inter-bank foreign exchange markets of Hong Kong, Tokyo, and Singapore. They find that the participants in the Tokyo market "have the most pessimistic views on intervention in terms of restoring equilibrium values, being conducted at the right moment, and achieving the goal." Of the respondents in the Tokyo market, 68.1 percent did *not* think that central bank intervention achieved its goal, whereas in the Hong Kong and Singapore markets, 60.8 and 58.7 percent, respectively, believed that it *did*.

Undesired Effects
When Japan hit an export boom in the past, it usually sent the inflow-ing revenues abroad straightaway, for example, by investing in US Treasury bonds. It was not until the foreign debt became due that the exchange rate appreciated, just as the model of section 9.2.2 would predict. This is what needs to be kept in mind when contemplating a large-scale intervention to bring down the yen. Intervention needs to

be perpetuated if it is to be effective; otherwise, interest and amortization payments will soon undo its initial effects.

There is also another potential "boomerang" effect that could take effect after a devaluation and that needs to be taken into account. From the model in section 9.2.2, we know that if efforts to devalue the yen succeed, this may spur exports and thus create another wave of incoming cash flow. The relationship between the real exchange rate and current account is not a simple one for Japan—after all, its current account surplus has kept rising despite the long-term appreciation of the yen. However, Müller-Plantenberg (2003) has recently shown that large real exchange rate changes did tend to bring about reversals of the temporary trends of the Japanese current account (rather than its level). Thus once devaluation succeeds to create another export boom, an appreciation of the yen should soon follow. It will not have to come immediately—as we know by now. But it will come.

9.6   Conclusions

Over a long period of time the Japanese exchange rate has followed the movements of the current account quite closely. Long swings in the current account translated into similar swings in the exchange rate. In general, export booms pushed up the yen, while slumps in net exports made it fall. However, it often took some time—usually up to one or two years—until the exchange rate had fully adjusted.

This chapter suggests that flows of international payments between Japan and the rest of the world have been a crucial driving force behind the yen. Importantly, these flows are related to the balance of payments. For instance, current account transactions that have to be paid for straight away lead to an instantaneous flow of cash, whereas debt-financed transactions can give rise to a flow of payments that is spread out over time.

Japan, the world's largest creditor, has used the proceeds of its current account surpluses primarily to lend abroad, investing heavily in foreign debt securities. This chapter shows how it is possible to estimate the maturity structure of this lending based on the information contained in the current account and debt balances. It uses the maturity structure of foreign lending to simulate international payment flows and shows that their movements are remarkably similar to those of the Japanese exchange rate.

These findings lead directly to the question of whether the present economic crisis in Japan could have been averted or whether something can be done to overcome it. Here the answer is a cautious one. It is pointed out that the strong yen and the deflationary pressure to which it contributed are not necessarily the result of bad policy making. A parallel is drawn to experiences in the 1990s when countries were hit by currency crises, even though they had, in more than one instance, followed sound fiscal and monetary policies. Likewise it is found that the large-scale acquisition of reserves is unlikely to fix the problem. Japan has, as a matter of fact, amassed foreign exchange reserves on an unprecedented scale over recent years.

Going beyond Japan, the findings of this chapter point to a number of potential economic fallacies. They concern fundamental questions such as whether the real exchange rate is driven by the nominal exchange rate, particularly at longer horizons, or vice versa; whether and how exchange rates are linked to economic fundamentals (Meese and Rogoff 1983); or why it is that deviations from purchasing power parity are so large and persistent (Rogoff 1996).

In recent decades the world has witnessed an ever greater integration of its national economies and financial markets. At the same time industrial countries have reduced their inflation rates and committed themselves to inflation levels close to zero. A conclusion of this chapter is that large external imbalances can have a strong and persistent impact on the exchange rates of different monies. Differences in inflation rates are both an outcome of this—as a result of the pass-through of exchange rates on import prices—and a requirement to overcome lasting real exchange rate misalignments. Thus Japan's inflation rate has stayed almost 2 percent below the weighted inflation rate of its trading partners for many years. While low international inflation rates are widely welcomed, one should not overlook that they have likely contributed to Japan's present condition, which is marked by deflation and stagnation.

9.7 Appendix

Data

The data used in this chapter were taken from the *Balance of Payments Statistics* and *International Financial Statistics* of the IMF and from the *Economic Outlook* of the OECD.

Software

The computations for this chapter were carried out using Ox, version 3.0 (see Doornik and Ooms 2000) and PcFiml (see Doornik and Henry 1997). The programs are available from the author upon request.

Acknowledgments

I would like to thank Eiji Fujii, Frank Westermann, as well as other participants of the Workshop on "Economic Stagnation in Japan" at the CESifo Venice Summer Institute 2003 for many helpful comments. I also thank seminar participants at the International Financial Stability Programme at the CEP (LSE) for their comments.

References

Abel, A. B., and B. S. Bernanke. 2003. *Macroeconomics*. Boston: Addison Wesley.

Bussiere, M., and C. Mulder. 1999. External vulnerability in emerging market economies: How high liquidity can offset weak fundamentals and the effects of contagion. International Monetary Fund Working Paper 88.

Calvo, G. A., L. Leiderman, and C. M. Reinhart. 1996. Inflows of capital to developing countries in the 1990s. *Journal of Economic Perspectives* 10: 123–39.

Cheung, Y.-W., and C. Y.-P. Wong. 2000. A survey of market practitioners' views on exchange rate dynamics. *Journal of International Economics* 51 (2): 401–20.

Dixit, A. K. 1989. Hysteresis, import penetration and exchange-rate pass-through. *Quarterly Journal of Economics* 104 (2): 205–28.

Doornik, J. A., and D. F. Henry. 1997. *Modelling Dynamic Systems Using PcFiml 9.0 for Windows*. Boston: International Thomson Business Press.

Doornik, J. A., and M. Ooms. 2001. Introduction to Ox: Ox version 3. London: Timberlake Consultants Press.

Eichengreen, B. 2003. *Capital Flows and Crises*. Cambridge: MIT Press.

Frankel, J. A. 1984. The yen/dollar agreement: Liberalizing Japanese capital markets. *Policy Analyses in International Economics* (Institute for International Economics) 9 (December). Cambridge: MIT Press.

Grenville, S. A. 1998. Capital flows and crises. *Reserve Bank of Australia Bulletin* (December): 16–31.

Johansen, S. 1988. Statistical analysis of cointegration vectors. *Journal of Economic Dynamics and Control* 12: 231–54.

Kenen, P. B. 2000. *The International Economy*. Cambridge: Cambridge University Press.

Keynes, J. M. 1929. The German transfer problem. *Economic Journal* 39 (153): 1–7.

Kraay, A., N. Loayza, L. Servén, and J. Ventura. 2000. Country portfolios. National Bureau of Economic Research Working Paper 7795.

Machlup, F. 1939. The theory of foreign exchanges. *Economica* 6 (24): 375–97.

Machlup, F. 1940. The theory of foreign exchanges. *Economica* 7 (25): 23–49.

Meese, R., and K. Rogoff. 1983. Empirical exchange rate models of the seventies: Do they fit out of sample? *Journal of International Economics* 14: 3–24.

Müller-Plantenberg, N. 2003. Current account reversals triggered by large exchange rate movements. Unpublished working paper. London School of Economics.

Müller-Plantenberg, N. 2004. Balance of payments accounting and exchange rate dynamics. Unpublished working paper. London School of Economics.

Robinson, J. 1937. The foreign exchanges. In J. Robinson, ed., *Essays in the Theory of Employment*. London: Macmillan.

Rogoff, K. 1996. The purchasing power parity puzzle. *Journal of Economic Literature* 34: 647–68.

Svensson, L. E. O. 2001. The zero bound in an open economy: A foolproof way of escaping from a liquidity trap. *Monetary and Economic Studies* (Bank of Japan) 19: 277–312.

Index

N/A